THEODORE OF MOPSUESTIA

Theodore, bishop of Mopsuestia (c.350–428), stands out as the pre-eminent exponent of the School of Antioch's literal, historical, and rational emphases in exegesis and of its staunch defense of Christ's humanity. At his death, he was hailed as one of the outstanding, prolific biblical theologians of his time. However, after his works and person were later condemned at the Second Council of Constantinople in 553, he is known today primarily as the "Father of Nestorianism."

This addition to the Early Church Fathers series provides in one place new extensive translations of Theodore's major extant works that have not been available in English up unto the present. It also summarizes the secondary literature and discusses at length the fundamental features of his theological thinking, especially regarding his method of exegesis and his functional stress on the union of Christ's natures as occurring in "one common *prosōpon*."

Frederick G. McLeod presents passages from Theodore's major works *On the Incarnation* and his *Catechetical Homilies*; his commentaries on Psalm 8, Adam's creation, John, Philippians 2, Galatians, Ephesians, and Colossians; and his rejection of the allegorists and Apollinaris; as well as providing all the anathemas of Constantinople II against Theodore's works and person.

This book will be invaluable to any scholar who wishes to read at first hand what this influential and controversial figure has actually written.

Frederick G. McLeod has a doctorate in Oriental Christian Studies from the Pontifical Oriental Institute in Rome and is recently retired from St. Louis University's Department of Theological Studies.

THE EARLY CHURCH FATHERS
Edited by Carol Harrison
University of Durham

The Greek and Latin fathers of the Church are central to the creation of Christian doctrine, yet often unapproachable because of the sheer volume of their writings and the relative paucity of accessible translations. This series makes available translations of key selected texts by the major fathers to all students of the Early Church.

CYRIL OF JERUSALEM
Edward Yarnold, S. J.

EARLY CHRISTIAN LATIN
POETS
Caroline White

CYRIL OF ALEXANDRIA
Norman Russell

MAXIMUS THE CONFESSOR
Andrew Louth

IRENAEUS OF LYONS
Robert M. Grant

AMBROSE
Boniface Ramsey, O. P.

ORIGEN
Joseph W. Trigg

GREGORY OF NYSSA
Anthony Meredith, S. J.

JOHN CHRYSOSTOM
Wendy Mayer and Pauline Allen

JEROME
Stefan Rebenich

TERTULLIAN
Geoffrey Dunn

ATHANASIUS
Khaled Anatolios

SEVERUS OF ANTIOCH
*Pauline Allen and
C. T. R. Hayward*

GREGORY THE GREAT
John Moorhead

GREGORY OF NAZIANZEN
Brian E. Daley

EVAGRIUS PONTICUS
A. M. Casiday

THEODORET OF CYRUS
István Pásztori Kupán

THEOPHILUS OF
ALEXANDRIA
Norman Russell

THEODORE OF MOPSUESTIA

Frederick G. McLeod

Routledge
Taylor & Francis Group

LONDON AND NEW YORK

First published 2009
by Routledge
2 Park Square, Milton Park, Abingdon, Oxon OX14 4RN

Simultaneously published in the USA and Canada
by Routledge
270 Madison Ave., New York, NY 100016

Routledge is an imprint of the Taylor & Francis Group

© 2009 Frederick G. McLeod

Typeset in Garamond 3 by
Prepress Projects Ltd, Perth, UK
Printed and bound in Great Britain by
CPI Antony Rowe, Chippenham, Wiltshire

British Library Cataloguing in Publication Data
A catalogue record for this book is available from the British Library

Library of Congress Cataloging in Publication Data
McLeod, Frederick G.
Theodore of Mopsuestia / Frederick G. McLeod. – 2nd ed.
p. cm. – (The early church fathers)
Includes bibliographical references and index.
1. Theodore, Bishop of Mopsuestia, ca. 350–428 or 9. I. Title.
BR65.T75746M35 2008

270.2092–dc22   2008002884

ISBN10: 0–415–43407–6 (hbk)
ISBN10: 0–415–43408–4 (pbk)
ISBN10: 0–203–89371–9 (ebk)

ISBN13: 978–0–415–43407–2 (hbk)
ISBN13: 978–0–415–43408–9 (pbk)
ISBN13: 978–0–203–89371–5 (ebk)

Dedicated to my Jesuit Province in New England and to my community at Saint Louis University for their spiritual, affective and material support, enabling me to bring this venture to a successful completion.

CONTENTS

CONTENTS

PREFACE

This book is one more in a series of writings on Theodore of Mopsuestia. My initial interest in Theodore was sparked after I published my critical edition and translations of five soteriological homilies of Narsai, a fifth-century East Syrian biblical theologian and poet. I then sought to trace his dependence on Theodore (whom he hailed as his special "Interpreter") in regard to how Adam and Christ's humanity are "images of God" and the "bonds of the universe." This led to a wider search to determine how much Theodore's christology influenced Narsai. Since many of Theodore's dogmatic works are lost, I found this to be an insightful way to enrich knowledge of each through the other. This enabled me to grasp in a far deeper way their understanding of christological terms and their reliance on typology, especially in their treatment of baptism and the eucharist. Then after publishing my book on *The Roles of Christ's Humanity in Salvation: Insights From Theodore of Mopsuestia*, I felt that I was ready, because of both my background in languages and my knowledge of Theodore's thought, to undertake this present work for the Routledge series on the Early Church Fathers. I am pleased that my proposal was accepted and has reached the final stage of publication.

I consider this to be a valuable work because so little of Theodore is readily available in any modern language. Although such scholarly books as those by Francis Sullivan, Rowan Greer, and Richard Norris, Jr., provide a wide range of the most significant passages from his works, I believe that there is a need to provide those interested in Theodore's thought a much more expansive coverage of his writings in a compact way. In Part I, I begin with what we know of Theodore's life and works. I then offer an overview of the secondary literature on Theodore. As regards his thought, I let Theodore explain his exegetical principles in his own words and then offer major examples of how he applies these in his treatments of original sin and Adam and Christ's humanity as the bonds of the universe and the special images of God. Because his approach to the union of Christ's natures is controversial, I then discuss what he means by "a union of good pleasure as in the Son" and how he justifies his unity "in one common *prosōpon*." I will conclude this section with a personal assessment of Theodore's importance within the Early Church. In Part II, I offer lengthy passages from his works *Against the Allegorists* and his commentaries *On Psalm 8, On the Creation of Adam, On John's Gospel*, and *On Philippians 2: 5–11*, as well as significant selections from the commentaries on Galatians, Ephesians, and Colossians. I have then translated all that has survived of Theodore's great works *On the Incarnation* and *In Opposition to Apollinaris* and present prominent selections from his *Catechetical Homilies*. I conclude with an English translation of the anathemas that the fathers at Constantinople II leveled against Theodore's works and person.

A few points of referencing need to be highlighted. In Part I, when I quote from the works of Theodore, I refer the reader to where this passage can be found in Part II by indicating the page number in parentheses at the end of the citation. It is there that one can obtain the reference to the edition that I have used. This procedure will allow the reader to view my quotations in a wider context. In the Introduction to Part II, I will discuss the texts I have used and my principles for translation.

Lastly, I am thankful for the very friendly and exceptionally thorough direction that I have received from Dr. Carol Harrison, the editor of this series, and for the assistance that Ms. Amy Laurens, Lesley Riddle, and Amy Grant have provided at Routledge's publishing house, and especially Andrew R. Davidson, for his careful professional editing of the final version of my manuscript, and Suzanne R. Peake. For anyone who has gone through the rigors of bringing a manuscript to publication, such gracious, graceful support is most helpful, if not necessary, for the successful completion of a detailed work such as this.

Part I

INTRODUCTION

1

THEODORE'S LIFE

Theodore of Mopsuestia lived from *c*. 350 to 428.[1] In their lifetime together Theodore and John Chrysostom were classmates, fellow monks, and close friends at Antioch in the late fourth century. Whereas John is esteemed today as a prolific and saintly churchman, Theodore is viewed as one of the outstanding christological heretics. Yet at the time of his death he was widely revered as one of the prominent biblical theologians in Late Antiquity and a leader of the famed School of Antioch.[2] He was hailed as the principal exponent of the School's literal, historical, and rational approach to biblical exegesis and respected as the most penetrating critic of Origen's allegorical interpretation. He is also acknowledged as the peerless spokesperson and systematic defender of the Antiochene efforts to protect and promote the full humanity of Christ. He is especially remembered and reviled for describing the unity of Christ's two natures as occurring in one *prosōpon* (person). Yet, despite his being an imposing intellectual force in his own day, little factual knowledge has come down to us about his life.[3] What is most ironic in all this is that such a towering, independent-minded church figure in his age has become in our day simply a name worthy of a sentence or two on how he influenced Nestorius in his christological thinking. This is doubtless primarily because relatively little of his surviving writings have been available in the major modern languages. Nevertheless, some central moments of his life have come down to us.

Theodore was born to a wealthy family in Antioch *c*. 350. As a young man, he was educated at one of the elite rhetorical schools[4] of his day, where he studied together with John Chrysostom. They subsequently entered a monastery directed by Diodore, who is recognized today as the real founder of what became known as the School of Antioch. Diodore stood out as a gifted theologian who

3

fearlessly defended the historical nature of the Christian Scriptures against the emperor Julian in the early 360s. He appears to have had a profound impact upon Theodore's scriptural and theological outlook. According to the sources, Theodore abandoned Diodore's school, with the intention of marrying, but, so it seems, was persuaded by a letter from John Chrysostom to return. During his years of studies at Diodore's school, he witnessed in the 370s the convulsion that Arianism caused in Antioch, with four antagonistic groups vying for religious ascendancy and with the leaders of his own theological community, Miletus and Diodore, being often exiled. After these controversies were generally resolved at the First Council of Constantinople, he was ordained a priest in 383. If Swete's account is reliable, he then left a little later to stay with Diodore in Tarsus until he was consecrated bishop of Mopsuestia in 392. Then because of his growing reputation as a scholar, most likely thanks to his monumental work *On the Incarnation*, he was chosen to represent the Orthodox position at a discussion with the Macedonians (also known as Pneumatomachians) over the full divinity of the Holy Spirit. According to the sources, the emperors Theodosius I and II were also highly impressed by Theodore's preaching, and Nestorius is said to have visited Theodore on his way to becoming the Patriarch of Constantinople. Theodore died in 428, widely hailed as one of the most dedicated learned churchman of his day.

Three years later, a violent dispute erupted between Cyril of Alexandria and Nestorius that eventually led to the convening of the Council of Ephesus in 431.[5] It took some time before its results were accepted. The fathers agreed that Cyril's second letter to Nestorius best expressed their will about why Nestorius was condemned. It appears that nothing was alleged at the council against Theodore, doubtless because he was no longer living and his memory was still widely esteemed, at least in Syria. Yet by the middle of the 430s Cyril had to defend himself against those who rejected the "Pact of Reunion" that he had agreed to in 433 with the Patriarch John of Antioch. Since this creed employed language redolent of Theodore's formulation, Rabbula, the Bishop of Edessa, and Basil, a deacon at Constantinople, began to press for Theodore's condemnation. Eventually, in 438, Cyril published his (now lost) attack against Diodore and Theodore. But by the time Cyril died in 444 the church in the East was starting to be convulsed by a new growing controversy, called Eutychianism – a view that so centered on the divinity of Christ that his human nature was marginalized. The conflict came to a head in 449 at the Second

Council of Ephesus (better known as the "Latrocinium" or "Robbers' Council") when the assembled fathers deposed those opposed to Eutyches, in particular Flavian, Theodoret of Cyr, and Ibas of Edessa. All this was reversed two years later in 451 when a new emperor convened the Council of Chalcedon that condemned Eutyches and Dioscorus, the Patriarch of Alexandria, and restored to their sees those removed from office in 449. The fathers at Chalcedon once again condemned Nestorius, insisting that Theodoret and Ibas had to agree with this act if they wanted to be reconciled. But in the extant official proceedings there is no indication that the fathers discussed Theodore or his writings as deserving of a similar fate. Yet his name was mentioned, but only in the letter that Bishop Ibas insisted had to be read before the assembled fathers as proof that he and his letter were orthodox. This was a critical point for Ibas because this letter had been earlier cited as evidence of his heterodoxy. His letter becomes significant because he praises "the blessed Theodore [as] a preacher of the truth and teacher of the faith" (Doran 2006: 171–2). Those opposed to Chalcedon interpreted this willingness on the part of the fathers to listen to the letter of Ibas, when taken together with what they were convinced was the Nestorian phrasing of Chalcedon's christological formulations, to be unmistakable signs that the fathers agreed with Theodore and his teaching. This letter and its approval of Theodore then became one among several focal points of controversy between those defending the Chalcedonian formula and those spurning it.

The conflict between the Orthodox and the non-Chalcedonians was increasingly ripping apart the political and the religious fabric of the Byzantine empire in the sixth century.[6] The emperor Justinian determined to bring both sides together. He felt that he could achieve this by condemning Theodore, Theodoret's anti-Cyrillan writings, and (what he dubbed) the "so-called" letter of Ibas. Theodore's condemnation was meant to indicate to the non-Chalcedonians that Chalcedon was not truly Nestorian and could be accepted as ecumenical. When Justinian realized that his imperial letter of 540 and his edict of 551 condemning Theodore, Theodoret's anti-Cyrillan writings, and Ibas's "letter" had little impact, he sought to convene an ecumenical council as a way to achieve his goal. He pressured Pope Vigilius to summon a council. The council, predominantly composed of bishops from the East, began on May 5, 553 under the Patriarch Eutyches, for the Pope refused to be present for the opening session and continued to absent himself for the other remaining eight sessions. The council concluded on June 2.

5

At the start of the council, Justinian (who assumed an active, "behind-the-scenes" role at the council) warned about an attempt being made to revive Nestorianism through an acceptance of Theodore of Mopsuestia's teaching. At the first session, the fathers listened to a recital of the Nicene–Constantinople creed and then 71 "suspect" excerpts and one creed that the adversaries of Theodore had excised from his writings.[7] No defense was permitted, nor any effort made to understand Theodore's excerpts in their own context. The fathers simply accepted these passages as clear evidence of Theodore's heterodoxy. This took place in an angry setting where two different accounts in the *Acta* describe how the fathers shouted out:

> Anathema to Theodore of Mopsuestia! Anathema to Theodore and his writings! These are wholly contrary to the church! These are truly contrary to the orthodox [teachings]! These are contrary to the Fathers! They are brimming with impiety! These are contrary to the synods and impugn the divine Scriptures! Theodore and Judas are one!
>
> (Straub 1971: 56)

If these outbursts really took place at the council sessions, they signal to what extent these fathers were stirred to a lynching frame of mind and help to explain why the end of the twelfth anathema condemns anyone who is sympathetic to Theodore's thought, including anyone who

> defends the [just] cited most impious Theodore and his impious writings – [specifically] those in which he pours out those blasphemies [just] cited and numerous others against the great God and Savior Jesus Christ – without anathematizing him, his impious writings and those who have accepted him and justified him or say that he has expounded in an orthodox way as well as those who have written on his behalf and his impious writings and those too who think or ever thought similarly and have persisted until the end in such a heresy, let such a person [or persons] be anathema!
>
> (ibid.: 236)

The fathers chose from the 71 excerpts read to them those they considered to be the most heterodox. These are formulated in their anathemas (ibid.: 231–7). After wavering back and forth – as he did both before and during the council – Pope Vigilius initially steadfastly refused to condemn Theodore as a person. But under Justinian's intense pressure he relented and finally signed the decrees. On his journey back to Rome, the Pope suddenly died in Sicily, thus avoiding the widespread angry confrontation that would have awaited him in the West when the council's proceedings became known. A schism quickly broke out in Africa and Aquileia, for the council's decrees were widely regarded in the West as a repudiation of the Council of Chalcedon. This breach was not ultimately healed in the West until the second half of the sixth century. Ironically, the unity that Justinian so wholeheartedly struggled to attain between the Orthodox and the non-Chalcedonians never materialized.

2
HISTORY OF SECONDARY LITERATURE

After Theodore's condemnation at Constantinople II, only the Christians belonging to the East Syrian Church, for the most part, valued Theodore's teaching and person. In the fifth century, Ibas, the Syrian bishop (436–57) of Edessa, played a large role in promoting this influence by having Theodore's works translated into Syriac. He also steadfastly defended Theodore after the Council of Ephesus and was later condemned for this at the "Robbers' Council" in 449. Though he was reconciled at the Council of Chalcedon, the letter he wrote to Mari the Persian in which he praises Theodore was condemned at the Second Council of Constantinople in 553.[1] Narsai (*c*.410–500?), who was the "rabban" (or head) of the Persian school at Edessa, until forced sometime in the mid 450s to flee for his life, labored ceaselessly to inculcate Theodore's teaching within his students.[2] As the co-founder of the famed School of Nisibis in the Persian empire, he formed the minds of the Syrian hierarchy, insisting that Theodore was to be their, as he was his, principal "Interpreter," because

> All who have grown rich from the treasure of his books have been very well rewarded and have acquired an ability to interpret as he has done. I who learned [to do this] in a stammering way have learned from him, and by my involvement with him I have acquired a way to be involved in the study of [scriptural] words. I consider my study of him has guided me to [interpret] in the right way what has been written [there].
>
> (Martin 1899; the translation is my own)

Even after Narsai's death around the beginning of the sixth century, the School of Nisibis continued to be a center of learning and dedication to the teaching and memory of Theodore that is still

8

maintained even today. In an article published in the *Journal of the Assyrian Academic Society*, M. J. Birnie (1996) describes the influence of Theodore on the East Syrian Church. He observes that from the time that Henana (+610) tried, as the head of the School of Nisibis, to replace the school's allegiance to Theodore, "there would be no room in the Church of the East for criticism of this Antiochene father."[3] This is clearly evidenced in the two papers presented at the "Non-official Consultations for Dialogue between Churches within the Syriac Tradition" that defend Theodore and his writings. The first, delivered at Vienna in 1996, is entitled "The Theology of Nestorius and Theodore," and the second, at Chicago in 1997, "The Person and Teachings of Theodore of Mopsuestia and the Relationship between Him, His Teachings and the Church of the East, with a Special Reference to the Three Chapters Controversy."[4]

After Theodore was condemned at the Council of Constantinople II, the Orthodox and non-Chalcedonian theologians manifest little concern about his person and works. One noteworthy exception is a comment that the Patriarch Photios makes in his *Bibliotheca* concerning Theodore's (now lost) work against Eunomius: "[I] read the twenty-five books of Theodore of Antioch against Eunomius in defense of St. Basil. His style is somewhat obscure, but the work is full of ideas and sound reasoning, and contains a wealth of evidence taken from the Scriptures. He refutes the arguments of Eunomius almost word for word, and amply proves that he is very ignorant of outside knowledge and still more so of our religion. I believe he is the Theodore who was bishop of Mopsuestia."[5] In the Latin West, Theodore's works seem to have initially had some influence in North Africa and Aquileia – two areas that spontaneously reacted in a strongly negative way to the official decrees of Constantinople II, for they believed that these decrees undermined those of the Council of Chalcedon. Facundus of Hermiane, who attended the Council, wrote on his return to Africa a long, spirited defense in Latin of Theodore, Theodoret of Cyr's anti-Cyrillan works, and the letter of Ibas (*PL* 67: 527–878). He claims to have had in his possession at least most of Theodore's works:

> Like wolves and dogs, the heretics have not preserved whole the sentences of Theodore . . . they have snatched a few obscure words from his sayings . . . . We, however, as you see, choose to draw closely from the spectrum [of his works] rather than incur the suspicion of fraud by being brief and obscure.
>
> (ibid.: col. 745B)

9

Although those Latins opposed to Constantinople II were doubtless much more interested in safeguarding the Chalcedonian doctrinal formulations rather than defending Theodore, their concern may have led them to translate at least some of Theodore's major works.[6] This may help to explain why Theodore's *Commentary on the Minor Pauline Epistles* and other Latin excerpts have survived. This commentary also benefited by the fact that the surviving manuscripts of this work refer to its author as being anonymous or St. Ambrose or St. Hilary. It was not until the late nineteenth century that H. B. Swete promoted the view that it was written by Theodore.[7]

Throughout the succeeding centuries, Theodore was considered to be heretical, known firsthand only by the excerpts used to condemn him and by those passages that survived in the catenae. J.-P. Migne published these in 1861.[8] Then, during the second half of the nineteenth century, liberal Protestant theologians who were imbued with Enlightenment views began to emphasize Christ as a human being.[9] Because Theodore was considered to be one who chose Christ's humanity over his divinity, Enlightenment scholars in the second half of the nineteenth century delved into Theodore's surviving fragments. I. A. Dorner (1866) regarded Theodore as a kindred theological spirit who had brought out the central importance that Christ's free human development plays in the attainment of salvation for himself and others. He saw this exemplified in Theodore's distinctive teaching about the "image of God," believing that it furnishes insights into human nature and salvation. According to Dorner, Theodore held that, as an imperfect creature, Adam failed to live freely, as God wanted, according to the law. Because of this, Adam was the cause of both personal and cosmic disharmony. The mission of Christ was to truly image God by showing to others how to freely overcome sin and death and achieve one's individual fulfillment and the restoration of all creation in a new harmony.

The next major development in the modern understanding of Theodore came in the late nineteenth century when two additional writings of Theodore then became available in the West. The first is Edward Sachau's (1869) edition of many new Syriac extracts, with a Latin translation, of Theodore's writings that he found in various manuscripts.[10] Then, eleven years later, H. B. Swete published the Latin text he realized was Theodore's *Commentary on the Minor Pauline Epistles*, the first volume in 1880 and the second in 1882. Shortly afterwards, in 1895, the renowned scholar Adolf Harnack (1958) focused upon Theodore's views of how salvation history is broken

10

down into two *katastaseis* (or ages) when humans are called to rise from their original mortal condition to an immortal, immutable existence that will take place in a later future resurrection. Harnack accepts Theodore's teaching that humans are naturally mortal and therefore weak and prone to sin. He regards Adam's fall as simply a necessary stage in the moral development of human beings and Christ's role as simply underscoring in an educational way how others are to achieve salvation. For Harnack, a person must be trained to act in a free moral way by choosing what is good and avoiding what is evil. According to this view, salvation is merely a moralistic and virtuous journey that all must undertake. Harnack thus favors what he considers to be Theodore's conviction that salvation is due primarily to the Man Jesus rather than to God and that Theodore's understanding of salvation is anthropological and soteriological rather than christological.

In 1932 and 1933, A. Mingana published a Syriac text and an English translation of Theodore's monumental work, his *Catechetical Homilies*. This work, published in two parts, contains the 16 homilies that Theodore delivered to catechumens preparing to receive baptism and the eucharist at Easter. These homilies provide clear explanations of how Theodore understood the theological significance of the Nicene Creed, the Lord's Prayer, and the sacraments of baptism and the eucharist. Together with Sachau's Syriac excerpts and Swete's translation of Theodore's *Commentary on the Minor Pauline Epistles*, Theodore's *Catechetical Homilies* offer theologians a much wider perspective for understanding Theodore's theological thinking.

In the first part of the twentieth century, the question returned to a point raised by Adolf Harnack: how much was Antiochene thinking influenced by Aristotelianism? L. Patterson (1926) thinks that Theodore's outlook was probably molded by the Peripatetics. Then 10 years later R. Arnou (1936) pointed out in an insightful article the similarity between the Antiochene understanding of the soul–body relationship and what had been taught by the fourth-century Christian philosopher Nemesius (1955) who lived in or near Antioch. Arnou claimed that the later Antiochene theologians moved away from an Aristotelian viewpoint to a Neoplatonic outlook, at least with regards to how the soul and the body relate to one another. R. A. Norris, Jr., sums this up well:

> Arnou may or may not be correct in the details of his analysis
> but his work remains important both because it calls attention
> again to an important respect in which Theodore's philosophical

anthropology bears on his christology, and because it implicitly questions the tendency to a facile identification of the Antiochene 'outlook' with Aristotelianism – an identification which has, in fact, never been carefully examined.

(Norris 1963: 251–2)

R. V. Sellers, in the two books that he published in the early 1950s, came to the conclusion that the Antiochenes were realists, interested "not so much in the metaphysical as the ethical point of view" (1953a: 59) and that their thought is closer to the Hebrew Scriptures than to a particular philosophical school (1953b: 166).

After theologians became more aware of Theodore's recently found *Catechetical Homilies*, they began to look more favorably upon his thought and confront the question of whether he has been rightly called a Nestorian. M. Jugie (1935: 257–71) pronounced that Theodore's *Catechetical Homilies* do not modify the traditional view of Theodore's christology. Wilhelm de Vries believed that his study into how Theodore regarded the sacraments of baptism and the eucharist reveals that Theodore viewed them as being purely symbolic anticipations of a future heavenly fulfillment, simply providing actual graces for living a virtuous life and obtaining forgiveness for one's sins. De Vries understood this to be a logical outgrowth of Theodore's Nestorian christological thought, his fundamental error being his patent "denial . . . that God has really become human, that God and the Man are one and the same in one person. This error has its roots in Theodore's rationalistic tendency" (1941: 92). This interpretation is adamantly opposed by both I. Oñatibia (1954) and Luise Abramowski (1961), who believe that de Vries failed to fully grasp Theodore's understanding of "participation" within his typology.

In 1939, Robert Devreese produced his edition of Theodore's *Commentaire sur les Psaumes I–LXXX* that had survived in Latin. The following year, J.-M. Vosté published his Syriac edition, with a Latin translation, of Theodore's *Commentary on John's Gospel*. This work has provided many important passages dealing with the unity of Christ as well as the full context for three excerpts cited at Constantinople II as grounds for anathematizing Theodore: Nathaniel's limited confession of Christ as divine (found among the 71 contained in the council's *Acta*),[11] as well as the anathemas that fault his interpretations of Christ's breathing upon the Apostles and Thomas's exclaiming "My Lord and my God" (1940: 235). Relying on the *Catechetical Homilies* and other Syriac texts, M. Richard re-examined those excerpts presented as reasons to condemn Theodore at Constantinople and concluded that the those cited by Leontius of Byzantium and Pope Vigilius were based on a text that Cyril of Alexandria had received from Theodore's adversaries, most probably the Apollinarians.[12] Richard (1943) compared these with Syriac texts and raised the basic question whether the excerpts attributed to Theodore may have been tampered with and, if so, whether they are, therefore, unreliable. Richard's study, when taken together with the positive impact that the *Catechetical Homilies* were making on other readers, may have affected E. Amann's (1946) sympathetic assessment of Theodore in his article in the *Dictionnaire de Théologie Catholique*. Robert Devreese carried Richard's critical analysis a step further. He believed in light of the new material then available that there ought to be a serious reconsideration of the evidence used to justify the condemnation of Theodore at the Second Council of Constantinople (1948: 103).

At the beginning of the 1950s, M. V. Anastos (1951) moved away from the dispute about the excerpts used to condemn Theodore to explore the relationship between immutability and freedom. He compared in a penetrating way how Justinian and Theodore understood this close nexus and the ramifications of this for understanding their positions. The focus of theologians, however, never shifted away from the radical concern that both Richard and Devreese raised about Theodore. Francis Sullivan (1951) was the first to respond in a closely argued but negative way in his article "Some Reactions to Devreese's New Study of Theodore of Mopsuestia." Soon afterwards Kevin McNamara (1952, 1953) published a two-part article that, while praising Theodore's intent, argued that Theodore ultimately failed to assert the unity of Christ's nature in a sufficiently orthodox way. John L. McKenzie (1953) joined the fray, questioning Sullivan's conclusion, at least as regards the excerpt dealing with Nathaniel. Then, in a brilliant analysis of the text, Sullivan (1956) showed that the excerpts cited at Constantinople II are truly authentic, excepting for three that belong to Diodore of Tarsus.[13] Sullivan then proceeded in a careful way to substantiate his main opinion that Theodore was rightly condemned and can be said to be the "Father of Nestorianism" (ibid.: 288). Sullivan's book sparked a spirited reaction by Paul Galtier (1957), who insisted that Theodore was advocating a true unity – not a moral union – when he affirmed that there was only one *prosōpon* in Christ. He found fault with those who judge Theodore solely in light of Cyril of Alexandria's language and anathemas rather than in Theodore's terms. He is convinced that the standard ought to be Chalcedon's faith declaration. Also during this time, McKenzie continued his controversy with Sullivan in a back-and-forth exchange of scholarly articles.[14]

At the beginning of the 1960s, John Romanides (1959–60) published an extended and instructive summary of the literature published on Theodore up to that point. He also set forth an Orthodox response to what he saw was the fundamental issue that underlies the dispute about Theodore. He believes that it centers on where freedom resides: whether in the will, as Theodore taught, or, better, as he believes as an Orthodox, in nature. He holds that, since God's transcendent nature exceeds all categories, it is not necessitated in any way to act. Who can say that God's nature is not free to unite itself to human nature? Romanides sees Theodore's failure as residing in his inability to break out of his rigid moralistic framework. This prevented him from truly appreciating Cyril's understanding of the union. Within two years, the Byzantine scholar M. V. Anastos championed a far different view in his article "Nestorius was Orthodox" (1962), which would apply to Theodore as well as to Nestorius. He reasons that if one judges Nestorius in light of the Chalcedonian Symbol, he can be said to be orthodox. Also Ulrich Wickert proposed that one can understand Antiochene theology through a close study of Theodore's commentaries on the Pauline epistles, in his *Studien zu den Pauluskommentaren Theodors von Mopsuestia: Als Beitrag zum Verständnis der Antiochenischen Theologie* (1962). This was followed by Günter Koch's investigation into Theodore's assumptions about salvation, in his *Die Heilsverwirklichung bei Theodor von Mopsuestia* (1965).

Several other major works were also published on Theodore in the 1960s. Most noteworthy, first of all, is Rowan A. Greer's *Theodore of Mopsuestia: Exegete and Theologian* (1961).[15] Greer argues persuasively for the primacy of a Hebrew influence upon Theodore's scriptural interpretation. He also seeks to connect the moral emphasis that Dorner and Harnack had detected in Theodore's view of Jesus' freedom, to Theodore's understanding of the graced kind of unity that exists between the Word and the Man in Christ. Shortly afterwards, Richard A. Norris, Jr. (1963), also published an invaluable study that explored what influence the various philosophical systems might have had on Theodore's thought, especially that of late Platonism. He is also insightful in his treatment of what Theodore means when he speaks of an "indwelling of good pleasure" and of a union in one *prosōpon*. Two other works shortly followed those of Norris. Arthur Vööbus (1964) returned to the traditional estimate of Theodore as a heretic. Although

Aloys Grillmeier in his first edition offered a balance treatment of Theodore, in his monumental two-volume work on *Christ in Tradition* (1975) he too regarded Theodore's christology as not fully expressing what the synods insist is essential for Christian faith.

In the 1970s, Joanne McWilliam Dewart sought to understand Theodore's theological thought regarding grace and the meaning of *prosōpon*. In her book *The Theology of Grace of Theodore of Mopsuestia* (1971), she studied how Theodore attempted to integrate his views on grace with his emphasis upon Christ's human free will. Then in her article for *Studia Patristica* (1975), she investigated the term that is critical for understanding Theodore's christological thought: his notion of "person." Afterwards, interest in Theodore shifted once again, but this time to an attempt to better understand the Antiochene method of exegesis, especially through Diodore and Theodore's commentaries on the psalms. The focus too was centered on how much the rhetorical schools have shaped the Antiochene exegesis. The principal figures here in order of publication are: Josef Martin (1974), Christoph Schäublin (1974), Rudolf Bultmann (1984), Frances Young (1989),[16] Dimitri Z. Zaharopoulos (1989), Bradley Nassif (1996), Herman J. Vogt (1997), John J. O'Keefe (2000), and Harry S. Poppas (2002). For those seeking an understanding of the various positions proposed by these scholars concerning the Antiochene method of interpretation up to 1996, Albert Viciano's (1996) article is helpful. This period has also witnessed the publication of translations of Theodore's works. There were three new versions of the *Catechetical Homilies*, with extended introductions, by Peter Bruns (1994), Simon Gerber (2000), and Sebastia Janeras and Joseph Urdeix (2000). Robert Hill has translated into English Theodore's *Commentary on the Twelve Prophets* (2003) and *Commentary on Psalms 1–81* (2006). George Kalantzis has recently published a new version of Theodore's *Commentary on John's Gospel* (2004).[17]

At the beginning of the 1990's, John McGuckin (1990) opened up a discussion of whether Theodore may have exercised some influence upon Augustine. A new encyclopedia article was published in 1991 by José Maria Lera, who shows himself sympathetic to Theodore's orthodoxy. There were also during this period two books examining the Antiochene understanding of the "image of God": one by Nabil el-Khoury (1990) and the other by me (McLeod 1999). As mentioned earlier, the Pro-Oriente Foundation hosted two non-official consultations to promote dialogue between the churches within the Syriac tradition.[18] Since 2000, I have published two articles: the first, "Theodore of Mopsuestia Revisited" (2000), and the second, "The Theological Ramifications of Theodore of Mopsuestia's Understanding of Baptism and the Eucharist" (2002), a study into how Theodore understands these sacraments as types. I have also published a book entitled *The Roles of Christ's Humanity in Salvation: Insights from Theodore of Mopsuestia* (2005), in which I explore the salvific roles of Adam and Christ as the heads of mortality and immortality, the bonds of the universe, and the images of God. For Theodore, these salvific roles help to reveal who Christ is as a person.

3

THEODORE'S EXEGETICAL METHOD

A considerable amount of research has been spent on determining the Antiochene method of exegesis, as well as Theodore's. As the previous chapter has indicated, scholars have helped to bring out to a fuller extent how Theodore's method of interpretation has been influenced by his rhetorical education, his philosophical and cultural outlook, his loyalty to a faith and scriptural tradition, and his own personality. Rather than simply repeating what Albert Viciano (1996) has already so well provided, I want to limit my comments here to what Theodore himself has affirmed, in his own words, about his usual method, and then examine specific passages that highlight how Theodore has applied this faithfully.

First, Theodore accepted without questioning – as did all the fathers – that the Christian Scriptures were the inspired word of God. This attitude was so pervasive that the fathers felt no need even to discuss it. Because they were so convinced that God had revealed Himself and His will within their Bible, they did not hesitate to accept what they believed to be all the truths found there. Dimitri Zaharopoulos specifies these: "Divine inspiration of the Bible was generally held by the fathers to require belief in the truth of all its assertions on matters not only of religious doctrine and ethics, but also of cosmology, astronomy, history and biology" (1989: 62). Theodore does express how God's Spirit inspires a prophet in doing so: "The Spirit wills that the [prophet's] tongue speak loudly and clearly not his own thoughts but those that He is revealing" (ed. Devreese 1939: 282). Whereas Theodore does not suggest any special role that inspiration plays in the Pauline epistles, he is much more forthright in what is acknowledged to be his first major work, his *Commentary on the Psalms*: "[The psalmist] calls the Holy Spirit the recorder because the Spirit has put His imprint on what has been affirmed in ink. For the Spirit, as does anyone who writes very well – that is, as does a recorder – inspires the [psalmist's] heart with thoughts that are revealed through [what has been written] in ink. For He enables [the psalmist's] tongue to speak loud and clear what is affirmed there and to arrange the letters to [fit] the ideas and articulate them distinctly for those willing to benefit from them" (ibid.).[1]

Although the fathers all agreed that the Scriptures were divinely inspired, they disagreed on how to determine what was the inspired message. Origen admitted that a commentator must fully respect what the text asserts. Yet he argued that a strictly literal interpretation cannot be applied in every case, especially when the text makes inappropriate, troubling statements about God. To deal with these situations, where a scriptural passage is difficult to reconcile with an all-wise and loving God, Origen chose to follow the exegetical lead of Philo, who introduced allegory as a tool for interpreting Scripture. Philo saw this as an accepted way to harmonize the Hebrew Scriptures with the sophisticated wisdom arising from Greek philosophy. Just as the Stoics used allegory to uncover the universal truths contained in Homer and the Greek myths, Philo and later Origen adapted this method, with restrictions, to interpret difficult passages in their Scriptures in a way that was acceptable to scholarship. In fact, Origen believed that every line of the Bible had a possible spiritual message. But, just as Philo's method was condemned by the Hebrew scholars at the School of Palestine and Babylon, so too did the Antiochene Christians, and Theodore in particular, strenuously reject the allegorical teaching of Origen.

The Antiochenes, beginning at least with Lucian, Eusebius of Emesa, and Eustathius of Antioch, strongly opposed Origen, believing that an interpreter should always stay with what the text actually states. Theodore became the leading spokesperson for this critical viewpoint, being especially concerned about what is the right standard for interpreting the Christian Scriptures. If one grants that the Spirit is revealing God's will in the Bible, then Theodore reasoned that one ought to seek the Spirit's intent within the actual words He has inspired. He concludes from this that there is no instance where an allegorical interpretation is justified, unless it is inherently connected to the text. In fact, Theodore is convinced not only that Origen's approach "is proven to be superfluous in every regard," but that the Scriptures themselves "condemn [Origen] by proving that he cannot accurately assert and prove [his position] – not in any one of these [cases mentioned] where he has rashly dared to oppose the Scriptures. Indeed someone ought . . . to declare him to be truly foolish and ignorant" (78). Theodore argues too that Origen cannot defend his interpretations as true possibilities. Rather they are products of a "nocturnal dream." For one ought to be able to justify in a critical way the meaning of a text by means of close, well reasoned arguments that others can fully accept. Finally, Theodore believes that Origen has been tricked into introducing into the Scriptures Philo's pagan exegetical method, which offers a false hope of answering a difficult scriptural passage:

> This wise one was tricked into declaring these things. He would never have willingly shown an interest in any interpretation that is filled with the insane blasphemy of the pagans, once he studied the true meaning of the text and inquired into the intent of each of its words.
>
> (79)

Theodore maintains over and over again that there is an essential nexus between the meaning the Spirit wants revealed and the written text. What is foreign or contrary to this is to be rejected. For one should "know that there is but one sense in all the words present in the divine Scriptures" (100). The aim, therefore, of Theodore's method of exegesis is to discern what is a text's literal or actual meaning. Besides this emphasis on the text itself, Theodore also stresses the historical dimension of the Christian Scriptures. When Theodore uses the term *historia*, it refers not to what one understands today as an event that has been established by the critical historical method. It simply means a narrative story that is recounting something that has happened. He was forcefully opposed to an allegory because it was upholding a possibility that can be imagined, not what actually happened or will happen. In his commentary on what is meant by the phrase "by way of allegory" (Gal. 4:25), Theodore insists that

> The apostle does not eliminate the historical [element in the] narrative. Nor has he detached the factual elements from the past, but has proposed them as happening at that time and made use of the historical [element in the] narrative in order to [express] his own understanding of an event, as when he says: 'Hagar [as Mount Sinai] corresponds now to Jerusalem' [. . .] such an emphasis on time will be superfluous, unless this has factually taken place as the apostle says it has.
>
> (120)

Theodore contrasts this emphasis with what an allegory tries to do:

> These [interpreters] are very eager to reverse the senses of the divine Scriptures, to appropriate everything posited there and create some silly fables on their own. And, in their foolishness, call such an "allegory." They thereby twist the apostle's [understanding of the] term, as though they were empowered to set aside the whole understanding of divine Scripture on the grounds that the apostle affirms that [these things are asserted] "by way of allegory."
>
> (120)

Theodore briefly sums up what he believes to be what Paul actually means by "allegory" in the present context: "This is [what] (Paul) means by 'what is said by way of an allegory.' He calls an allegory the comparison that can be made between what happened long ago and what exists at present" (121).

The Antiochene emphasis upon the historical was doubtless heightened by the emperor Julian's attack against the historicity of the Gospels. Julian claimed that the Gospels were wholly like the pagan myths that have no historical bases and should be interpreted as an opportunity to discover the universal, spiritual truths hidden in them. Unfortunately very little has survived of Diodore and Theodore's heated opposition to Julian's claim.[2] But they certainly recognized the inherent danger involved in removing the historical basis of their Scriptures. Theodore also realized that, since God is the Lord of history, then what he has revealed must be historically true. This made Theodore aware of, and sensitive to, any attempt to weaken the real historical basis of the Bible, as he doubtless believed an allegorical exegesis was unwittingly doing. An imaginative projection may be inspiring but it has no basis whereby it can be critically substantiated. The inability of exegetes in his day to prove the messianic claims they were making about the psalms may explain why Theodore was so adamant in restricting the number of messianic psalms to four. It is interesting to note here that Rudolf Bultmann's observation (1984), that the Antiochene emphasis upon *historia* may be derived from the Christian faith conviction that their religion is historical, appears quite insightful.

Theodore's spirited rejection of allegory does not mean that he excluded every kind of spiritual interpretation. He doubtless accepted Diodore's explanation of what is meant by *theoria* (seeing the actual spiritual fulfillment of a text) and *allegoria* as these relate to *historia*:

"We do not object to *anagogē*[3] [a search for a higher meaning] and a more lofty *theoria* ... For *historia* does not exclude a more lofty *theoria*. Rather [*historia*] is the basic substructure for higher insights. This alone must be held to, lest *theoria* be ever looked upon as subverting that upon which it is founded. For such would no longer be *theoria* but *allegoria*" (Diodore of Tarsus 1980: xcii). As Diodore has done here, Theodore grants that a psalm may reveal a prophetic outcome that God will bring to pass in the future, and that Scripture readily admits the presence of types. For instance, Psalm 8 is considered to be truly messianic; Adam to be a true type of Christ; baptism and the eucharist to be anticipating a future heavenly life. So, in addition to conceding the legitimate usage of metaphorical language and other figurative kinds of speech, Theodore also approves of some spiritual interpretations, but within strict parameters.

For a messianic psalm and a type to be interpreted as truly valid in a Christian sense, Theodore requires that both the psalm and the future event that it points to – and the same is true of a type and its archetype – must be explicitly acknowledged as being actual persons, places, or events whose relationship is historically verified in and by the Scriptures. This can be used as a reliable standard because God who is the God of truth has revealed these to be "organically" bonded to each other as a seed is to its flowering plant:

> The God of the Old and New Testaments is one and the same as the primordial God who is the Master and Creator of all things. He guided the events of both former and present times with one end in view. He had resolved from of old to make known the future age (*katastasis*) whose beginning He had determined [would occur] in accordance with His plan for Christ our Lord ... Thus by comparing the two [states], we should know how boundless are the benefits that we are going to receive.
>
> (Theodore of Mopsuestia, *Commentary on Jonah*,
> *PG* 66: 185)

As regards a type, Theodore requires that it must not merely point to the existence of its archetype, but also be similar to it, in a truly inferior, imperfect sort of way. Theodore describes this when he observes how the Letter to the Hebrews distinguishes between the Jewish and the Christian sacrifices on the basis of how a shadow differs from an icon (or image):

When one sees a shadow, one may know that another reality exists. But one cannot point out its distinguishing elements. For while the shadow shows the close proximity of an entire body, there cannot be a shadow without a body. But it does not portray the body that it is revealing – which is what an image is naturally fitted to accomplish. For when an individual sees an image, one knows who is being represented because the likeness is exact, that is, on the likelihood one knows this one. However, one can never know whose shadow is represented. For the shadow has no representative likeness with the body from which it comes.

(164)

The same outlook is expressed when Theodore points out how Psalm 8:2 is fulfilled by Matthew 21:9, where the phrase "From the mouth of infants and nursing babies" is applied

in the case of our Lord and is, in fact, fulfilled when at his entrance into Jerusalem, little children ran up to him with palm branches and olive leaves, shouting: "Hosanna in the highest, blessed are you who come in the name of the Lord." What is said about Christ is applicable to what [the prophet] has uttered in the present psalm. He also condemns those Jews of a rebellious spirit who are not afraid to attack clear prophecies. So the blessed David, [inspired] by the grace of the Spirit, sought to merge here the prophecy affirmed about Christ with those events spoken of above where he was honored – [a passage] that no one doubts pertains to him.

(81–2).

Stylistic techniques

When applying his literal, rational, and historical exegetical method to a text, especially to authentic prophecies and types, Theodore also employs techniques that he most likely learned from his days in Libanius' rhetorical academy.[4] A few citations will highlight his usual attitude:

[The task] of a commentator at this point is to consider, as much as one can, those passages that most find difficult to interpret, whereas a preacher will speak about things that are clear – though he may sometimes find some superfluous matters useful. Yet when explaining his [position], he ought, nevertheless, at the same time to speak concisely, if his explanation cannot be made clearly without a lot of words . . . For it is the task of an interpreter, especially one who is accurately explaining [the text], not only to affirm what he says with authority but also to reject through his words the contrary opinion.

(95–6)

This is reiterated in his comment on how he will interpret a psalm:

So when I interpret a psalm, I fully respect its text, only taking care, as is my custom, to state briefly the exact meaning that a word has. I first state, as is my custom, its argument – [a step] that does not differ, as you know, from what I have said in my introduction.

(79)

Theodore's almost rationalistic outlook may seem to bolster those who venture to hold that the Antiochenes were Aristotelians. Yet this is difficult to confirm other than that they may have been exposed to Aristotle's teaching on logic and the virtues in Libanius' academy and in the cultural milieu of that day. As regards Theodore's attitude toward the pagan philosophies, he attacked Origen for introducing Stoic exegesis into the Scriptures. He is also caustic about pagan philosophical thinkers when he includes them among those whose works are to be renounced at baptism as being dangerous: "Angels of Satan are also those who under the guise of philosophy have devised the dangerous teachings of the pagans and so corrupted many that they do not adhere [any longer] to what our religion affirms" (223). Like the fathers of his day, Theodore regarded philosophers as the defenders of paganism. In his study on what philosophers may have influenced Theodore, R. Norris has uncovered traces of some Neoplatonism, most likely coming through Nemesius. But he concludes that "Theodore is not a Neo-Platonist and this fact is nowhere more evident than in his emphasis on the practical, as opposed to the contemplative, reason" (1963: 136). From what has been seen, Theodore's rational bent appears to be due more to his own personal intellectual proclivity, as it has been molded by a superior rhetorical training and by a firm commitment to the Antiochene tradition.

4
EXAMPLES OF THEODORE'S EXEGETICAL METHOD

To exemplify how Theodore applies his exegetical method, we will first examine his Genesis commentary. He wrote at least one commentary in response to either Augustine or Jerome, regarding whether Adam had been created immortal, and in what sense Adam was the cause of an inherited sin. The Fall of Adam had become an important issue at the beginning of the fifth century, mainly in the West, because it raised such questions as what kind of sin is removed when infants are baptized and how the Greek text of Romans 5:12 ought to be translated: whether as "in whom all have sinned" or as "inasmuch as" or "because" all have sinned. Theodore argues that Adam was originally created mortal and that Christ's humanity is the first to experience immortality. Since immortality is so closely involved with his understanding of salvation, this was not a minor disagreement over how to rightly interpret the creation story. Theodore bases his argument on what the Genesis account actually states. In opposition to the allegorists who interpreted Adam, paradise, and the serpent in a spiritual way, he insists that Adam is a historical figure and that any allegorical interpretation is foolishness:

> For by so entangling the historical narrative [with extraneous material], they no longer possess a historical narrative. Since this is a fact, let them assert what is their source for declaring who was the first man to be fashioned and in what way the disobedient (Adam) exists and how the sentence of death has been introduced . . . Where, therefore, have they derived this knowledge that they have accepted? How can they say that they have learnt to speak thus from the divine Scripture?"

(120–1)

As regards those who claim that Adam was immortal and lost immortality by sinning, Theodore appeals over and over to what Scripture states:

> For God does not say to those who are wholly mortal by nature that "You will be mortal," but that "You will surely die" (Gen. 2:17), thus threatening to introduce the reality of death, except that He has postponed its actualization according to His customary kind way [of acting] . . . [This does not mean] that humans then became mortal but rather that they have incurred the sentence of death because their transgressions made them worthy [of this].
>
> [God] did not use the word "earth" [here], as those most wise defenders of original sin do, those confused fathers [preoccupied] with sin and who depict [Adam] as an immortal being who is now receiving the sentence of death for the first time. But the divine Scripture has revealed that this condemnation confirms [the fact] that [Adam] is mortal by nature.
>
> (89–90)

Theodore argues even further:

> But it is most insane to conceive of such a view, as it is evident that [God] knew that he was going to sin and that he was, therefore, assuredly going to die. How utterly lunatic is it to believe that God first made him immortal for six hours – for such was the time period from his fashioning from the earth on the sixth day up to his committing sin – and then, after he ate contrary to the divine command, [God] expelled him from paradise and destined him because of his sinning to be mortal. Surely, if He had wanted him to be immortal, why did He not intervene by blocking his sin, so as to prevent him from being so sentenced? Why too did He not change the immortal state of the devil, the source of all evils, into a mortal one?
>
> (86)

As regards the question of what was the effect of Adam's sin, Theodore points out that those holding that Adam's sin has been transmitted to all his descendants have introduced a novel teaching. For it portrays God as a vindictive kind of God who "condemned Adam to be mortal and, because of his one failure, punished him and all those not yet born with death" (87). He insists that God does not punish one for the sin of another. For sin is due to one's own failure: "God does not, as some erroneously declare, punish one for another's failure, but everyone is going to receive a reckoning for his own faults" (87). Theodore also inquires why the just, such as Abraham, Moses, and the prophets, are punished. He responds to his own question: it is because all have been created mortal.

> Therefore, this [clause] "even to those whose sins are not like the evil deeds of Adam" signifies that death rules over all who have in any way sinned. Although the [specific] kind of Adam's sin and that of all others are not the same – [suggesting that] all those born afterwards did not have to die – but, because they have sinned in some way or other, they have all received the sentence of death. For death is decreed as a penalty not for any one or other sin but for all sin.
>
> (91)

Theodore is insistent that all humans have sinned, except for Christ. This is the reason why his humanity was chosen to be the dwelling of God's Word and the mediator who would reconcile all to the Father. Theodore locates this tendency to sin within human mortality. He writes: "As long as we are living in this world in a mortal and changeable nature, it is now no longer possible [for us] not to have a movement contrary to the will of God" (Tonneau 1949: CH 5.17/124–5[1]); and "Even if we make a real effort at being virtuous, it is not possible for us to be altogether without sinning many times. For without willing these, we are forced to fall because of the weakness of our nature" (Swete 1880: 147).

Adam and Christ as heads of human existence

To understand Theodore's position on the effect that Adam's sin had upon humanity and all creation,[2] we need to consider how he interprets Paul's assertion that Adam is a true "type of Christ" (Rom. 5:14). This will exemplify how he seeks theological meaning in the typical/archetypical relationship between Adam and Christ's humanity. Theodore's interpretation of the Genesis story was probably influenced by the first two chapters of Colossians (especially 1:15–17): "(the Son) who is the image of the invisible God, the firstborn of all creation because in him were created all things in heaven and on the earth, visible and invisible . . . And he is before all things, and

26

all things are bound in him." It appears that Theodore saw that these archetypal roles of Christ's humanity also apply to Adam as the type. For both serve as heads and bonds of the universe and images of God. As discussed above, when the Scripture relates two realities to each other in a typical way, they are seen to be similar to one another, but with the archetype completing and fulfilling its type. The first role that Adam was called to play in creation and salvation was to be the head of mortality, not merely in the sense he was the first human to be created but that in some "organic" sense others are bound to him as a head is to its body: "Adam is the one who has begun the present life for all. We all are thereby one human being by reason of our nature. For each of us fulfills a membership role, as it were, in common" (119). The same can be said of Christ in the flesh as the archetype, not merely because he is the first to become immortal but also because all those who come after him can share in this existence and become members of his Body:

> So also Christ is the one who has begun the future life, with all sharing in a common way in his resurrection and, after his ascension, in his immortality, seeing as we have become one with him. For each of us has a communal membership role with him due to our actual resemblance [to him].
>
> (119)

Adam and Christ as the bonds of the universe

Not only are Adam and Christ *qua* man the true heads of existence, one mortal and the other immortal, but they are also the bonds of the universe. This helps to substantiate the view that the "bodies" of which they are the heads are much more than a mere metaphor. Theodore holds for a "natural" kind of unity between humans and the rest of creation:

> For [God] made [Adam] to be a being composed of an invisible, rational, immortal soul and a visible mortal body. His soul possesses a likeness to the invisible [angelic] natures, while his body is closely akin to the visible [material] beings. For God willed to gather all of creation into one "reality," so that, though constituted from different natures, creation might be gathered into this one bond.
>
> (Sachau 1869: Fol. 22a/Latin: pp. 7–8)

Theodore explicitly calls this "reality" a body: "God made the whole of creation one cosmic 'body,' containing all things, both visible and invisible" (92).

When Adam sinned, this idyllic world of harmonious union came to an end. Adam no longer served as the divinely appointed "way" for creatures to know, serve and worship God: "The [human] soul became detached from its body, and [his role as] the bond uniting creation to himself was dissolved. The intellectual natures were consequently angered at this turn of events and were no longer friendly toward us" (Swete 1882: 268). When the angels

> regarded everything as hopeless and nourished a growing antipathy for us [. . .] The Lord said that He would restore us by raising us up and making us immortal, so that no one should ever fear that the common bond [uniting] creation would ever again be changed and be dissolved . . . Then [our role as] the universal bond will remain [secure] with no possibility of a future dissolution, and thus our friendship with creation will remain unbroken.
>
> (92–3)

It is evident that Theodore's teaching on Christ as the bond of the universe flows from what he believes to be the Pauline statements on how Christ in the flesh will recapitulate everything and unite all once again to the Father:

> But after death was introduced because of our sinning, there occurred a dissolution of both elements; for the soul was separated from the body, and the body when detached underwent a total disintegration. The bond uniting creation was thereby dissolved. [God] later "restored" or rather "recapitulated" in Christ everything in the heavens as well as on earth by making, as it were, a certain bonded kind of renovation and reintegration of all creation through him. For by making his body incorruptible and impassible by his resurrection and returning it to its soul in an immortal state, so that it can never again revert to a corrupt state, [God] was seen to have restored His bond of friendship with all creation. This was much more fully achieved in Christ, with every creature esteeming us. For God the Word was dwelling [in our nature], with all convinced that the divine nature manifests itself through him because of His inhabitation. Therefore He termed this to be "a restoration of all" because all things are gathered into

28

one, with [all] seeking this oneness through a harmony among themselves. For the Maker intended [this to be so] from of old and from the beginning fashioned everything for this end that He might now bring this to pass with the greatest of ease through Christ. This will happen in the future age when all humans and spiritual powers will look to him in the way that God intends and will then acquire a firm, harmonious peace among themselves.

(121–2)

Adam and Christ as the chosen images of God

Once again we have seen how Theodore has discovered a true typological relationship existing between Adam and Christ's humanity. Both have a real bonding role to play in creation, but with Christ's far surpassing Adam's first role because he provides a lasting reintegration of creatures in a perfect, peaceful union with God. We turn now to the third salvific role that Adam and Christ's humanity play in salvation. Since both are designated by Scripture as special images of God, Theodore accepted this as God's revealed word on how He is to be known by His creation. In Patristic times, the notion of "image" was understood in two major ways. The first argues that, since God is transcendently spiritual, humans can image him only in spiritual ways. Then some, drawing upon insights gleaned from Neoplatonism, were able to explore and fully justify a Christian form of mysticism. Theodore, however, emerged as the foremost proponent of a second viewpoint, which saw a concrete, visible aspect that was essential to God's revealed message about how Adam and Christ's humanity are God's image.[3] First he derides the former view:

> I am amazed, however, by those who have accepted this [as referring] to the divine nature. First of all, they do not pay attention to the fact that the blessed Moses is speaking about a human being when he states: "God made him to be His image" (Gen. 1:26); as also does the blessed Paul: "A man ought not to veil his head, seeing that he is the image and glory of God" (1 Cor. 11:7). This would never have been asserted of human beings, if this were peculiar [only] to God. Even more so they have not realized that every image, as long as it is seen, reveals what is not seen. Therefore, it cannot be that there ever exists an image that is not seen.

(123–4)

The chief purpose of image, in Theodore's understanding of how the Scripture views "image," is functional. For an image helps one to recall and reveal someone who is absent, in order to cherish someone's else memory: "For generally speaking, images are clearly made by those who intend to [show] either honor or affection, so that they who can still see may possess a memento of those who are no longer seen" (124).

Theodore appears then to have interpreted the Genesis (1:26–27) statement about Adam being created God's image in light of Colossians, which affirms Christ to be the bond of the universe, as well as the visible image of the invisible God:

> [The Genesis author] reveals, by repeating his statement of how the human being is the most important creature because he is [made] in God's image . . . because of his constitution wherein all beings are collected, in order that they may have access to God through him as the image of God, when they fulfill the laws that are decreed here regarding their service to him. They are reconciled to the Legislator by their care for this one. For since God needs nothing and is invisible, they offer the honor due Him by being useful to him who is in need and visible to all.
>
> (Sachau 1869: Fol. 29a/Latin: p. 18)

Adam, however, is not faithful to his task of being the image of God in creation. It is Christ's humanity that will be the perfect image who will restore the full dignity of God's image and enable all those who follow his lead to become immortal: "We were from the beginning [made] in God's image. Yet we lost this honor by our failure, but we have now received the honor of a [restored] image by the gift of God, and because of this we have become immortal and will dwell in heaven" (Tonneau 1949: CH 12.21: 356–7).

Isaak August Dorner (1863–66) recognized the importance of "image" for understanding Theodore's thought regarding human nature and salvation. However, he was limited because of the works available to him. Much more can be said about Adam and, above all, Christ's role in manifesting the invisible God. In commenting on Colossians 1:15, Theodore insists that the role of image applies to Christ's humanity, for he is the visible image in whom the invisible God dwells:

> Yet we see that [God's] invisible nature [dwells] in him *qua* image in that he is united to God the Word and will judge all the earth

when he appears in the future age, as rightly befits his nature, arriving from heaven with great glory. He will clearly fulfill the role of [God's] "image" for us because we all believe the divine nature in whom the fullness of creation is restored [dwells] in him as His "image," although we do not consider that his authority to judge belongs to his visible nature.

(123)

When Theodore speaks of the "Son" as God's visible image in Colossians, he holds that this refers to Christ's humanity. This is clear from his commentary on how Christ *qua* man is "the firstborn of all creation":

Some very learned people have added that [the phrase] "the invisible image of God" is affirmed of the divine nature, since the one "firstborn" could be neither seen nor accepted as applying to humanity. For they would rightly discern that this [title] cannot be applied to the divine nature. But if the "firstborn" were just a creature, he ought then to be rightly called the "first-created." But if they say that he has been "begotten," there will apparently be great confusion about this, since the uncreated One is also said to be the "firstborn of creatures." For the one who is said to be the "firstborn" can certainly be spoken of as being the firstborn for those who essentially preserve their likeness to him. The apostle clearly reveals this, when he says to the Romans: "He predestined those He foreknew to become conformed to the image of His Son, so that he might be the firstborn among his many brothers" (Rom. 8:29). He clearly affirms that he is their firstborn brother. And those who are conformed to him according to the likeness that they have with him from God, rightly consider him to be their firstborn, as he is pre-eminent in this regard. For he did not say that they are "sons who are conformed," but "sons of the image," [thus] clearly speaking about the Son's image as it refers to his visible nature. But they question how the assumed man can be seen to be the "firstborn of all creation," because he is not before all creation, but has accepted being so in the final days. They do not understand that [the term] "firstborn" is said not only in a temporal sense but also frequently in the sense of being specially honored, since [the term] "firstborn" is also said of those born after him. One born prior to [an individual] who has been specially honored certainly [can be said to] come after

31

him. This is both verified by natural reason and approved by the divine Scripture.

(124)

Theodore exemplifies how Christ's humanity can fulfill his image function in regard to God the Word in a lengthy quotation that has survived. He likens Christ to the honor paid to the image of a king or emperor, which is reverenced within a city because of the way it is meant to symbolically represent the king's presence. Since this likeness is cited as proof of Theodore's heretical outlook, it is quoted now at length:

> So too those rulers who have their image [mounted] within the cities are thought, through the cultic adoration [shown them], to be honoring the images of those [leaders] who are not present but are to be treated as being present.[4] Both of these [roles] are fulfilled by Christ. For all his followers who seek after virtue and are prepared to fulfill their obligations toward God love Him and greatly honor Him. Even though His divine nature is not seen, they can fully express their love for Him by means of the one who is seen by all, with all judging that they see [God] through [his humanity] and are always [able to be] present to Him.
>
> And so [his followers] bestow every honor upon him as the imperial image, since the divine nature is in him and is seen to be in him. For if the Son is said to dwell [in him], then the Father is also with him. For [the Father] is believed by everyone to be in every way inseparable from the Son. The Spirit is not absent, because He also came to [Christ in the flesh] at the moment when He anointed him and is always with the assumed one. It should not be surprising to all those pursuing virtue that the Father is said to be with the Son: "For we will come, both I and the Father, and we will make our mansion with him" [John 14:23]. All are certain too that the Spirit is inseparable from [the Father and the Son].

(141)

From the above examination of how Theodore has specifically applied his exegetical principles to passages in Scripture, we see not only how consistent but also how very illuminating has been his treatment. His first and primary aim has been to determine what the text states and then to justify his own interpretations by means of a clear-sighted and rigorous use of critical reason. He believes that the historical narratives in the Scriptures are reporting actual facts involving real, existing people. This has enabled him to take a strong stand regarding the original state of Adam and his role in introducing sin and death into the world. He believes that Adam was originally created mortal and, because of sin, kept humanity in a mortal state that left human beings prone to sin. For, being the head of human mortal existence, he affected all those, humans and non-humans, bonded to him by nature. He was responsible for keeping all who are born in a state that, although not sinful in itself, was imbued with sin. To show how he believes that God had intended from the beginning to lead all sinful humanity and all creation to a union with Himself, Theodore skillfully portrays this through his clear treatment of how Adam and Christ are typically and archetypically related to each other as the heads of a mortal and immortal existence, as the bonds of the universe and as the specially chosen images of God. These roles highlight how Christ's humanity functions in unitive and revelatory ways in salvation. Christ not only reveals the existence and will of God but also unites all creation within his humanity and serves as the way for all to be united to God. But, if all creation is bound to Christ's humanity as members of a body to its head, the question then arises how Theodore understands the union and unity existing between Christ's humanity and the Word of God.

5

GOD'S INDWELLING OF GOOD PLEASURE

Theodore describes the unified relationship that Christ's humanity possesses with God the Word as an "indwelling of good pleasure in one *prosōpon*" (130). He means this as a way to solve the dilemma he faced on how to express the unity of two natures in one "person." He blends a scriptural description with a common Greek word for "person." He was keenly sensitive here to the task of steering between two extremes. First, he had to explicitly reject the opinion of Paul of Samosata: "An angel of Satan is Paul of Samosata, who says Christ our Lord is a mere man and denies that the Only-Begotten [Son] who exists before the ages is a divine person (*qnōmā/hypostasis*)" (165). The other extreme he sought to counter was the christological stance of Apollinaris, his primary christological adversary in the late fourth century:

> An angel of Satan is also Apollinaris who undermines our [faith] confession in the Father, Son and Holy Spirit. Under his outward guise of orthodoxy, he has rendered our salvation incomplete, when he asserts that our intellect (*nous*) has not been assumed and does not participate as the body does in the reception of grace.
>
> (166)

Apollinaris had argued logically that, since two substances cannot become one, the Word of God must have assumed the rational soul of Christ, thereby effecting a true union of the divine substance with an incomplete human nature. Theodore rebukes this unsophisticated attempt by Apollinaris to say that the resulting "person" is fully human as well as divine: "The one born of the virgin is not the God from God [who is] consubstantial with the Father; unless perhaps He is that [rational] 'part' (the *nous*) of the one born, as [Apollinaris] calls the Deity, [regarding Him] as that 'part of Christ' [when he acts] in inferior [non-divine?] ways" (150).

34

For his part, Theodore counters the charge by the Apollinarians that he teaches that Christ is a mere man: "For [Christ] is not merely God and not merely man, but is truly in both of them, being by nature also God and also man" (218). Although Theodore can easily assert this, he is still faced with the predicament of how to express a true unity of the Word and Christ's humanity that preserves at the same time the complete integrity of Christ's two natures, especially the activity of Christ's human free will. This latter role is fundamental in Theodore's theological synthesis. For Theodore insists that Christ's free human actions have an essential role to fulfill in God's plan for salvation. Christ is viewed as being a true mediator, being truly man as well as truly God, but, to fulfill his mediating role as a human, Jesus had to freely – together with the Spirit's graces – live a sinless life from the moment the Word dwelt within his nature at his conception. So, if Apollinaris were correct in assuming that the Word replaced Christ's rational soul, then Jesus would not have been humanly free to play his human role in salvation:

> Therefore, if [Christ in the flesh] has not received a [rational] soul but rather it was the Deity who conquered, then nothing he did would benefit us. For what advantage would there be for the perfection for our way of living by having the Deity [acting] as the human soul? For then our Lord's struggles would seem to have no advantage for us, but rather to have been [accomplished] for the sake of show.
>
> (142)

Theodore also cites Luke's statement about Jesus growing in age, wisdom, and grace before God and other humans as evidence that supports his conviction that Jesus truly possessed a human intellect:

> For these two schismatic sects [the Apollinarians and Eunomians] are aware that this [Lucan] testimony is contrary to their teaching when the latter asserts that [the Word] did not assume a soul, and the former that He assumed a soul but not a *nous*. If there should be anyone who asserts that there exists a human soul without a *nous*, how then did Jesus grow in wisdom? Does he maintain that the Deity grew in wisdom? Not even these are so rash to assert this to us in their foolishness. Is it not clear that the "Body"[1] has grown in wisdom? For he has clearly assumed a rational soul, as he was able to grow in wisdom by acquiring this in his *nous*.
>
> (156)

Theodore's rejection of a substantial and operational mode of union

Theodore categorically excludes the possibilities that the Word and Christ's humanity can ever be united in either a substantial or an operational[2] way:

> For, if we learn how the indwelling takes place, we will know both its mode and its modal difference. Some declare that the indwelling [of the Word] has occurred in a substantial way, and others in an operational way [. . .] But to say that God dwells in a substantial way is wrong. For then one would be restricting His substance to only those in whom He said that He would dwell, [meaning] that He will be distant from all others – which is absurd to say about an infinite nature who is present everywhere and limited by nothing. So, if one states God is present everywhere by reason of His substance, one [must] also attribute His indwelling to all, not merely to humans but also to irrational and inanimate beings, [that is] if we maintain that He dwells by means of His substance. Both of these [interpretations] are clearly false. For to say that God dwells in all [in this way] is to assent to an outright absurdity, and to attribute substance to Him is not applicable. Therefore to say that the indwelling occurs by reason of substance should be [taken] as utmost folly. Someone can also assert the same about [God being present] by means of His operational activity. For His operational presence would again be limited to only those [experiencing His power]. How then will we account for the fact that God foresees all things and [providentially] governs all things and acts upon everything in a way that properly accords with [each] or what also fits and consistent [with this], [acting] through those who communicate God's activity to the universe? For, since He endows all things with the power for each to be its own self and to work according to its own nature, we [can] say that He does dwell in all things. Thus we can clearly state that it is in neither a substantial nor an operational way that God has effected these kinds of indwelling.

(129–30)

To obtain a clearer understanding of what Theodore means by a "union of indwelling," we must seek the answer in the New Testament. For this is always the source from which he draws out his understanding of reality. He appears to be especially indebted to John's Prologue, the baptism accounts, and the story of the Transfiguration as well as the first two chapters of Colossians, for both the language and the reason why he speaks of the union as an "indwelling of good pleasure as in His Son." For instance, he believes that it is particularly significant that, immediately after John declared that "the Word was made flesh," he asserts that "He dwelt among us" (John 1:14):

> So, if the statement "The Word was made flesh" is said [to connote] some change, how then is [the phrase] "He dwelt" to be understood? For it is very clear to all that "He dwells" is different from "He is dwelt in" . . . For He dwelt in us by assuming our nature by dwelling [in it] and by dispensing everything [needed] for our salvation through him. How, therefore, did the indwelling Word of God become flesh? Clearly He has not been changed nor transformed; for [otherwise] He would not have been said to be indwelling.
>
> (136)

What then does Theodore mean by "indwelling"? He first of all points out that a reader must carefully distinguish between an indwelling in a general or universal sense and in a particular aspect of this:

> If a universal is taken in its given sense, it does not express its specific forms. Rather these are, on the contrary, different from each other by nature and degree . . . A universal term contains its specific subsets within itself. But we have to learn how to rightly qualify these specific forms. Likewise the term "indwelling" is a universal, with a particular kind of indwelling [needing] to be determined by each [specifically]. To be in agreement, therefore, upon the meaning of the term "indwelling" [in general] does not mean an acceptance of a [specific] kind of inhabitation. On the contrary, the meaning is determined by examining [the exact denotation of] the word.
>
> (Sachau 1869: Fol. 2a/Latin: p. 35)

This is what Theodore does. He specifies his meaning:

> For we do not [want to] delay [here] to draw out what we have explained at length, so as thereby not to provide any further occasion for [our] calumniators to disparage [our efforts]. For

[our aim is to point out that] God the Word has dwelt in him from the time he was fashioned in his mother's womb, and that He has dwelt in him not by reason of any general [kind of] inhabitation or grace as He is thought to be present in many, but according to a certain excelling grace whereby we say that both natures are united and that one *"persona"* (*prosōpon*) is effected by reason of the union.

(Swete 1882: 307–8)

But what is this "excelling grace" that Christ's humanity has received and how does it differ from the way that God dwells within the saints? For both kinds of indwelling are graced, although Christ's is admittedly at a higher level. To speak thus implies certainly a moral union. But Theodore insists that the Word's indwelling in the humanity of Christ is radically different because it is an "indwelling of good pleasure – as in His true Son":

Therefore, when He is said to dwell either in the apostles or generally in the just, then He dwells there as He is pleased [to do so] with the upright, just as [He does] when He is pleased with the virtuous. However, we do not maintain that the indwelling took place in [Christ][3] in this way – for we would never be so mad – but "as in [His] Son." For since He was very well pleased [with him], He dwelt [within him] in this way. What then is [meant by] "as in [His] Son"? [It should be understood] in the sense that, when He dwells [within him], He has united Himself wholly to the assumed one and made him share in every honor that [the Son] shares because he is the one in whom [God's] Son by nature dwells in such a way that He is accounted to be one person (*prosōpon*) because of his union with him. Thus He shares all power with him, so that all things will be accomplished by means of him and that He will pass judgment by examining all through him when [Christ] will come [at the end of time], but with the clear understanding that they differ according to what properly belongs to their natures.

(131–2)

Instead of appeasing his critics, such a response has only reinforced the conviction of Theodore's opponents that he was simply espousing a moral unity, or at least one that does not adequately affirm a substantial unity between the Word and Christ's humanity.

Much depends in the passage just cited on how one translates and understands the phrase "as in a s/Son." For Theodore intends this added phrase to specify what he means by "an indwelling of good pleasure." The phrase can be translated in one of two, equally permissible, ways. A noun not preceded by the Greek article is usually rendered by the generic "a," meaning here "as in a son." However, the article can also be omitted when speaking about a person. In the present case, this would mean Theodore is speaking about the "Son of God."[4] Theodore actually explains this to be so in one of his extant citations:

> Therefore, he did not say: "He spoke to us in the Son," but in [article absent] "the" son. For what is said in an absolute sense [without the article] can thereby signify both [senses], the first signifying "the true Son." I thus call the "true Son" that one who acquired his sonship by a natural generation and, in the second case, to be the one who received this [sonship] by being designated as such and who truly shares this dignity because of his union with Him.
>
> (137–8)

It would seem, therefore, if this translation is the correct one, then "an indwelling of good pleasure as in His true Son" is an allusion not merely to God's proclamation in Matthew 3:17 that "This is my beloved Son in whom I am well pleased," but also to a strictly literal translation of Colossians 1:19, "because in him [a reference to the 'Son' in v. 13] all fullness was pleased to dwell," and Colossians 2:9, "because in him dwells all the fullness of the Deity in a bodily way." If this is a correct reading of Theodore's text, this means, therefore, that Theodore's indwelling differs from all others because God was pleased to fill the humanity of Christ with the fullness (the divine *plērōma*) of God. So to translate the above phrase "as in a son," therefore, as some have done, makes no sense in the context of the passage. Rather it signifies that, even though God foreknew how Christ in the flesh would live out his life in conformity with His divine will, He totally initiated this union in which Christ's humanity is filled with the divine *plērōma* to such an extent that it is able to truly share not only in the graces of the Spirit but also in both the power and honors of the Word.

Theodore indicates in two passages how he understands what is meant by God's divine *plērōma*. Both clearly reveal why Christ's graced indwelling is so radically different from all others with whom God is well pleased:

[John] says that is "From his fullness that we have all received"; that is, that we are receiving the grace of the Spirit who enables us to receive from [Christ's] abundant riches. He is speaking here of his human nature, because he possesses all the graces and makes known the majestic nature of the One who exists in him. Because [Christ's humanity] is united to God the Word through the mediation of the Spirit, he has been joined [with Him] in a true Sonship. We, however, receive a portion of the grace of the Spirit [present] in him, and by his mediation we are made participants in an adopted sonship [and daughtership] together with him, yet we are far distant from this dignity.

(Vosté 1940: 37/26)

Theodore also understands Christ's possession of the divine fullness to be more than his role as a mediator of the Spirit's graces. As seen above in the treatment of how Christ's humanity recapitulates the universe, the divine *plērōma* refers to how Christ can be said to be filling up all that is:

"For in him all fullness was pleased to dwell." He also calls the *"plērōma* of God" the church and, indeed, all things, seeing that he is also in all things and fills all. This is clearly known [to be the sense] from what he said when writing to the Ephesians (1:22): "He gave him to be the head over the whole church which is his Body, the fullness of him who fills all in all." He says this because God took pleasure in him; that is, all fullness is dwelling in Christ, namely that He has judged it to be good to join to him all creation that is filled by him.

(125)

Theodore is clearly following what he believes to be Paul's thought, that Christ is the head of all those who belong to the Body of his church and to all the rest of creation who are bonded to his human nature. To claim then that the humanity of Christ has been graced only in a superior way to what the saints have received fails to recognize Theodore's real intent.

Before proceeding any further into how Theodore expresses the union of Christ's two natures and what he intends by this, we need a brief summation of what he intends by his "indwelling of good pleasure." For this phrase indicates that the Word has lovingly united Himself to Christ's humanity at the very moment of Jesus' conception. Theologians may seriously question the philosophical as well as theological adequacy of his language. But he is relying, as he always does, on how the New Testament both expresses and grounds the reason why Christ's humanity shares in the divine honors of the Word of God:

> For just as He is said not to be dwelling in all when He is present to all by His substance, but only in those to whom He is present by His good pleasure, so [in this sense] He can be said to dwell. But this [mode] of indwelling is not equally found everywhere but depends upon how God dwells by His good pleasure. Therefore, when He is said to dwell either in the apostles or generally in the just, then He dwells there as He is pleased [to do] with the upright, just as [He does] when He is pleased with the virtuous. However, we do not say that the indwelling took place in (Christ) in this way – for we would never be so mad.
>
> (131–2)

6

THEODORE'S UNDERSTANDING OF *HYPOSTASIS* AND *PROSŌPON*

It is always difficult to speak about who Christ is because of the uncertainty of language. For a scholar must always face the possibility that the words used to express ecumenical decrees may differ in meaning from how most understand them in a twenty-first-century context. This is especially true as regards what is specifically meant by the terms *nature* and *person*. For today many, if not most, would express the reality of a "person" in the broader way that conciliar fathers looked upon "nature." It is crucial, therefore, to know, as clearly as one can, what one's terms signify and whether they are understood in the same way by others. This is especially pertinent for Christians, who understand Christ to be a divine person subsisting in a human and a divine nature. Since this is a fundamental mystery of their faith, human language will never completely encompass this reality. Scholars are particularly sensitive to this in the present post-modern age when the severe limitation of words to convey meaning is now recognized. Thus, in order for the reader to relate accurately to what Theodore struggled so fiercely to express about how he viewed the Christ of faith, it will be helpful to reflect upon the different significances that the term *person* possesses in the present culture. Afterwards we will then discuss how Theodore understood his christological formulations.

Boethius (*c*.480–*c*.524) defined how many Christian theologians have understood the term *person* throughout the centuries as a *rationalis naturae individua substantia* ("an individual substance of a rational nature"). It is basically a metaphysical definition. Later theologians refined this by making explicit other concepts contained therein, such as "existing," "complete," and "incommunicable." The significance and relevance of this metaphysical definition is sharply etched in today's abortion controversy. For, if one accepts that there is present at conception a living mass of dynamic cells that possesses

42

its own DNA, then this definition would justify calling this "clump of cells" a living person whose existence must be respected. Many today reject this definition, partly because modern philosophers and scientists cannot deal meaningfully in a direct way with what is proposed to be an underlying substance and are unable to prove in a scientific way that this living mass is a human person. They prefer to consider a person in a more tangible way. They choose to regard a person from the external ways a person acts and speaks in a unique, rational, and free way. This provides over time knowledge on which to base a judgment of what kind of responsible agent such a person is. But this is in fact a functional approach that enables one to declare with confidence who a person is by a recognizable behavior. Such a view presumes that the inner person is capable of showing itself in external ways and that such an individual's consistent exterior way of acting is revelatory of the inner person.

Also today many choose to define a person psychologically in the sense that a person is conscious of being the same individual from the time he or she emerged from one's mother's womb up until the present, as well as being aware that he or she is not only the source of but also the one responsible for his or her free actions at this moment. It is easy to understand the confusion on the part of those who interpret the ecumenical councils' metaphysical definitions of Christ in light of their modern psychological understanding. The Word then becomes not merely the subject of attribution that justifies in a logical, grammatical way why Mary can be said to be "the mother of God," but also the subject of operations that can – without distinctions – appear to be stating that, whenever Jesus speaks, it is the Word who is actually speaking, even when he affirms that "the Father is greater than I" (John 14:28).[1]

Another modern view emphasizes how a person is and becomes such by the ways he or she relates to others. The aspect of a person being stressed here is the essential need that a person has to be with others within a community in order not only to grow as a person but even simply to be a person. In other words, a "person" is not merely an individual but one possessing a relationship to others that must be implemented in fulfilling ways. This is borne out by the deep-seated, age-old need that all have for a traditional family or clan, and a national and religious identity. For Christians, this is typified, theologically speaking, in the way the Persons within the Trinity are defined by how they relate to each other in the same divine nature. The post-moderns too point out that individuals determine who they are by the ways each differs from and relates to others. In this sense, a "person" can be described as one having necessary, essential relationships to others.

Although the next two views of a "person" are applied in a broad way to a true individual in various communal relationships, they are mentioned to round out present modern-day viewpoints. They are arbitrary legal designations. First, one can speak of a moral person, in the way a corporate group can be treated as a responsible "person" and be liable to be sued for all its harmful actions. Second, the American Supreme Court has determined in an arbitrary, legal way its Roe v. Wade and Roe v. Connor rulings that a fetus is not, constitutionally speaking, a "person" until it is viable outside its mother's womb.

Meaning of terms in the early Church

Although there was considerable fluidity as to how the basic christological terms were understood in the fourth and fifth centuries,[2] there appears to have been a growing consensus about what was intended by such terms as *ousia, physis, hypostasis,* and *prosōpon* in a theological context. Whereas Theodore does not define or discuss these terms at great length, except for a few passing comments in his surviving writings, these are sufficient in their contexts to clarify his meaning. *Ousia* (substance) and *physis* (nature) require only brief comments. *Ousia* refers to the deepest underlying substratum of an individual. *Physis* signifies an *ousia* but with its unique properties, in the major ways that a species delimits and particularizes its genus. For example, Theodore employs the word *ousia* to express the general nature or substance of the Trinity. But whenever Theodore refers to the Word's and Jesus' natures, he invariably employs the word *physis*: "For when we distinguish the *physeis* [natures], we say that the *physis* of God the Word is complete . . . And the *physis* of the man is complete as well" (135). Because Theodore understood *physis* to connote a complete, concrete nature, he was dumbfounded by Apollinaris' assertion that the Word replaced Christ's rational soul.

As easy it is to distinguish *ousia* and *physis* from each other, it is as difficult to define what is meant by *hypostasis* and *prosōpon*, not only in the theological works around the turn of the fifth century but also in Theodore. Helmut Köster points out that the term *hypostasis* differs in its connotations during this period, depending on whether it is derived from the transitive verb *hyphistamai* or the intransitive *hyphistēmi* (Kittel 1968, vol. 8: 589). If *hypostasis* is taken in a transitive sense, it signifies "subsistence" and "actualization." This is how Theodore understands *hypostasis*. But he also presumes that, since existence is not a free-standing term, it must always inhere in a concrete living being. For something has to be existing if it is to be known as existing. This realistic outlook explains why Theodore can interchange, even in the same sentence, an abstract for a concrete term. Richard Norris (1963: 209) notes that "errors using this language were in fact the common habit of his time, which was quite accustomed to references to the 'Man' in Christ." Graham Warne (1995: 59–60) expands upon this when commenting on a similar Jewish practice:

> The Hebrews used one single term to express both a concrete observable reality (to which they could readily relate), and a non-concrete, or figurative meaning . . . That which was concrete and observable provided the means whereby the non-concrete could be perceived. The human person, therefore, was characterized by function, rather than by metaphysical abstraction.

Theodore reveals how he understands the term *hypostasis* as different from nature in his remarks on how the soul and the body each has its own hypostatic nature:

> We say that the nature of the soul is one and that of the body another, understanding that each of them has a *hypostasis* (*qnōmā*) and a nature (*kyānā*) and granting that while the soul is distinguished from its body, it remains in its nature and in its *hypostasis*.
>
> (136)

Theodore enlarges upon their differences in another passage where he distinguishes between the *qnōmā* (*hypostasis*) of an animal and a human soul and their bodies. He affirms that an animal's *qnōmā* ceases to exist at death, whereas the human soul does not, because its existence is immortal:

> But this is not true for human beings. For its soul exists in its own *hypostasis* and is far superior to its mortal body. In fact the body acquires its life from its soul and likewise dies and is dissolved whenever the soul departs. But when [the soul] leaves, it does not perish, but remains forever in its *hypostasis*, because it is immortal.
>
> (160)

It is clear from these passages that Theodore understands *hypostasis* as signifying an extraneous power granting life to concrete natures and, at its departure, death ensues, unless the nature is immortal.

An interesting example may highlight Theodore's thought on this matter. It contrasts how *hypostasis* applies only to living realities. In commenting upon John's Prologue, he writes:

> Why does [John] call this One the 'Word'? We say in response that in no other instance does the Scripture employ this term 'word' in the sense of being a *qnōmā* (*hypostasis*). Here he names the Son to be the Word in [the sense of being] a *qnōmā* when he designates Him in a singular and absolute sense without [any] addition or definition.
>
> (98)

In another passage, Theodore explains why the term "word" should be understood as a personal title for the Son of God and not simply as a word present in or uttered by the rational soul:

> [The Word] was with [the Father] from eternity, being like the word that always comes forth from the soul and exists with it. Because the word [that proceeds] from the soul is seen to be something other than it, even though it exists by the soul's *qnōmā* (*hypostasis*). For it does not have its own *qnōmā*, but is seen [to exist] in the soul. But, when applying this comparison, so that we would not assume that the Son does not have [His own] *qnōmā* apart from the nature of the Father, the evangelist has briefly added that "the Word is God."
>
> (Tonneau 1949: CH 3.14, 74/75)

Theodore, therefore, carefully notes in this comparison how the Word of God differs from the "word" being uttered by the rational mind. A mental word exists in the soul that utters it, whereas the Word exists in His own *hypostasis* and shares the same nature as the Father's *hypostasis*.

By understanding *hypostasis* then as a term signifying that a nature is really existing, Theodore and later Nestorius were unable to fathom how Apollinaris and later Cyril of Alexandria could espouse the existence of only one *hypostasis* in Christ, namely that of the incarnate Word. For this would mean for Theodore – and also Nestorius and the Monophysites – that Christ has but one nature. For they could not comprehend a *hypostasis* separated from its nature. Cyril, however, understood *hypostasis* in the intransitive way mentioned above whereby it is used primarily to signify a substantial individual in a concrete way. He wanted to bring out that the Word and Jesus were truly singularly one, in such a way that what is said of Jesus can also be attributed to the Word as the subject of attribution. As later clarifications will bring out, Cyril's actual intent was to distinguish between a person as an existing, single individual and its nature, thus allowing for the possibility that there could be two natures truly subsisting in one sole substantial being. This is a distinction that Theodore failed to grasp and probably could not do so in his framework.

Theodore's understanding of *prosōpon*

Theodore's understanding of the christological terms becomes even more clouded when the discussion centers upon his principal word for "person," *prosōpon*. At the Council of Nicaea (325) *hypostasis* and *ousia* were seemingly used in a synonymous way when the fathers anathematized: "those who say . . . that [the Word of God] came to be from things that were not or from another *hypostasis* or *ousia*" (Tanner 1990: 5).[3] Theodore may have taken this to be justifying his view that *hypostasis* cannot be distinguished from "nature." So too there was a similar linking for *hypostasis* and *prosōpon* in a synodal letter that is doubtless reflecting the thought of the lost Tome for the Council of Constantinople I (381). Here the fathers professed their belief in "a single Godhead and power . . . three most perfect *hypostaseis* or three perfect *prosōpa*, so that there exists no place here for the disease of Sabellius wherein the *hypostaseis* are confused, with the result that their peculiar characteristics too are destroyed" (ibid.: 28).[4] The same coupling of these two terms is later found in the Council of Chalcedon's dogmatic declaration about the unity of natures in Christ: "The property of both natures is preserved and comes together into a single *prosōpon* and a single *hypostasis*" (ibid.: 86). These citations reveal that the fathers at Nicaea, Constantinople I, and Chalcedon considered these terms as possessing some equivalency with one another. Granted that *hypostasis* and *prosōpon* are related to each other, how then do they differ in Theodore's understanding?

Whereas one can argue that the word *hypostasis* is employed in the documents above in the metaphysical sense that seeks to affirm that the union of Christ's two natures is a substantial one, the term *prosōpon* is much more problematic, especially when the fathers at

Constantinople II solemnly decreed:

> If one accepts the one *hypostasis* of our Lord Jesus Christ in the
> following way as signifying the presence of many *hypostaseis* and
> thereupon tries to introduce into the mystery regarding Christ
> two *hypostaseis* or two *prosōpa*, and then, after having inserted two
> *prosōpa*, speaks of one *prosōpon* according to dignity, honor, and
> worship, as Theodore and Nestorius have written in their madness,
> and then falsely charges that the holy Synod in Chalcedon
> employed the phrase "one *hypostasis*" in the same sense as their
> impiety, without confessing that the Word of God is united to
> His flesh hypostatically and that, therefore, his *hypostasis* or his
> *prosōpon* is one – for this is how the holy Synod in Chalcedon has
> professed the one *hypostasis* of our Lord Jesus Christ – let such a
> person be anathema!
>
> (172)

This condemnation is clearly rejecting Theodore's stance that each
nature has its own *hypostasis* and its own *prosōpon* and that the unity
of natures is to be declared to be in one *hypostasis*. It is evident that
the fathers at Constantinople are interpreting Theodore in their own
language and framework.

Despite the conciliar negative view of Theodore's language, one
must remember that his predilection for the word *prosōpon* is not
unique to himself and can be justified as acceptable in official conciliar
documents prior to Constantinople II. But why did he regard it as the
best way to express the union? The next chapter will consider how the
two natures can be said to relate to each other in a functional, unitive
way; our present aim is to make sense of what Theodore intends by
saying:

> Likewise we say here that the substance (*ousia*) of God the
> Word is His very own, and the man's his own. For the natures
> are distinct, whereas the *prosōpon* is one because of the union.
> So too, whenever we attempt to distinguish the natures here, we
> say that the man's *prosōpon* is complete and that the divinity's is
> also complete (*teleion*). But whenever we look to the union, then
> we assert that both natures are one *prosōpon*, with the humanity
> receiving at [his] creation the divinity's honor and with the
> divinity accomplishing everything expected of him.
>
> (135)

But what exactly is this union of Christ's two hypostatic natures in one *prosōpon* (*prȩwpā* in Syriac)? It is clear that a hypostatic nature means for Theodore that a nature is really existing, that a person encountering the earthly Jesus would say that he is really human and not a god who has assumed human clothing. The meaning of *prosōpon* is not as clear-cut. For the term *prosōpon* connotes, by its very nature, the outward appearance of a "person," particularly when *prosōpon* denotes a "mask" or a "role" an actor plays in a theatrical exhibition. Theodore's enemies, however, are convinced that he is ultimately maintaining that the Word and Jesus are two independent individuals subsumed under the moral umbrella of what he calls one "person" in appearance only. Yet Theodore regards *prosōpon* as connoting, if not denoting, much more. For, if Theodore had intended to speak merely about Christ's visible appearance, he would have employed the Greek word *morphē* or *schēmā*.

Theodore's commentary on Philippians 2:5–11 expresses clearly how he understands *morphē* and *schēmā* in relationship to the common *prosōpon*. This hymn is one of the most interpreted christological passages in all of Scripture, as it portrays Christ Jesus descending from and re-ascending to heaven. Ever faithful to his exegetical principles, Theodore first establishes the theme he believes Paul is developing here. He maintains that Paul introduces the descent and the ascent of Christ in order to justify the importance of humility. In so doing, Theodore sheds light on the difference that he holds between a *schēmā* and a *prosōpon*. Because the text here is a Latin version, it is important to realize that the critical Greek text for this New Testament passage – which Theodore undoubtedly followed – reads as follows: "[Christ Jesus] emptied himself when he took the outward form (*morphē*) of a slave, coming to be in the likeness of human beings and found to be outwardly (*schēmati*) as a man" (2:6–7). Theodore's Latin translator, however, has chosen to render *morphē* and *schēmati* as *forma*.

Granted the nuances presented above, we are now prepared to understand Theodore's intent when he assigns two outward forms, that of God and that of the slave, both to Christ's *persona* (that is, his common *prosōpon*). The *persona*'s outward form of a slave reveals the nature responsible for Jesus' external humble deeds, while that of God (who by His nature is incapable of acting in humble ways) gives His divine blessing to the statement that all must practice humility to attain salvation. Thus, although the two forms or external ways of acting are different from one another, they are, nevertheless, attributed to and united together in the one *prosōpon*. Such a viewpoint is best exemplified by the Synoptics, who portray Christ acting as one in human and divine ways. Whereas *schēmā* is indicating the present outer form that Christ as man and God may now take, it is seen to differ from the unity that a common *prosōpon* denotes, that is, the unity as it is acting as one. Its external activities mirror and reveal the inner workings of the human and divine natures. Christ *qua* man engages in humble tasks, while Christ *qua* the form of God (that is, the Word of God) is approving of humility. But both are attributed to the same reality.

Theodore may not explicitly call the unity of the above forms a substantial unity. But he clearly regards it as such, when he continues his interpretation:

> [Paul] immediately adds: "in Christ Jesus" (Phil. 2:14), thus speaking, as he customarily does, about one *persona* in a singular sense. He makes mention of two relations[5] and natures, maintaining that "the one existing in the form of God" . . . accepted the form of a slave, clearly stating that the outer form of God is one and that of the slave another, meaning thereby that one is assumed, and the other the assuming One. Lest there be any consideration given [to the possibility] that "the form of a slave" can be thought of as referring to any other than Christ, because it is [Christ] who has been the object of this [designation], [Paul] affirms that "the one who exists in the form etc." is to be understood [as referring] to Christ's *persona* . . . When [Paul] speaks, therefore, about what ought to be said of the divine nature, he has joined together in one and the same *persona* what properly belongs also to [Christ's] humanity, in order to enhance his humility.
>
> (110–11)

In taking this stance, Theodore is convinced that he is only repeating Paul's teaching:

> For we have learnt from the apostle that there is an inner and outer man, and state their unity by combining the inner and the outer in a common way. We do not call them by a simple term, as if they are united in the same[6] *hypostasis*. Rather we say that there is one *prosōpon* and affirm these two are [united] as one.
>
> (136)

Theodore's three analogies

Theodore recognized that his assertion about there being in Christ two *hypostaseis* (real existing natures) with two *prosōpa* (their natural powers to reveal themselves outwardly) in one common *prosōpon* is difficult to grasp. In fact, it may strike one as unintelligible, if not utter foolishness. For how can two become one? Theodore answers the dilemma by presuming that, if two different natures can manifest themselves as one in a visible way, then they must be inwardly functioning together and are truly one. This is certainly the way that the Synoptic evangelists depict Christ as acting as one in human and divine ways. Theodore does not appeal to this explicitly in his extant writings; he does, however, offer three analogies – two of these from Scripture and a third from the soul–body relationship – to illustrate, if not explain, how two *prosōpa* can become one.[7]

In the first example, Theodore notes how Christ's humanity has been described in John's Gospel (John 2:19–21) as the Temple in whom the Word has dwelt from the first moment of his conception and will continue to do so forever.

> At the very moment he was fashioned, he was already assumed to be God's Temple. We cannot agree that God was born from a virgin, but we do hold that the one who is born is simultaneously the same One present in the one born and that God the Word is both the Temple and in the Temple.
>
> (149)

Theodore's second analogy likens the union of Christ's two natures to the relationship between a husband and his wife (Matt. 19:6–7), who, although two, form one body. Theodore's third analogy clearly expresses the kind of unity he is espousing. Here Theodore compares how the soul and body are mutually united to form one human being to how the Word and Christ's humanity can be united to constitute one *prosōpon*.

This third analogy must not be applied too rigorously. For the soul and body are each incomplete natures that are simultaneously united in a necessary union and result in a new nature. Since this is so, the analogy cannot be applied to the Word, seeing that He exists already before the union and has entered it freely, without a new nature resulting. Nevertheless, the soul's union with the body is aptly suggestive of how a spiritual reality can function together with its bodily partner in an organic-like unity. Theodore affirms this relationship thus:

> Since we speak about a human being as made up of a soul and a body, we maintain that the soul and the body are two natures but one human being that is composed of both . . . So too the soul is united to its body, with a single human being resulting from [the union of] both. There still remains a difference of natures, with the soul being one and the flesh another. The former is immortal; the other mortal. One is rational, and the other irrational. Yet both are one human being. Each by itself is never absolutely and properly said to be a human being, though perhaps with some added notion, such as a human being with an inner and outward [self]. But [such a partial self] is not human in an absolute sense, but [a self] with an inner and an outer [aspect], so that one [the soul] may appear to be inwardly a human being and the other outwardly so. We also speak in a similar way about Christ our Lord, O illustrious one, that the form of the servant subsists in the form of God. Nor is the assuming One the assumed one, nor is the assumed one the assuming One. The unity, however, between the assumed and the Assumer cannot be separated, seeing that it is incapable of being sundered in any way.
>
> (153–4)

Theodore is convinced that his centering the union of Christ's natures in one *prosōpon* maintains the integrity of both within a true unity. He designates this as an "exact union" (*sunapheia akribēs*), which his adversaries interpreted as being a Stoic phrase signifying the combination of two independent subjects within what is truly a moral union. But, in her usual methodical way, Luise Abramowski (1981: 70–103) has assembled numerous passages in the early fathers where the term *sunapheia* expresses their understanding of the unity present in the Trinity and christology. Theodore's other term *akribēs* can be interpreted as meaning "exact," "accurate," "precise," "complete," and "strict." There is no question, at least in Theodore's own mind, that his phrase expresses an authentic, substantial kind of union. For, if this prosopic union were dissolved, then Jesus would be seen to be merely a human being:

> Clearly, therefore, we do not think that the divine nature of the Only-Begotten was born of a woman since she received her

fashioning from Him. [The fathers] do not say that she [gave birth] to the One generated from His Father before all time, since [the Son] is always from Him and eternally present with Him. But they follow the sacred Scriptures that affirm the natures in different ways, while [at the same time] teaching that there is one person (*prṣwpā*) because of the "exact union" that took place, so that they would not be thought to be dividing the perfect sharing that the assumed one [now] has with his Assumer. If, therefore, this union is dissolved, then the one assumed is seen to be no more than a mere man like us.

(161)

In summary, since Theodore regards his union of good pleasure as prior in a logical sense to the union of Christ's two natures and to any activity on the part of Christ's free human will, it is clear that he regards the Word as the One who freely causes this union to take place on what we consider to be the metaphysical level. This is where two existing or hypostatic natures combine together as one. But, when Theodore attempts to describe this unity as one reality, he cannot, like Cyril, call it a hypostatic union. For to say that there is one *hypostasis* means in his framework one really existing nature. He prefers to accept as true what he believes the Gospel accounts are affirming, that two natures acting outwardly as truly one must also do so inwardly in a mysterious way. His one common *prosōpon* may be describing the union in a functional way, but it is based on the premise that an individual reveals its inner self by how it speaks and behaves over a period of time. But even more fundamentally, he is convinced that the New Testament accounts are justifying why one can trust their functional christology as actually revealing who Christ is as a true inner "person." It is the way that many today understand what is meant by the term. So as long as one uses a title that combines the divinity and humanity, such as the "Lord Jesus Christ," Theodore has no problem in applying both divine and human attributes to this unity. We turn now to consider how Theodore explains how the one common *prosōpon* can be said to have one will, power, operation, and authority and to receive one adoration.

7

THE FUNCTIONAL UNITY OF
CHRIST'S NATURES

Theodore considered the real problem in christology to be not so much whether the unity of Christ's natures is to be centered in one *hypostasis*, on what we would call today a metaphysical level, but rather how his two natures can be rightly said to operate together as one individual. The fathers at the early councils established dogmatic formulations that they believed accurately expressed the substantial unity of Christ as a single individual. While fully recognizing the need for this kind of true personal unity, Theodore insisted that any formulation must preserve and express the full integrity of Christ's humanity, especially his human free will. He believed that Christ's humanity had an essential role to play in God's plan for universal salvation. The dilemma he faced was: how could he justify his assertion that Christ has but one will while also affirming that his human will did still function in a truly free way; and how too could he maintain only one Son of God, while at the same time distinguishing between the Word as the Son of God by nature, and Christ in the flesh as the Son by grace?

It is important to keep in mind, when interpreting how Theodore responds to the above questions, that he has never asserted that Christ is a mere man. In fact, he explicitly denies this, calling it a lie:

> [My opponents] say: "Those asserting Christ to be a pure man ought to be called *hominicolae* (those overly obsessed with Christ's humanity)." This is an open lie on the part of those who would want to say this [about us]. For no one has ever heard us say these things. I think that such an open lie cannot be [seriously] maintained, not because they are not knowingly given to lying, but because they can be so easily refuted.
>
> (128–9)

In two other instances, he is careful to distinguish: "If someone wants to ask who do I finally say Jesus Christ to be, I say: 'God and the Son of God'" (139); and "He was not merely God and not merely man, but is truly 'in both of them,' being by nature also God and also man" (163). When pressed further, Theodore will nuance how Christ can be rightly said to be God and man in his understanding of a true unity:

> When, therefore, they ask: "Is Mary the mother of the man or of God?" let it be said by us: she is both. For she is indeed [the mother of the man] by nature, and for the other by a relation. For she is the mother of the humanity by nature, seeing that a man has come from Mary's womb. But as regards Mary being the mother of God, even though God was present there when the man was born, His nature was not limited there. Rather He was willingly disposed [to do so]. Thus it is right to say that it is "both," but not for the same reason . . . The same answer ought to be given, whenever [my adversaries] raise the question: "Has God or the Man been crucified?" [The answer] is "both," but not for the same reason. For it is the latter who has been crucified, as he is the one who underwent suffering as he hung on the cross, after having been arrested by the Jews. The former [can be said to be crucified] in the sense that He was with him in the way that we have stated above.
>
> (142)

Granted that Theodore believed he was affirming a true unity when he maintains that Christ's divinity and humanity are united in one *prosōpon*, he then had to admit the presence of a common operating will on (what we would call today) the psychological level. If one can speak thus about a divine being, this would be the dimension of Christ as a person in which his one common *prosōpon* is conscious of being a responsible individual. Theodore expresses this in the following two quotations:

> The Word knew from his foreknowledge that a man would be born from a virgin without intercourse and would be inseparably united to Himself with an identical will, since [the Word] had united [the man] to Himself because [the Word] was pleased with him. He showed plainly that the man and his activity are precisely similar to His own, because [the man's] rule and power are inseparable

from His own; and the adoration [shown him] is equally the same in practice;

(143)

and perhaps more emphatically:

> When our Savior said to the leper: "I will it: be clean"; he shows here that there exists one will and one operation according to one and the same power. This takes place not on the level of nature but on the level where he was favored to be united to God the Word.

(143)

Theodore makes no effort to explain how the will of the Word and that of the humanity come together as one will. Rather he simply presumes that this takes place, as seen in his commentary on Romans 7:11:

> [Such statements about the desire to do good but ultimately doing evil] ought not to be taken as a contradiction, even though the apostle used [the phrase] "to me" equally in both of these [statements]. For he said "to me who wants to do good" as it pertains to the soul, and "yet evil is close at hand to me" to the body. Because he was speaking about two natures, he employed "to me" in both of these statements as [referring] to two distinct realities, aptly distinguished by their natures, yet being one; that is, he is speaking of these two as being one person because of the body's bonding to the soul. So also when our Lord speaks of his humanity and his divinity, he uses this "I" as referring to the common "person" (gwa *prçwpā*); and in order to let us know by this [statement] that he is not speaking about the one and the same nature, he indicates this [difference] by making distinctions.

(104)

In other words, Theodore is arguing from the way Paul uses language to assert that human and divine activities can be rightly attributed to the "ego" of Christ's common *prosōpon* as the ultimate source of this (common) activity, while at the same time being sensitive to the need to identify which of the two natures serves as the immediate instrument of this activity. He believes that every specific action must be correctly affirmed as flowing directly from its own proper nature.

Theodore, therefore, looks upon a union in one common *prosōpon* as being more than a mere moral union, at least on what we designate the psychological level, at which one's "ego" is conscious of being a true individual and acting as the ultimate subject of all of one's actions. He is convinced that his way of speaking satisfies the personal unity that the New Testament writers express when they portray Christ as both human and divine:

> The union of natures according to good pleasure specifies how both of the natures can be said to have one name, will, operation, authority, lordship, rule, dignity and an undivided power, because each of the two is said to be and is a person (*prosōpon*) by reason of [their union]. Why then is it necessary to say more? . . . But a union [effected] by good pleasure keeps the natures unmixed and undivided and makes it clear that there is one person (*prosōpon*) for both, as well as one will and one operation, with one authority and rule flowing from these . . . Since he was united to God the Word who, as we have said, was benevolently disposed towards him, this one who was born from the virgin's womb remained an undivided Temple, having the same will and the same operation with Him in all things, seeing as there is no closer unity [than this].
>
> (144)

Theodore never explores at any length, at least in his extant writings, the nature of this common will, other than that the divine and the human wills function and are one in a similar way to how the soul and the body function and are one human being. This is wise since the New Testament does not supply a detailed answer but simply states that Christ's natures are united as one in an unmixed way. He accepts this to be an unanswerable mystery, for, if one does not cease one's inquiry at this point, then a person can conclude that the Word is the subject of all of Christ's human actions, or make Christ in the flesh at least appear in one's writings to be an independent individual, uniquely inspired and graced by God. This problem of reconciling the Word's freedom with that of Christ's humanity is similar to the one that the Dominicans and the Jesuits faced, in the *De Auxiliis* dispute in the late sixteenth and early seventeenth centuries, over how to reconcile God's efficacious grace with human free will. An excessive stress upon the necessity of efficacious grace can ultimately lead to predestinationism, whereas overemphasizing human free will can nourish the belief that one is alone self-sufficient for the achievement of one's salvation. When this controversy became bitter, the Roman Curia had to intervene, requiring both sides to acknowledge the positive aspects of the other's position and await the Vatican's final decision. Needless to say, this resolution has yet to be rendered, because, similar to the union of Christ's two natures, the quandary raised by grace and free will cannot be fully answered in a rationally satisfying and convincing way. It is difficult, therefore, to fault Theodore, when he simply accepts that two natures can be distinct on one level but yet be united on another, in an analogous way to how the spiritual soul is united to its physical body.[1]

In the union of Christ's natures, Theodore recognized that, despite the gulf that exists between the two, the divine and human wills each have a particular role to play in regard to the other. First, he admits how overpowering is God's will:

> "I can do nothing, as you [can] see, by my own nature, since I am a man. I accomplish works, but it is the Father who resides in me" who does everything. For "I am in the Father and the Father is in me" (John 14:10–11). God's Only Begotten Word is also in me. It is clear that the Father who is with Him remains in me and it is He who is effecting my works.
>
> (152–3)

Theodore is insistent that this kind of assistance has remained unbroken from the time of Christ's incarnation: "Never, not even for an instant, can this form of a slave be separated from the divine nature that has assumed him. For the distinction of natures does not void the exact union" (219). Passages such as this must be kept in mind when reading others, such as the following, where Christ *qua* man is depicted as acting in a free, active way.

So, while careful not to minimize the Word's role in guiding and assisting the human will, Theodore was steadfast in his defense of Christ's human freedom, for this stands at the heart of his theory of salvation. In sharp contrast to Adam, who initially sinned and kept humanity in a mortal existence, Christ in the flesh lived a sinless life throughout and became the head of an immortal existence. So, although his humanity was specially aided because of his union with the Word and the graces coming to his human nature from the indwelling Spirit, the assumed one conquered sin and death. Theodore clearly brings out in several notable passages the role that Christ's humanity has played, and will continue to play, in God's divine plan for salvation:

Since [the assumed man] conjoined himself [to God] with an irrepressible love for the good, God the Word actively assisted his resolve. He then persevered, not yielding to [any] inferior tendency. With this kind of purposeful thinking with which God the Word actively provided him, he then pursued with the greatest ease the most perfect virtue, both by keeping the law before baptism and, after baptism, by pursuing with grace his public life. He submitted his [life] as a type for us, since it establishes for us the way to [find] fulfillment.

(133)

So, although sensitive to the initiative that the Word takes in the union, Theodore insists that Christ in the flesh can still freely act in a human way:

There is always present to me the power of operating whenever or howsoever I will want [to act]; [. . .] I also [can] act whenever I want, as there is no set time for those things to be done by me for human salvation. And just as [the Father] has the power of operating, so do I . . . For I also have the power to act in an equal way whenever I want.

(103)

Theodore, however, is careful to establish the balanced harmony that needs to exist between the voluntary involvement of Christ's humanity and the assistance of God's grace:

We will not say that this man had no voluntary role [to play]. For he preferred the good. In fact, he purposely desired to accomplish the greatest good and to hate evil. But his pure resolve was protected by divine grace, with God perfectly knowing from the very beginning what kind of person he is and, by dwelling in him, providing him with considerable cooperation, so as to strengthen him [to work] for the salvation of all of us.

(141)

The issue of the unity of Christ's two wills becomes problematic when the question is raised: can Christ be attracted to temptations? For, if Christ's human will is so allied with the Word's, how can any temptation even make him pause to consider it? Yet Theodore does not hesitate to say:

For our Lord was much more troubled in his struggles with the spiritual passions than with those of the body. But, because of his superior reasoning power, he conquered [lustful] desires. For the Deity was clearly mediating and aiding him so that he could succeed in these instances. Hence our Lord appears to be the one especially battling against these. Since he was not deceived by an avaricious longing for money nor tempted by a desire for glory, he provided no opening to his flesh and thus [could] not be conquered. So, if he had not received a [rational] soul but it was the Deity who conquered, then nothing that he did would benefit us. For what advantage would there be for the perfection of our way of living in having the Deity [acting] like the human soul? For then our Lord's struggles would appear to have no advantage for us, but rather to have been [done] for the sake of show.

(142)

In other words, Theodore is arguing here that it is important that Christ's human will be truly free to experience and resist temptations, to bring out that humans have a necessary, essential role to play in their salvation, and that the assumed man can truly be a typical model for others.

Theodore is willing, too, to recognize a development in Christ's humanity, even while he strongly insists that an inseparable union was established from the initial moment of his conception:

Up to the time of his crucifixion he was allowed to excel in virtue for our sake by relying on his own resolve, nevertheless with God urging him on in these efforts and aiding him to completely fulfill what was at hand. For [the Word] was united to him from the moment [the man] was fashioned within the womb. When [the assumed man] attained the age when humans acquire the power to discern between good and evil, he had already earlier acquired the power to discern such differences much faster than all others who [can] attain this critical power, but generally not all at the same time. For some devote themselves more quickly to the [attainment of] greater practical wisdom regarding what needs [to be done], whereas others acquire this over a longer period of time through training. What stands out in [Christ's] relationship to all others is that his [growth] occurred much more swiftly for him than it is customary for others of [his] age, yet in a way fully appropriate [to his state]. But he also possessed something greater in his relationship to others: he was not born as humans usually are in a natural way, through the union of a man and a woman, but rather he was formed by the activity of the divine Spirit.

(132–3)

As the above passages indicate, Theodore understood a prosopic union to be dynamic – one that allows for human growth in Christ without contradicting his fundamental unity with the Word:

"Jesus advanced by age and wisdom and grace before God and other humans" (Luke 2:52). For he advances "by age" with the passage of time; "by wisdom" by acquiring knowledge over time; "by grace" by pursuing virtue in ways consistent with practical and theoretical knowledge. God's grace increased his virtue, and thus he has [been able to] progress "before God and human beings" [at least] before those who see his progress. For [God] not only observes this but has also testified [to this], and works with him in what he does. Clearly he has completed a virtuous life in a more perfect way, and with greater ease, than it was possible for all other human beings. Seeing how fully God the Word foreknew what sort of person [the man] would be when He united Himself to him from the moment of his fashioning, [the Word] enabled him to cooperate with Him in a far greater way for the successful accomplishment of righteousness, by dispensing through him what [is necessary] for the salvation of all, by urging him on to more perfect [tasks] and by diminishing those struggles [affecting his] soul and body, thereby equipping him fully for a greater and more rapid fulfillment of virtue.

(134)

One Son

Theodore was keenly aware that he was being criticized for holding that there are two Sons in Christ: the Word as the Son by nature and the "Man" as the Son by grace. His opponents were doubtless reacting to such a statement as this:

I call the "true Son" that one who acquired his Sonship by a natural generation. In the second case, he is the one who has received this [Sonship] by being designated as such and who truly shares this dignity because of his union with [the true Son].

(138)

Theodore also seems to regard Christ's Sonship as similar to what other humans can obtain: "So he calls him 'Son,' not only after he has distinguished [him] from God the Word, but also because he is said to be included under the term for sonship with all others who share this sonship by grace" (139). But Theodore strongly rejects the accusation that he teaches two sons:

> They have presented their [charges] to readers, as proof of our impiety, according to their own way of thinking. One such statement is that we assert two sons. In this way they have us affirming in our work [*On the Incarnation*] that one should think and say [that we hold] two sons and that we vigorously defend this way of speaking, while clearly insisting that one must not say that two sons are asserted anywhere in Scripture. Therefore, those listening to these charges must regard them as not only inept but also weak. For it is impossible for such a [charge] to be substantiated as true on the basis of any strong, creditable argument.
>
> (149)

Although Theodore may seem to regard Christ's human sonship by grace as being on the same but superior level as other humans, he presents the difference, however, as being radical, for only the assumed man has the Word of God dwelling within his human nature:

> Since he has also shared the grace of Sonship because he has not been naturally generated from the Father, nevertheless he enjoys pre-eminence over all others. For he has acquired his Sonship from his union with Him, who has granted him a more dominant sharing in His [Sonship].
>
> (139)

Theodore spells out this difference:

> Note here how, in his understanding of "Sonship," the apostle appears to be including the assumed man with most [others], but not in the sense that he shares his Sonship just as these do, because of his similarity [with them]. For [all] have received their sonship by means of grace. But only the Divinity possesses Sonship by His own nature. However, [the assumed man's] extraordinary [gift] of Sonship clearly exceeds all other humans because of his

union with [God]. He received this when he heard this title "Son" [of God] conferred upon him . . . For he was the first one to be worthy of being designated the cause [of salvation] for others.

(138)

Although one can rightfully argue compellingly that Theodore's statements about Christ's human activity and his moral development make him too human, contrary to what a true substantial unity requires, this may be the inherent problem for any position emphasizing the full humanity of Christ. But such statements must be reconciled with what he affirms about the divine *plērōma* being bestowed upon him as the "Son of God," and about the unity found in the common "ego," as well as about his willingness to attribute human and divine statements to the same reality. We see this expressed whenever he speaks about how the Word manifests Himself outwardly as the Son of God:

For if the Word of God is the perfect Son of God by nature, having been generated by the Father, who then is the one existing outside of this nature? It is not because he makes Him outwardly present that he is said to be "Son." Rather it is because he is exactly united with God the Word that he is entrusted with the title "Son of God." It is evident that what is said of the Son of God is also understood to be applicable to the one who was assumed as complete. Nor are we forced because of this to say "two sons" . . . For we too refer to the assumed one as possessing the title "Son of God," even though he is a complete human being.

(156–7)

This ability to share in a pre-eminent way in the Sonship of God is due to the activity of the Holy Spirit:

"Christ in the flesh" is the first to be generated in the Spirit and, because of the Spirit's mediation, is united to the Only-Begotten, from whom he has received the true dignity of Sonship and will [now] communicate to us the gift of the Spirit by whom we too are regenerated and are enumerated among His children according to the measure of each one's virtue.

(Vosté 1940: 47/Latin: p. 33)

Theodore is certainly implying a true unity of Christ's humanity with the Word that surpasses a merely human union.

8

ASSESSMENT

Theodore of Mopsuestia stands out as a tragic figure in the late fourth and early fifth centuries. He possessed one of the great theological minds in the early Byzantine period, but unfortunately he is remembered as the "Father of Nestorianism." Admittedly, troubling questions have been raised about whether he has sufficiently safeguarded Christ's full divinity in his surviving writings. But, for anyone reading the selections provided in Part II, this is not as clear-cut as some think. Paul Galtier's critique (1957, esp. pp. 177–83) is still valid against those who are convinced that Theodore is justly labeled a major heretic, when he argues that Theodore ought to be judged not solely by the standard of Cyril of Alexandria's terminology and theological framework but primarily by that of the Council of Chalcedon. But, even granting that Theodore's statements about Christ's human freedom, when taken out of the overall context of his thought, may be logically pushed to the conclusion that he regarded Jesus as a truly independent individual, it is hard to justify his personal condemnation 125 years after his death, especially as he died before an official consensus was reached on how to affirm in an acceptable orthodox way the unity of Christ's natures.

From what has been highlighted in the previous chapters, Theodore can be characterized as basically a conservative biblical systematician who derived his theological teaching from what he found explicitly stated in the Scriptures. He was principally committed to maintaining the role of Christ's humanity in salvation against those he feared were overemphasizing Christ's divinity. He sought to defend what he believed to be the central roles that Christ's humanity plays in God's creative and redemptive plan for the cosmos. He focused upon the ways that Christ in the flesh sums up and recapitulates all created beings within his humanity. As such, his humanity clearly serves as the mediating link or bond with God. Also, because of his victory over sin and death, Christ has become the head of a new, immortal existence and the head of his Body, the church, enabling all those united to him, as do the members of any body to their head, to share in his exact union with the Word of God and become children of God. For, just as a body shares in its soul's power, achievements, and honors, so too do those who are one with Christ as the "Son of God." Such an understanding of how Christ's humanity recapitulates all creation offers profound insights into how Christ *qua* man can be said to stand forth as the universal mediator and the spokesperson for all creation. The question, however, regarding Theodore's christology as such is: how exactly does he unite Christ's humanity to the Word?

To express accurately Christ's functional role as the divine mediator, Theodore has relied upon language provided by the New Testament that describes how the Word was pleased to dwell in Christ's humanity from the moment of his conception. This choice of words emphasizes God's free, loving initiative in establishing the union of His Word with a human nature. Theodore may have preferred to stay with this scriptural way of referring to Christ as both divine and human, but the controversies of his day impelled him to define more exactly his position in cultural terms of his day that have serious philosophical ramifications for any christology. Since he regarded the term *hypostasis* as affirming a real existing single nature, he had to assert that, since the Word and Jesus are both really existing, then their two natures must each have its own *hypostasis*. So when one affirms there exists only one *hypostasis* in Christ, that of the Word, Theodore would interpret this to mean that Christ has but a single real nature, the divine nature of the Word. If this be so, then it follows in Theodore's understanding of how all creation is bound in Christ's human nature that every created being must also logically be pantheistically absorbed into the divine nature.

To avoid this difficulty, Theodore chose the word in his day that expresses a "person" in a functional sense. For *prosōpon* connotes, if not denotes, the outer ways that the inner person of an individual reveals itself. It presumes that there exists an underlying unity between the outer and inner person, which is fully substantiated by God's revealed Scripture. By choosing the expression "one common *prosōpon*," Theodore has shrewdly finessed the problem of how two natures can become one. He is simply stating that the outward human and divine actions of Christ truly reveal the inner workings of the human and divine natures subsisting as one. Since he could not conceive of how "person" and "nature" could be understood as capable of being separated, he saw no other way to affirm how the two can belong to the same living reality than to accept the fact that this is actually so on the substantial as well as the operational level. In other words, Christ's inner "person" reveals itself in two outward, visible ways that enable one to infer that there exists an inner mysterious unity of two natures that is not merely functional but has a real metaphysical basis. This is how the three Synoptics portray Jesus Christ in their Gospels as acting as one in human and divine ways. Paul does the same when he asserts in Philippians that the form of the slave and that of God are united in one and the same reality. Theodore, of course, has to confront the problem of identity when he interprets Christ's assertion in John's Gospel that "The Father and I are one." The same can be said in reverse for Cyril when he tries to explain how a hypostatic Person can be said to function as one in two radically different natures.

Theodore does actually express the presence of a substantial unity when he proposes a single "ego" for his "one common *prosōpon*." He justifies this on the basis of what he found in Paul's comments in Romans 7: 15–20. If one can speak analogously – according to our human way of understanding – then one can speculate as to how Christ operates on two psychological levels: i.e. on one level where the one common *prosōpon* acts as having one will that combines the divine and human wills, and on another level where the divine and especially the human nature can each will in their own natural way. In the former case, Theodore maintains that the "ego" of the common *prosōpon* can be said to possess one will and one operation and acts as the subject of unity to whom divine and human properties can be attributed. Nevertheless, when Theodore speaks concretely about this common *prosōpon*, he uses such titles as "our Lord Jesus Christ" – which denotes the union of both natures as one. Whereas he would reject the statement "the Word suffered and died" unless it were nuanced, he has no reservation in affirming this of the Lord Jesus Christ or of the assumed one or the assuming One. The use of such dual titles enables him to achieve in his writing his goal of protecting the exercise of Christ's human freedom within the union of Christ's natures. But it weakens his stance on the personal unity of Christ as a single individual.

To grasp the fundamental difference between Theodore and Cyril's christologies, one must examine how each understands the intricate relationship between a "person" and "nature" as the subjects of both attribution and operations. Probably influenced by what was traditional in his day, Theodore readily accepted the teaching that the activity of the Trinity flows immediately from the Persons' common divine nature. This points out how one can conceive of a difference between a person and that person's nature, even though the *hypostasis* of each Person in the Trinity is inseparable from their common divine nature. The situation is different in the case of Christ where the two hypostatic natures radically differ, according to Theodore, in their union within the one common "person." Nevertheless Theodore sees that the "ego" of Christ's common *prosōpon*, albeit truly the ultimate source of Christ's actions as a composite, must operate through his individual natures as the primary proximate causes of actions. In other words, Theodore has to allow a role to both the divine and especially the human nature to function freely in such a way that an action can be attributed properly to each nature as well as to the composite. His silence on how this is possible suggests that he recognized that no one can sort out how each of Christ's natures functions freely in its own way, while at the same time being controlled in a harmonious, mysterious way by the "ego" of his one common *prosōpon*.

Although one can justify Cyril's understanding of Christ's hypostatic union on Johannine and creedal grounds, there still remains an ambiguity present. As the Antiochenes and Monophysites show, one can understand Cyril's formulation in a strictly literal way, in the sense that the Word as God was really born of Mary and suffered and died. For, if there exists no significant distinction between a "person" and a "nature," then one cannot maintain that there is a difference between "person" as a subject of attribution and as a natural subject of operation. Theodore was keenly aware of such a distinction because his defense of Christ's humanity required this. For him, the New Testament way of speaking about Christ necessitated an inclusion of a human role in all of Christ's actions, even though they are effected ultimately by the Father in their common *prosōpon*. His concern, therefore, was not so much to avoid the vagueness present in such statements as "the Word was crucified" but to honor the role that Christ's humanity has contributed to the redemption of all humanity. This explains why he is so is painstaking in the care he takes to assign attributes to the correct nature that is at that moment acting.

Since Theodore died before the term *hypostasis* became the catchword for expressing the unity in Christ as a single individual and before a compromise clarification was accepted at the Pact of Reunion in 433 and at the Council of Chalcedon, one can only speculate over how exactly he would have responded to the proceedings from the Councils of Ephesus and Constantinople II. Judging from his habitual way of responding, he might certainly raise the objection, as Paul Galtier (1957) has done, of whether it is logical and also just to judge his thought on the basis of Cyril's language and theological framework. He would doubtless insist that the New Testament ought to be the ultimate authentic standard. He might be willing to concede that Cyril's stress on a hypostatic union can be argued to be present in John's Gospel. But he would very likely point out the difficulties in trying to do the same for many Synoptic passages where Jesus is depicted in very human ways. For instance, it would be hard to substitute the Word, even in Cyril's understanding, for Jesus in Luke's statement that "Jesus is said to have grown in age, wisdom and grace before God and men" (2:52).

Since Part I has highlighted how Theodore has focused upon the functional, communal, and mediating aspects of Christ's understanding of "person," one can argue that this stress can be considered as complementary to Cyril's metaphysical approach, in much the same way that the Synoptics' emphasis is balanced by John's Gospel. Both approaches, understood in the right way, can enrich one other; for Theodore's christology can enlarge Cyril's individualistic stress upon Christ as a "person" (and vice versa). But Cyril's focus is so centered on the Word's *hypostasis* as the best and only way to express the unity of Christ's nature that it becomes difficult to incorporate how Christ is the true visible image and mediator between God and His creation as well as the head of both creation and his Body the church. As the Synoptic accounts show, one must be sensitive to what Christ, humanly speaking, has done and is now doing as the resurrected Christ. In this sense, Theodore's christology can help to reveal the mystery of who Christ is as a "person" by how he has acted for others. Most Christians find the christological disputes of the past irrelevant in the twenty-first century, so they may find a functional approach far more meaningful and inspiring than knowing how to define Christ in a formalistic way. For the notion of "person" is broader than Cyril's metaphysical definition. It also includes essential functional, communal, relational, and psychological dimensions that ought to be acknowledged as acceptable ways to speak of Christ as a Person. This emphasis can be said to be the lasting legacy Theodore strove to bequeath to the Christian tradition.

Part II

TEXTS

9

GENERAL INTRODUCTION TO THE TEXTS

Few of Theodore's extensive writings have survived intact in his original Greek. The only complete work in Greek is Theodore's *Commentary on the Twelve Minor Hebrew Prophets*.[1] Considering that both his works and person were anathematized at the Second Council of Constantinople in 553, this is not surprising. In fact except for the East Syrian Church, where Theodore's memory as an orthodox biblical theologian was and still is esteemed, he has been stigmatized as a major Christian heretic.[2] When Edward Sachau (1869) published his 73-page collection of Syriac extracts, he began a process of increasing the number of Theodore's works available in modern languages. Twelve years later, H. B. Swete (1880, 1882) published a Latin translation of Theodore's *Commentary on the Minor Pauline Epistles*, with an Appendix containing, with some new additions, those excerpts found in Migne's *Patrologia Graeca*. Theodore's Pauline commentary was able, amazingly, to survive in Latin because, as Swete has observed, it was "originally either anonymous or ascribed, as we find it in our present MSS, and by all the extant writers who quote it, to S. Ambrose" (1880: li–lii). Then Alphonse Mingana (1932–33) published both the Syriac text and an English translation of Theodore's *Catechetical Homilies*.[3] This was later followed by J.-M. Vosté (1940), who published a Syriac version, with a Latin translation, of Theodore's *Commentary on John's Gospel*.[4]

No other complete work of Theodore's has come down to us. The closest is the Latin version that Robert Devreese (1939) has published containing Psalms 1–80 of Theodore's *Commentary on the Psalms*.[5] Lucas van Rompay (1982) enlarged upon this by providing a Syriac version, with a French translation, of Psalms 118 and 138–148.[6] As noted above, the largest number of excerpts, some quite lengthy, are found in Migne, Swete, and Sachau. These contain valuable passages that reveal Theodore's thought on Genesis, original sin and the incarnation, especially where he is replying to Apollinaris. K. Staab (1984) has gathered a considerable number of Greek excerpts from Theodore's commentaries on Paul's major Epistles, specifically from Romans, Corinthians, and Hebrews.[7] In the chapters to follow, I have translated from each of the above major works usually large continuous portions of texts that I consider significant for anyone seeking to understand Theodore's exegetical, christological, and sacramental thought as well as his style of writing and his customary manner of argumentation. These provide, I believe, a wider context for making a just assessment on those excerpts cited as grounds for condemning Theodore. These will allow the reader to evaluate the principal aspects of Theodore's thought in their own way.

Five other collections contain valuable excerpts: (1) those that Augusto Guida (1994) believes belong to Theodore's response to the Emperor Julian; (2) the citations that Françoise Petit (1987) has gleaned from the catenae that express Theodore's understanding of the "image of God"; (3) the fragments that William Macomber (1968) has located, expanding the number of excerpts that have survived from Theodore's Gospel commentaries; (4) a significant passage that L. Abramowski (1958) cites as coming from Theodore's *Contra Eunomium*; and (5) other excerpts from the *Contra Eunomium* that R. P. Vaggione (1980) has been able to gather. These last five collections provide us with texts that are welcome additions to the excerpts present in Migne. As regards the textual histories of these editions, I leave it to those so interested to confer the scholarly introductions of the works cited above.

Although it is difficult to assign all these works to specific time periods, a few dates can be established with relative certainty because of internal evidence.[8] J.-M. Vosté argues persuasively for the following order, relying on external as well as internal testimony. Theodore's first major work appears to be his *Commentary on the Psalms*, in all probability published in the latter years of 370, with his *Commentary on the Twelve Minor Prophets* shortly after this. He probably wrote his principal work *On the Incarnation* sometime following his ordination as a priest in 383. Vosté believes this occurred in the middle of the 380s, whereas Swete proposes a wider period from 383 to 392. If Theodore left Antioch after his ordination to reside with Diodore in Tarsus, this would mean that he probably had Diodore to advise him in writing this work. The next work whose date can be established is *Against the Macedonians*, written doubtless before or around his consecration as bishop in 392. The picture then becomes cloudy. Vosté speculates that Theodore would most likely have written his next great work, the *Catechetical Homilies*, when he served as the bishop of Mopsuestia, perhaps between 402 and 403. After some wavering, Vosté proposes that Theodore wrote his New Testament commentaries on Matthew, Luke, John, and Paul between 400 and 415. Because Theodore remarks in his work against the Apollinarians that he wrote his book *On the Incarnation* 30 years earlier (196), this would strongly suggest that he wrote his work (perhaps his second) *Against the Apollinarians* in the early 410s. Then too, because he calls his adversary on the question of original sin "most wise" and "most brilliant," this would indicate a time around 410.[9] Vosté feels confident furthermore to assign the fragments belonging to Theodore's work *Against the Allegorists* to this later period because he believes that it manifests a maturity of thought, though I suspect that his references to the Arian dispute indicate that it may well belong to an earlier period, probably around his *Commentary on the Psalms*. Finally, Theodore's commentaries on the Hebrew Scriptures date, so it seems, from the earliest period of Theodore's writings, except that at least some of his work on Genesis could well belong to the 410s because of the original sin dispute. So too his *Reply to Julian the Emperor* (which is more important for the question that it raises about the historical foundation of the Christian Scriptures than for the relatively few excerpts that have survived) also doubtless belongs to the early period. In summary, whether Vosté's calculations are correct or not, the excerpts and works that have come down to us reveal, as we discussed in Part I, a consistency of thought, with perhaps only his views on inspiration and the Adam/Christ typology suggesting some notable development.

All the translations found in Part II are my own. Although so much of Theodore's work has come down to us in Syriac and Latin rather than in his original Greek, I have given preference to the Greek text. I do so even when this appears within a Latin work, such as Swete's edition of Theodore's *Commentaries on the Minor Pauline Epistles*. In such a case, I will note in my translation what has been taken from the Greek and what belongs to the Latin version. I have made the Syriac text my second choice. Although sensitive to how Syriac translators may not always provide an accurate translation, I believe that they were more committed to the memory of Theodore and more sensitive to the nuances of his Greek text than a Latin translator. For instance in Swete 2: 312, the Latin reads *in loco sensus*. This can be translated "in place of sense." But as the Syriac translator was keen to recognize, doubtless because he was aware not only of Theodore's thought but also of Apollinaris' teaching that claimed that the Word of God assumed the rational soul of Christ, he was careful to translate (what was doubtless the original Greek) word *nous* as the "rational mind."

Although the Latin translator is correct in translating *nous* as *sensus* – this is the first meaning given in Liddell and Scott – he has missed the correct nuance that *nous* was meant to convey in Theodore. Whether my assessment is correct or not, I have translated the Latin versions only when there are no available Greek or Syriac texts.

As regards the accuracy of my translations, I have remained as close as I could to the text. Yet I have tried to balance this with a desire to make my translation as idiomatic and readable as I can for an English-speaking reader. When one considers that the Syriac and Latin versions are already one step away from the original, it is important to bring out as clearly as possible Theodore's thought. For instance, I have broken down many of his own (or his translator's) lengthy sentences into two or three sentences, while maintaining, as best I can, the sequence and dependency of these upon the main clause. I have also changed participial clauses into dependent clauses and have occasionally inverted these as well as have transformed nouns into verbs, if these express Theodore's thought in a smoother and more agreeable way for the reader. Whenever I have introduced words to the text, I have placed these within brackets. I have occasionally changed one noun into an adjective modifying a second noun. I believe all this has succeeded because the sentences in each section seem, at least to me, to cohere with and promote Theodore's overall thought in a particular paragraph. The presumption here is that Theodore has intended to make sense in his writings and has combined all the sentences in a paragraph to promote the point he wants to make. So whatever blocks the flow of thought can and ought to be questioned as to whether it has been accurately translated.

I have been careful to note in each chapter where one can find a particular passage in the work I have translated. In the text, I indicate in parentheses when I have moved to a new page of the version being used and, where it applies in Sachau, Vosté, and van Rompay, also to their translations. There is a slight variation when I refer to Tonneau's edition of the *Catechetical Homilies*. I have chosen this work as it is more accessible than Mingana's and has the Syriac text on one side of the page and the French translation on the opposite. To accommodate those who may have other translations of Theodore's 16 homilies, I also give the number of the paragraph in the homily where the text is located. For example, CH 8.2/188–9 means that the text is found in paragraph 2, Homily 8 of the *Catechetical Homilies* (abbreviated "CH"). The numbers 188 and 189 are respectively the page numbers for the Syriac and French translations in Tonneau's edition.

10

IN OPPOSITION TO THE ALLEGORISTS

[The following selection contains most of what has survived of Theodore's "Treatise Against the Allegorists." I have translated this passage from Lucas van Rompay's Syriac version (1982). This section is significant for the reasons that he offers in opposition to Origen's use of allegory, rejecting it as a pagan way to interpret the Christian Scriptures.]

(7/10) Therefore, just as we have done in discussing those other usages from the divine Scriptures, we have not only explained those passages that are obscure but also preserved intact the textual meaning of those that are presented in an obscure way or that seem to be enigmatic in some other way. [Origen[1]] proceeds by clarifying many points regarding the historical narrative that are apparently not contrary to the meaning of what is said. And he was not considered to be speaking in favor of one position over another, even though he shows himself opposed, while at the same time apparently in full agreement with the written text. This is necessarily the case when his explanation is seen to be in accord with the written text and the stated meaning of the words [contained there], howsoever they may be presented. By examining these, he would explain these passages in light of the narrative. (8) But then to twist the entire narrative or to change the written text, how is this not completely insane and evident wickedness? For, if one can rightly assert without shame, this wanton frenzy [for allegory[2]] is like that [shown] to [the pagan] idols. [lacuna] They introduce [interpretations] that do not agree at all – not even in a single instance – with what is written. And they rashly use the words of the divine Scriptures to deceive and lead the multitudes astray, in order that they might appear virtuous guardians of the priestly narrative – which they call an "allegorical interpretation."

Whenever they speak of their allegorical interpretations, I say again and again that these are truly dependent on the pagans who have invented these [kinds of interpretation] in order to set aside their fables as they are [now] setting aside the true facts present in the divine Scriptures. If, on the other hand, they affirm, as the apostle has declared, that he was never disobedient [to the truth found in the Scriptures], I agree with them on this point. But clearly their interpretation is worthless because it diverges from the blessed Paul. As we have abundantly shown in our own interpretation, he did not employ an allegorical interpretation in order to rise above its historical narrative. Nor have these [texts] been, as it were prophetically, illumined by [interpreting] these in a typical way. For, [in] an allegory, someone draws out of the text another meaning that transcends the meaning of the text, in order to demonstrate thereby [a meaning] that someone maintains has been implanted there. Such an interpretation, however, does not supplant the historical narrative and the meaning of the text, but it remains the same as the original. For example, if we say that age is honored by God, because He has suffused it with all sorts of virtues, the fact that Joseph has also appeared to be honored because of all his [lacuna]. The same is also asserted in the Epistle to Galatians where he says that justification by grace is better than that accomplished by adherence to the Law. And on what basis does he says this? (9/12) Ishmael is born according to the order of nature but Isaac in grace. And this latter was much more honored than the former, insofar as the justification that the New Testament bestows by grace is rightly honored more than that given to those who live according to the ordered way of the Law.

The blessed Paul calls this an allegory – which I fully accept. But, when one makes use of it throughout all the Scriptures, I do not think that there exists in the divine Scriptures a [single] historical text from which one cannot derive great profit by teaching its readers not to disregard what is written. But, on the other hand, when a prophecy is revealed there, it is fittingly seen from the sense of the verses; that is to say – if one can speak openly – that it is deduced from the historical narrative itself. So has the blessed Apostle proceeded when he says that what is accomplished by grace is better than what seemingly happens according to some precept [the text is corrupt here]. The same is true regarding his words in his Epistle to the Galatians, when he argued on the basis of what was declared there as happening to [Hagar and Sarah] as being applicable to the [two covenants]. In fact, it is clear that he has deduced that the two [are connected] from the text. For there is a link between what took place [between Hagar and Sarah] and what has been accomplished [covenantwise]. He teaches us in this way to hold on to all these [relations] and to make use of them.

So the [term] "allegory" seems to be used thus by the blessed apostle and this fits in well with the purpose of the divine Scriptures. It also possesses advantages (10/13) of all kinds for our reading an historical text. But this is not the [intent] of these virtuous ones who have introduced allegory into the divine Scriptures, as the pagans have done [in their writings]. However, they do not recognize [their mistake] as the pagans finally did when they became aware of how contrived were their fables dealing with their gods. They invented the allegory to show the absurdity of their fables, making enormous use of the allegorical method for two [reasons]. First, because the fables contain no truth, they could change the external aspects of an allegory. Second, they made those whom they call their gods to share in the absurdity with which their fables are filled. However, it is not fitting for us to do this or anything like it, because [the stories] in the divine Scriptures are not deceitful fables composed to please those who come upon them. So we are careful not to be found going beyond the narrative element of what has been written, as these are doing. For [our Scriptures] possess wondrous advantages for those who come upon them. For this reason, we also say that, when they mention something obscene that occurred in the past, we have need [to know this] for our own instruction, in order to [know] not what to do but what not to do. For they appear to be warning us with their reproaches and objections against doing as these do, to teach us not to act in a like manner. For the divine Scriptures look to and are aimed [at achieving] what is for our own well-being. It is truly for this purpose that we do what is set forth in their text, observing not only what has been said but above all [honoring] those who have been worthy of [receiving] divine grace. [There follow several examples to exemplify this from the Scriptures.]

(11/14) But then it did not seem right to the illustrious Origen to inquire into these [examples]. Rather Philo the Jew is declared to be superior to them. From the time [Philo] was instructed in pagan learning, he regarded the meaning of the divine Scriptures to be inferior and contemptible. He is also the first to have introduced the allegorical narrative that the pagans [drew] from Gentile learning. For he presumed that [the Scriptures] would in a similar way also be strengthened by the allegorical method, although he was unaware of how dangerously he was altering the divine Scriptures by suppressing the historical elements within the text. As a result, these [elements] appear to be falsehoods, like those [promoted] by the pagans, and would not be true. But this does not come close to the astonishing way that Philo has plotted against the divine Scriptures by daring to introduce a number of human musings into Moses' teaching; that is, into the divine Scriptures. For he has boldly declared that the world was established in an ordered way at creation similar to (12) what Moses teaches us about this [event] in his account. Because he rejects the historical texts in many instances, he has made what is stated in the accounts agree with his views. But he is obliged to acknowledge some things over which he is confused; [such as] the former glory [of Israel], the expectation that the Jewish people had toward this [restoration], and the truth they bestowed upon this [belief]. But, because of his passion for vainglory, he introduced pagan teaching into the divine Scriptures, without any regard to how he thereby casts shame upon the divine Scriptures.

As regards these questions, since the illustrious Mar³ Origen did not find anyone who could teach him about what is true in the divine Scriptures, he turned to Philo to serve as his guide for interpreting allegories, in order to shamelessly change everything written there according to this [method of] interpretation. Because of this, he showed himself to be skillful in [explaining] church teaching with great exactitude. So, if he had failed only one time, he would not have been reprimanded for his error. But his wickedness is [even] greater, as he has not always proposed the same meaning on every occasion, [offering it] on one occasion in this way and on another in a different way, taking pains to demonstrate all this from the divine Scriptures. But more than all else, these [Scriptures] condemn him by proving that he cannot accurately assert and prove [his position] – not even in one of those [cases] where he has rashly dared to oppose the Scriptures. Indeed someone ought either to tell [his followers] that they are teaching in opposition to [the Scriptures] or, as in this case, to declare him to be foolish and ignorant. For it is astonishing that such a way of thinking as his has been allowed to be introduced into [the Scriptures]. For [example] he has taken great care to demonstrate [his opinion] that these bodies with which we are clothed will not rise at the resurrection in the world to come, as the blessed Paul clearly states so well: "This corrupted being will put on (13/16) incorruptibility, and this mortal one will be clothed with immortality" (1 Cor. 15:53). [lacuna] Someone else may possess a more accurate knowledge (17) about his remaining books. But it is not up to me at this time to compile all his foolishness; that is, his passionate but rash statement about the soul entering the body from outside and, to a lesser degree, about the soul's life that [his followers[4]], like the pagans, have dared to link to and associate with what the divine Scriptures [say] about the Son and the Holy Spirit. Someone can very readily respond to all this, as do all those who agree with him regarding these points, that they find the proof supporting their impiety within his books. For they say that the Son's nature greatly differs in relationship to His Father's. These demonstrate this by arguing that he is saying the same thing as their teaching. These [followers] also assert that the divine Trinity is not one, citing Origen as a witness of what they hold [here] and in all [other] instances, although he was wholly in opposition to what they held [lacuna] in their interpretation of the divine Scriptures. This wise one [Origen] was tricked into declaring these things. He would never have willingly shown an interest in any interpretation filled with the insane blasphemy of the pagans, once he studied the true intent of the Scriptures and inquired into what is the meaning of every word . . . He would then have been able to know that there is but one sense in (18) all the words of divine Scripture and to have found in them, as it should be, the invincible truth of the Church's teaching.

We have, therefore, spoken about these matters, O illustrious Cerdon, in accordance with what you have asked concerning those who are industriously corrupting the sense of the divine Scriptures, doing this in an empty-handed way in my opinion, even though we can still say much more about these ignorant ones who are unacquainted with even how (14) to enter into the divine Scriptures and who believe that they have found an authorized road on which to advance without effort . . . [lacuna] those who judge rightly about what you have inquired. So, when I interpret a psalm, I fully respect its text, only taking care, as is my custom, to state briefly the exact meaning that a word has. I first state, as is my custom, its argument – [a step] that does not differ, as you know, from what I have said in my introduction.[5]

11

PSALM 8

[I have translated the following psalm from Robert Devreese's (1939) Latin text. It is one of only four psalms that Theodore believes are truly messianic predictions of Christ. It is also valuable for the ways that it highlights Theodore's understandings of a type and of the prosopic union of Christ's natures.[1]]

(42) [Greek] In this psalm the blessed David prophesies to us about Christ. [Latin] For he proclaimed under the Spirit's inspiration what was later fulfilled regarding Christ, thus refuting his depraved Jewish opposition by affirming [Greek] how "children, both those nursing and other infants, would praise him in an inspired way" (Matt. 21:16). [Latin] These [children], in fact, fulfilled this [type] regarding our Lord, in that these prophecies and their outcomes fulfill what has been foretold. [Greek] Some say that the blessed David was speaking of an ordinary man when he composed this psalm at the Tabernacle festival when the fruit was being harvested and assigned to the presses. [Latin] Whether this [timing] is true or false does not appear to be especially significant for us in trying to arrive at a greater understanding of the psalm. For if the time is known when the psalm was sung, one can cite this evidence as an added point that is true, but it cannot provide knowledge of what is said and disclose what is to be understood. For, even if the time is not known and the statement is thus false, this in no way changes our understanding [of the psalm]. Nor will our knowledge of what is being said be [made] any more difficult or hindered.

(43) It should also be noted against those heretics who accept, as we do, the Old as well as the New Testament, that this prophet's psalm does reveal a major difference between God the Word and the man assumed, and sharply distinguishes between the One assuming and the

one assumed, with there existing as much difference [between them] as between God and all others.[2] There is no doubt that the Jews have accepted this psalm as dealing with God and a human being who is rightly said to be far inferior. As we have said, there is between the assumed man and God the Word as much diversity as there can be, but not a difference of honor. The honor to which the assumed man is entitled far surpasses [that of] every other creature. This man has received this pre-eminent honor because he is united to God through a prosopic union. But, because we are now scrupulously selecting individual points [of interest], we do not agree that our interpretation is straying too far afield. For we are resolved to act thus in all the psalms, namely that we leave aside whatever is factually extrinsic [to the text] and we will speak only about what pertains to our interpretation.

"O Lord, our Lord, how admirable," to the end [of the verse] "of the earth." Having been led by the revealing grace of the Holy Spirit into a contemplation of future things, [David] is filled with an overwhelming astonishment and emits a cry of amazement at the beginning of the psalm: "O Lord," he says, "our Lord, how admirable is your name throughout the whole earth." By means of this cry, elicited from an overwhelming sense of admiration, he is above all indicating that the preaching of the Gospel will extend to the whole earth and that, after the [Gospel] faith has been announced and the Gentiles have renounced their idols, they are going to believe. For the fact that the Gospel has been taught throughout the earth is proof that the name of the Lord has been made worthy of admiration. By asserting "How admirable is your name throughout the whole earth," he thus announces, together with his amazement at [God's] majesty, the events he saw would come to pass. He is saying that the preaching of the Gospel would be received throughout the whole earth. And Your name, O God, will be (44) celebrated wherever its proclamation will reach. This is made manifest by what follows: "Since your majesty has been elevated above the heavens." So he says that the honor of Your name is found in all parts of the world, as the grandeur of Your glory has reached from the lowest level of the earth to the heights of the heavens. All human hearts have acquired this knowledge of You as the Creator God of the heavens.

"From the mouth of infants and nursing babies" (Ps. 8:2). This [verse] applies to our Lord and, in fact, is fulfilled when the little children came running up to him with palm branches and olive leaves as he entered Jerusalem and shouted, saying: "Hosanna in the highest, blessed are you who come in the name of the Lord" (Matt. 21:9).

What is said about Christ [can be] attributed to what the [prophet] has uttered in the present psalm. He also condemns those Jews with a rebellious spirit who do not fear to attack clear prophecies. In this way, the blessed David, [moved] by the grace of the Spirit, sought to join together here the prophecy affirmed about Christ with those events mentioned above where he is to be honored – [events] that no one doubts pertain to him.

"On account of your enemies [you have presented a way] to also destroy their hostile defender." [David] is asserting here that God was responsible for this praise that flows "from the mouth of infants," to both overcome the infidelity of His enemies [that is, the Jews] and silence their shamelessness. For God's power and grace brought together the young children, so that their actions might fulfill what had been predicted about Christ and that the psalm's testimony about the immense honor [to be shown] to Christ might be openly mentioned. In fact, he calls the Jewish people "the hostile defenders." For, since they did not receive him but, in fact, persecuted the Son of God, they have revealed their open hatred, all the while pretending to be defenders of the Law given by God.

"Since I will look upon the heavens" up to "you have established" (Ps. 8:3). [David] is saying that I will know and will believe that You are the Creator of all things. But instead of [declaring] "I will understand" and "I will know," he inserted [the phrase], "I will look upon." These remarks are so clearly said of God the Word (45) that no one can raise a word in contradiction. But, if He is the One [affirmed to be] our Lord in the Gospel when the scribes and Pharisees said: "Do you not see what they are saying?", by chastising the little children they are attempting to restrain them from praising him so wholeheartedly. He responds, "Yes, have you not read: 'From the mouths of infants and nursing babies you have achieved praise for yourself'?" (Matt. 21:16). He shows by this that the blessed David's prophetic prediction was being implemented in fact by deeds.

It is certain that what has been prophesied about him most surely pertains to him, since he adds the following verses, in which he says: "What is man that you are mindful of him" up to "under his feet." These words that we have quoted indicate that they are one and the same: God the Word of Whom the principal assertions are made, and the man of whom He is mindful and whom He visits and has made "a little less than the angels," whom He crowns with honor and glory and whom He has set "over the works of his hands." Here in this [verse] is shown how markedly the natures differ. So lowly and ordinary is the state of that one whom God has deigned to call to mind that the blessed David is simply stupefied and amazed by all that we have gathered and mentioned. So when he says "What is man that you are mindful of him?" etc. he clearly indicates the vileness of our nature and that it is not of such great worth that God would be so mindful of him that He would unite Himself to his nature, making it thereby equal in honor to Himself. This is the reason why the prophet was so wondrously stupefied by the goodness of God. For He allowed such a humble and vile nature to share in His own dignity. Therefore, it is sufficiently evident that it is God the Word who was mindful, who called, who made a man to be "a little less than the angels," and who crowned him "with glory and honor." Who indeed is this man on whom such great honors have been conferred? We learn from the Apostle Paul who says, "He testified, however, saying: 'What is man that You are mindful of him' up to 'under his feet'" (Heb. 2:6–8) and, in addition, says: "That one who has been made a little less than the angels we have seen to be Jesus who has been crowned because of his suffering and death with glory and honor."

(46) [Greek] This psalm shows us, therefore, that there is a great difference between God the Word and the assumed man. This distinction is found in the New Testament when our Lord ascribed to Himself the principal points of the psalm, which affirms that He is the Maker of creation and that His splendor far exceeds that of the heavens, and evokes wonderment in all the earth. At the same time, the apostle understands the next assertion to be about the man Jesus, who was deemed worthy of such great kindness. How is this not clear? For the divine Scripture has wisely taught us that God the Word is one, and the man another, and shows us that their difference is complete. For there is One who calls to mind, and another who is deemed worthy to be remembered. It is the Former who sees, visits, considers, whereas the other is (47) blessed by being deemed worthy of this. Whereas the Former acts kindly and makes the other to be less than the angels, the latter is kindly received and accordingly made less. The Former crowns with glory and honor, and the latter is crowned and blessed with such honors. The Former has set him over all the works of his hands and subjected everything under his feet, and the latter has been made worthy to be made the Lord of those things over which he previously did not have power.

When, therefore, we hear the Scripture affirming that Jesus has been honored, or that he has become known [as he is], or that something has been conferred on him, or that he has received mastery over everything, we do not understand these [honors] as referring to God the Word but to the man assumed. [It makes no difference] whether these things have been conferred upon him by the Father or, as we hold, by God the Word. We are not mistaken [here]. For we have learned to say this is so by the divine Scripture's teaching authority, relying upon the testimony of what this psalm says concerning this man. For the blessed apostle affirms: "For, as regards this man, He has subjected everything to him, and there remains nothing not subject to him." In this psalm, God the Word is understood to be the One who has subjected all things; and so too a little later on: "Now, however, we no longer see all things subject to him" (Heb. 2:8) – which is doubtless [a reference] to the man. But God the Word (48) is also said to be the Lord of all, so, when [Paul] affirms in his epistle to the Corinthians: "When he has abolished all rule, authority and power, he must reign until he puts all his enemies under his feet" (1 Cor. 15:25), this has to be understood of the man. He immediately supports this [conclusion] by [citing] a passage from the psalm. It is clear that he has taken "He subjected all things under his feet" from the psalm and then adds [to this]: "When, however, he says 'all has been made subject to him,'" he is without a doubt excluding the One who made everything subject to him. If this verse "He made everything subject under his feet" (Heb. 2:8) was [only] peculiar to the Apostle, it would then be superfluous to add "when, however, he says." But, because he was making use of the psalm's testimony, he later states: "When, however, he says." But who says this? Without a doubt, [it is] the blessed David. The close similarity of words shows that this is so, because [Paul] inserted the testimony of the psalm into [his Epistle to] the Hebrews, saying to them: "Now, however, we do not yet see everything subject to him." This is similar to his statement: "He must reign until he puts all his enemies under his feet. The last enemy, death, is destroyed" (1 Cor. 15:26). Then a little later, he says: "When, however, all things will have been subject to him." Without a doubt, these are not now subject to him, because he says: "All has become subject to him. Then even the Son will also be subject." We ought to take this [as a reference to] the man; and [the clause] "who has subjected all things to Himself" we understand [to be referring] to either the Father or God the Word. We do not readily [admit] being mistaken here, because it is the divine Scripture that reveals that God the Word has made all things subject to the man. This is indicated further on in another place where the Apostle is speaking either of God the Word or of the man. He applied the psalm's testimony to what he says [in his Epistle] to the Hebrews: "What is man that you are mindful of him?" He also affirms to the Corinthians: "How death [has come] through a man, and through a man the resurrection of the dead. And, just as all die in Adam, so also will all be brought to life in Christ" etc. But, if someone says that the blessed David is speaking of man in a generic sense, this will be seen to be contrary to what the Apostle Paul affirms when he spoke in opposition to this. He will then reinforce what we have rejected above. For, if the blessed David had said that a man in general was made worthy of such a great benefit, (49) the blessed Paul would not then have wanted to approve of the assumed man's honor being imparted by God. Rather he would have wanted to demonstrate what uniquely pertains to [each] nature, seeing that there is such a vast difference between the Word and the man. So our faith remains sure that after the ascension he received so much honor that he far transcends all creatures and, because he is united with God the Word, he ought to be adored by all, as the blessed David says: "You have subjected all things under his feet."

"Sheep and oxen, all the flocks" up to "of the sea." By saying indeed "You have subjected everything under his feet," he showed that he is speaking of a more exceptional person than is our way of judging. But, because of the infirmity of the hearers of that time, he adds "sheep and oxen" etc. as applying to an ordinary man. He wanted his way of speaking to be appropriate to their capacity [for understanding]. Thus, by prophesying about Christ and enumerating God's benefits for us, he concluded the psalm with the cry of one saying in amazement: "O Lord, our Lord" up to "the earth."

12

THE CREATION OF ADAM AND EVE

[I have translated the following excerpts from Migne's *Patrologia Graeca* (*PG* 66: 1005–12) that treat of Theodore's views regarding Adam's original state and the effect of his sin upon creation. However, I have followed the order in which H. B Swete (1882) presents these. I have also included other excerpts on these topics that are found in Staab (1984: 113–212) and Sachau (1869). These passages are important as they exemplify how Theodore applies his exegetical principles to Scripture and how he responds to the question of whether Adam was first created immortal or mortal and what the impact of his sin was upon humanity.]

Book 3 (*PG* 66: 1005) [Latin]. The response of these most wise men[1] is that God did not know that Adam was going to sin. But it is most insane to conceive of such a view, as it is evident that [God] knew that he was going to sin and that he was, therefore, assuredly going to die. How utterly lunatic it is to believe that God first made him immortal for six hours (for such was the time period from his fashioning from the earth on the sixth day up to committing his sin) and then, after he ate contrary to the divine command, [God] expelled him from paradise and destined him because of his sinning to be mortal! But, if He had wanted him to be immortal, why did He not prevent him from being sentenced [to death] by impeding his sin? Why too did He not change the immortal state of the devil, the source of all evils, into a mortal one?

Moreover [God] would hardly be bestowing the resurrection as a great reward – as the blessed Paul has expressly affirmed in the passages above – upon those from Adam up to the coming of Christ our Lord, who were [guilty] of so many impieties and iniquities, if He was going to hand them over to endless punishments without [any opportunity for] amendment. For how will the resurrection be regarded as a gift if it is to be conferred as a punishment without [any chance] for conversion for those going to rise? . . . (1006) Who is so mad to believe that such a great good is to be made the matter of infinite punishment for those who are to be resurrected? It would be altogether better for them not to rise than to experience after their resurrection so many and such terrible kinds of infinite punishments.

[Latin] But this brilliant proponent of original sin has been unable to grasp any of this. Indeed he has never been trained in the divine Scriptures, for, as the blessed Paul says: "Nor did he learn the sacred (1007) writings from infancy" (2 Tim. 3:15). So, when he often speaks in emphatic terms about the senses of Scripture and dogma, he has shamelessly proposed his many opinions regarding the Scriptures and dogmatic matters in inept ways that are peculiar to him or in common with others. For, being mesmerized with his own skill, he has allowed no contrary viewpoint to be expressed, except by those who silently obstruct those who are knowledgeable about the divine Scriptures. Most recently he has adopted the novel teaching wherein he maintains that a raging, wrathful God condemned Adam to be mortal and, because of his one failure, has punished him, and all those who are not yet born, with death. By arguing in this way, he is neither afraid nor embarrassed to dream up such views regarding God as no one among sane thinkers, and those involved in a concerned way for justice, have ever attempted to do. However, he has failed to remember God's divine words: "Have I any pleasure in the death of the wicked, says the Lord God, [seeing that my desire] is that they should turn from their ways and live?" He shows thereby that God does not, as some erroneously declare, punish one for another's failure, (1008) but everyone is going to receive a reckoning for his own faults. The blessed Paul has also offered remarks that are in accord with these: "God," he says, "will repay each according to their own deeds" (Rom. 2:6); and "Each one of us will carry our own burden" (Gal. 6:5); and "Why do you judge your brother? Or you, why do you despise your brother? For we all will stand before Christ's tribunal" (Rom. 14.10).

But this astonishing man is convinced that God was aroused to such great fury on account of this one man's sin that He sentenced him to the most fearful punishment and has leveled an equal condemnation upon all of his offspring without exception, even though there were so many righteous ones [whose number] no one can readily enumerate. Of these one ought to mention above all – which seems especially absurd [to do] – Noah, Abraham, David, Moses, and countless other just ones who were subjected to [such a] punishment because of the failure of that one man and that one sin [committed] by his eating from a tree! If this be so, God would then be extending His wrath beyond the bounds of justice, in that He would be casting aside all the many virtuous deeds [done] by the just and be subjecting them to a monstrous punishment solely on account of Adam's sin.

(1009) If he carefully considers nothing else, he ought at least to look at Abel in an open way because he was the first just one to die. For, if God determined his death to be a punishment for humans, how was this not utterly unjust? For the one responsible for the sin lives, and Eve who encouraged his wickedness also lives with him. I pass over here the devil, who is still existing even now in an immortal state, while the first just one, who promoted virtue and was the first to cultivate divine worship, was subjected before all [others] to the punishment [imposed] for sinners. This wisest of men ought also carefully to consider Enoch, who is not dead. He was not endowed with such great virtue or piety that he lived a life better than all [others], such as Moses, the prophets, the apostles, and all the rest, of whom the most the blessed Paul says: "Of whom the world was not worthy" (Heb. 11:38). Why is it that Enoch alone should live his life without having to undergo death [rather] than these [others] who have died? From the beginning God had already inwardly determined that these would first be made mortal and then later enjoy immortality. By acting in this way, God wanted this to be done for our benefit . . . In a clearer way he said God showed the same [aim] when He transported Enoch [to Eden] and made him immortal. For, if God has imposed death as a punishment due to sin, and not previously predetermined within Himself to infallibly arrange for everything [to happen] to us as it accords with His purpose, then Enoch would never be experiencing an immortal life [before] Christ our Lord experienced it.

Our Lord has been made the source for all human blessings, so that, just as Adam was the first to originate the state of mortality, our Lord has begun the second state, that of immortality. As our first fruits, he possessed the natural features of the first Adam, as he was born from a woman, was wrapped in swaddling clothes and little by little grew in age, as [Luke] says: "For Jesus grew in age, wisdom, and grace before God and humans" (Luke 2:52). He was also circumcised, (1010) was presented to God in the Temple as the Law prescribes, became subject to his parents, and freely lived in a lawful way. Then, in order to make satisfaction for all others, he underwent death as the payment that our nature owes, in order that, by dying in accordance with what is required of human nature and then by rising from the dead by means of divine power, there would be a new beginning for all other humans who have died in accordance with their nature. He has thus [enabled] them to rise from the dead and be changed into an immortal existence. For, just as we all have been made conformed to Adam according to our present state, so we will be made conformed to Christ our Lord in the future [age]: "For he will transform the body of our humiliation, so that it will be made conformed to the body of his glory" (Phil. 3:21) and "Just as he was earthly, so we also are earthly; and just as he is heavenly, so will we be heavenly; and just as we have borne the image of the earthly one, so we will also bear the image of the heavenly one" (1 Cor. 15:48–49), showing thereby that, since we have become sharers in the first state of Adam, we will also necessarily realize a sharing in the future state of the second Adam, who is Christ our Lord according to the flesh, inasmuch as he who possesses this same nature [as ours] has risen and taken up all that belongs to this nature. He has endured death, accepting it as part of our nature; and by rising from the dead he has made our nature to be perfectly free from death. Moreover, he accepted death, but not sin. For he remained totally free from [sin]. He assumed what belongs to nature, namely, death; but in no way did he accept sin, which belongs not to nature but to the will. So, if sin belongs to nature, as this most wise man has so eloquently maintained, then, because sin exists wholly in nature, he should then accept this as a necessary [part of nature].

(1005) He preferred [not] to speak to the great number of passages that demonstrate that Adam was completely a mortal being formed from the earth, but about (the passage treating Adam's) eating. Nor was he able to turn from this to the truth, for instead of [relying] on true dogma he connects the challenge [to eat] to the seducer's lie . . . For God does not say to those who are wholly mortal by nature that "You will be mortal," but that "You will surely die" (Gen. 2:17), threatening to introduce the reality of death, except that He postponed its actualization according to His customary kind way [of acting]. So when He affirms, "Whoever sheds human blood, his blood will be shed as recompense for this" (Gen. 9:6), He does not say that whoever kills a human being will become mortal, but rather that he is worthy to be condemned to die. So also when He earlier said, "You will surely die," [this does not mean] that humans then became mortal but rather that they would incur the sentence of death because their transgressions made them worthy [of this].

Note too that God is seen to have imposed His divine condemnation on Adam after he sinned, when He affirms: "Because you listened to your wife's words and have eaten from the tree that I commanded you not to eat, the earth is cursed now because of your deeds. In sadness you shall eat from it all the days of your life. Thorns and thistles shall it bring forth for you; and you shall eat the chaff from the field, and with the sweat on your brow you shall eat your bread until you return to the earth" (Gen. 3: 17–19). In this way, He threatened [Adam] with a future life full of hard labor if he was to obtain from the earth the food [needed] to nourish and sustain him. He was now without the overwhelming bounty that was available to him when he enjoyed the tremendous abundance of paradise. Thus, when God ordered him to work and maintain paradise, He was not assigning him (1006) to work the earth as a punishment, indicating thereby that he was changing humans from an immortal to a mortal nature. Rather He was forewarning that the earth's fruitful bounty would be filled with hardships, in contrast with the former abundant wondrous delights of paradise. For, since [Adam] had been made wholly mortal, he then needed the fruits of paradise, as he now does in his searching for the fruits of the earth. But, having been deceived by the earlier delights and [not mindful of the threatened] punishment, he is terribly distressed when he hears about his most painful, toilsome future.

[God] then concludes at the end, "For you are earth and you shall return to earth," signifying thereby that his nature was mortal. He did not use the word "earth" [here] as those most wise defenders of original sin do, those confused fathers [preoccupied] with sin, who depict [Adam] as an immortal being who is now receiving the sentence of death for the first time. But the divine Scripture has revealed that this condemnation confirms [the fact] that [Adam] is mortal by nature. For this most often brings home to humans their corruptible nature subject to decay, for, as [the psalmist] states: "He remembers that we are dust. For a human being's day is like hay; and as a flower of the field flourishes, so will he flourish. But when the wind passes over it, it will no longer be there" (Ps. 103:15–16). He wants to bring out here that we are all corruptible and subject to decay, like hay that flourishes for a little while but will perish shortly afterwards. For we live our life for only a brief time, until we finally reach that point when we no longer exist. Also as Abraham has said, "I am but earth and ashes" (Gen. 18:27) before God, as if to say: "I am not worthy to speak with such a mighty God, I who am a human fashioned from the earth and who will be wholly [subject to death] in the future." So [when he says:] "Because you shall be earth and shall return to earth," he should have said more, if he was to become mortal at the start of creation.

Romans 5:12–14 (Staab 1984: 118). [Paul] says that, when the Law was introduced, it did not free us from sin. For, as long as the Law existed, governed, and ruled human beings, it increased sin, for observing the law could only contribute to this. To prove what he has discussed, he asserts that "Sin is not imputed when there is no law." The law is so far removed from sin that, if the law did not exist, no sin would exist. He designates the law to be whatever determines [right from wrong] by means of either conscience or a legal prescription. For no one would be said to have committed sin, if it were not clearly seen to be present and then judged by [a standard of] good. Then he continues, "Inasmuch as all have sinned," and then, following up on this, he adds: "But death has ruled from Adam up to Moses, encompassing even those whose sins are not like the evil deeds of Adam, who is the type of the one to come." Therefore, this [clause] "even to those whose sins are not like Adam's evil deeds" signifies that death rules over all who have in any way sinned. Although the [specific] kind of Adam's sin and that of all others are not the same – [suggesting that] all those born afterwards did not have to die – yet, because they have sinned in some way or other, they have all received the sentence of death. For death is not decreed as a penalty for any one or other sin but for all sin, as is observed in the following: "We boast not only so [about our salvation] but also in God through our Lord Jesus Christ." For he affirms here that we boast not only because God has reconciled us to Himself through the Christ but also because He has forgiven all the former evils, whatever these may be. When Adam sinned and death also became a reality through this, sin entered into his offspring, and death ruled rightly over all humans. For since all have sinned – even if their sin was not the same as Adam's but done in some other way – it was necessary that death rule over all equally. So, when the Law was introduced, it could not take away sin from humans. But rather just the opposite happened: the opportunity for our sinning then increased, because sin cannot be judged as such without laws. But when there seemed to be no hope whatsoever for a change for the better, because of the multitude of sins committed, Christ then redeemed us from all these evils. Thereupon [Paul] briefly added, "who is the type of the one to come," in order to state that what happens to Adam typifies what will come to pass in regards to Christ. For, just as evil consequences have occurred because of Adam, so have we received through Christ an opportunity to enjoy superior benefits.

Romans 7:5 (Staab 1984: 125) Because we are naturally subject to death and, because of this, have a powerful tendency to sin, we committed every sort of sin, even though we were taught by various laws what we should avoid. What then ought to be done in order "to make death bear fruit"? He says that the punishment of death has securely constrained us. Since we are so overwhelmingly disposed to sin because of our mortality, we have become subject to [death's] punishment because of our failures, with the law incapable of assisting us. On the contrary, [the law] has become a public sponsor of sins insofar as we do the opposite of whatever the [laws] command us [to do].

Romans 8:19 (Staab 1984: 137) God made the whole of creation one cosmic body, containing all things, both visible and invisible, as [Paul] affirms in his epistle to the Corinthians: "We have become a spectacle to the cosmos, the angels, and human beings." Although these differ among themselves, with some visible and others invisible, [God's] intent is that all things be bound into one reality. For He created the human being to be fashioned with a visible body that is related to the material creation – for it is constituted of earth, air, water, and fire – and of an invisible soul that is akin to those invisible [spiritual beings]. He has also made [Adam] to be the pledge of His friendship to all. The visible beings assist him, as we now realize from our experience. The rational natures[2] also serve us, so that things might work out for our benefit . . . At that time when Adam came into being and heard God's threat that he would die if he sinned, [the angels] wondered what would be the outcome of this for him. Then when he sinned, he became [liable to] death because of his decision. His soul became detached from its body, and [his role as] the bond uniting creation to himself was dissolved. The intellectual natures were, as a consequence, angered at this turn of events and were no longer friendly toward us, as we were guilty of so many evils. Then as time passed, succeeding [generations of] humans turned more and more to evil and made themselves liable to the sentence of death, [so much so that] [the angels] regarded all as hopeless and nourished a growing hatred for us. Hence they did not want to do anything more for us, [showing] this by turning away and becoming hostile toward to us, and by loathing us as enemies of God. What then was to become of such as these? The Lord said that He would restore us by raising us up and making us immortal, so that no one should ever fear that the common bond [uniting] creation would ever again be changed and be dissolved. When they received this promise, [the angels] were cheered, knowing that divine grace will restore what has caused us to falter and will repair our friendship with all those whom we have defrauded through our wickedness. Then [our role as] the universal bond will remain [secure] with no possibility for a future dissolution, and thus our friendship with creation will remain unbroken.[3]

Genesis 1:27–2:1 (Sachau 1869: Fol. 28a–29a/15–17). Who is this [Adam]? From where [does he come]? And how does he differ from all others? Since [Moses] had to repeat the narrative, he said: "And God made the human. He made him in the image of God. He made them male and female." But when [Moses] spoke about the other creatures, he said that [God] simply willed that they exist. This then happened, and His will act was fulfilled. By repeating the narrative he also shows the pre-eminent nature of that one who has been made in God's image. For, by thus repeating his narrative, he has made known the human being's superiority over every one of the remaining creatures. It was for this reason that he declared here "He created him to God's image," in order to show that [the human being] is the one who excels by reason of His fashioning because all beings are bound together in him. Because [human beings] are God's image, they [can] draw near to God by fulfilling the directives commanding them to serve him. They please the Lawgiver by caring for him. Since God needs nothing and is not visible, they respectfully honor Him by serving the one who is needy and visible to all.

Then as he customarily does, [Moses] also adds something when he repeats his narrative. He thereby indicates exactly what has taken place, as he did in [his treatment] of the luminaries, when he affirmed in a general way earlier: "God made the lights in the heavenly firmament in order to shed light upon the earth and to separate the night from day." Then when he repeats the narrative he says: "And God made the great lights: the great light [of the sun] to govern the daytime and the feeble light [of the moon] to govern the night and the stars." In the middle of this narrative, he has clearly taught us which luminary was to govern the day and which one was to govern the night. Thus he has interpreted the command of God here in a general way [when He spoke of how] He made the human being and how this [affirmation] [is to be understood] in an inclusive way as male and female. Therefore when he repeats the narrative that states "God made man in the image of God," he adds "He made them male and female," thereby distinguishing their common nature . . . He added "He made them male and female," not rashly, but because they came into being as male and female at the same time as God had willed that some of these [creatures] be drawn from water and others from the earth. But a human being has not come to be in this way. For the woman was not formed from the earth as the man was. Rather the man was created from the earth, and the female from him. So it was necessary to make known here that "He made them male and female," seeing that they were made in different, not equal, ways, thus indicating that, although their way of coming to be differs in accordance with the will of their Maker, yet these two are one being. There is one nature for both the male and the female, just as it is for all animals made from the earth. For [God stated] it was "good," after he affirmed that the male came first and then added that the female came to be afterwards. For this is the order of their creation, namely that the male came to be first and then the female . . . And Moses also adds: "And God blessed them and said to them: 'Grow and multiply and fill the earth and subdue it and dominate the fish of the sea and the birds of the sky and all the beasts of burden and all the animals of the earth and all the reptiles that creep upon the earth.'" For what he has spoken about is said to have happened by God's command. So, in his repetition of the narrative, he makes known that everything has been completed when he adds that they have been empowered by God's blessing to multiply in their procreation.

13

COMMENTARY ON JOHN'S GOSPEL

[The present selections have been translated from the Syriac text that J.-M. Vosté (1940) provides. They are especially significant because they exemplify how Theodore reconciles his christological thought with the way that the Evangelist John has portrayed Christ as fully divine as well as human.]

Preface (5/2) Our aim, therefore, in this book, is, together with the assistance of the Lord God of all, not to omit anything that others find difficult [to grasp] when interpreting the words [of Scripture]. Nor will we spend time on any reading that one perchance finds to be evident. Nor do we repeat or imitate the error of the sophist Asterius,[1] who, so it seems, wants to be more honored than to enlighten in his book, where he delights in having written reams about this subject. But he did not realize that he was not providing his reader with any help for an accurate reading of the Gospel, because he spent time only on what is evident, while stretching out what he was saying in a skillful way but at excessive length. In every chapter where we offer our interpretations, we strive not to draw out our comments by adding superfluous words. [The task] of a commentator at this point is to consider, as much as one can, those passages that most find difficult to interpret, whereas a preacher will speak about things that are clear, though he may sometimes find some superfluous matters useful. Yet when explaining his [position], he ought, nevertheless, at the same time, to speak concisely, if his explanation cannot be made clearly without a lot of words. This is applicable when we come across verses that the deceitful heretics have corrupted through their sickly impiety. We are not reluctant to say so, since the one who is being talked about is clearly known to us, although we will be very careful in doing this. For it is the task of an interpreter, above all one who diligently explains [the text], not merely to speak thus with authority but also to reject any opinion opposed to his words. I will, therefore, first state my own understanding of the entire book; then with God's power, I will proceed to explain my words.

(6/3) There was published then at that time the books of the other evangelists who also composed Gospels: Matthew, Mark, and Luke. Soon this small [message of] hope was diffused everywhere. All the faithful strove with great passion to learn through reading [these Gospels] what was our Lord's way of living on earth. One finds these and other accounts similar to these in the three evangelists, the only difference among them being that one thought that he ought to write about the nativity of our Lord in the flesh and speak of what occurred at his birth. Another, on the contrary, immediately began from John's baptism. The blessed Luke, in fact, began with what occurred at the birth of John and then proceeded from the birth of our Lord (7) to John's baptism.

The faithful in Asia judged that John would be, in their opinion, a trustworthy witness superior to anyone else for writing a Gospel. Because he was with our Lord from the beginning and was endowed with higher grace because of his love [for Christ], they brought him the books of the evangelists, seeking to learn from him his opinion about these writings. [John] greatly praised the veracity of these [Synoptic] writers, yet saying that they omitted a few things, that they needed to have mentioned certain miracles, and that they are almost wholly lacking in [doctrinal] teaching. He also said that they ought to have written about the coming of our Lord in the flesh, in such a way so as not to fall short of speaking about his divinity (4), lest with the passage of time those humans who knew him only through these accounts would believe that our Lord was to be known only in this way. For this reason all the brethren asked him to write in a scrupulous way what he thought was especially needed and what he regarded as omissions by the others. Since he did not refuse, he immediately undertook the task without delay, for he thought it would be shameful if many would suffer grave harm because of the negligence of one person. His intended desire was, therefore, to write a Gospel. He then immediately started from the beginning to teach about [Christ's] divinity.

Book One (11/7) "In the beginning was the Word." As it seems to me, no one should be faulted for saying that the blessed John the Evangelist did not grasp the [full] power of this "Word" when he spoke. For it was only later that he understood by reflecting upon its meaning. For as I think, the suitability of this term surpasses not only human skill [to grasp] but also our whole human nature. (12) For [the task] was not only to be capable of recognizing the divine substance, but, even more than this, to express what is understood.

One can likewise speak concisely about the incomprehensible substance of God the Word as though he would be speaking concisely about another but be unable to explain with ten thousand words about what is understood. For, as often as I consider the [term] "Word," I am amazed at how far the heretics have striven in their fight against its whole importance. So it seems to me that anyone who shamelessly persists in opposing this does not differ from those Greek philosophers who, wanting to destroy all religious teachings among humans, have even dared to say about the sun that it is not a luminary and promise to provide demonstrations of this! For, if there exists something prior to the beginning, we would concede that the Son is not the first nature. But if one is first in every way in the sense that he is said to be the beginning, then he is not the beginning either because something other is prior to it, or because it is necessarily the first among those present (take this to be what we think). [John] has clearly said that God the Word was in the beginning. But if someone wants to inquire into [the exact meaning of] this phrase "in the beginning," as the philosophers and Scripture customarily do, he will discover that both equally indicate the Only Begotten's divine substance. For, as in many other [instances], if someone traces exactly how [the philosophers] employ these words, he will discover that their way of speaking is not alien to that of Scripture. For, whereas one's religious doctrine may differ, this does not entail a different outlook regarding the usage of the words used. For, although [the philosophers] have erred in many matters, nevertheless common sense forced them not to twist how words are used. (13) For this reason, the divine Scriptures have also equally made use of proper words for their suggestive power.

(8) But let us examine this word ["beginning"] in another way. Before examining it, let us consider how it is used among humans. We call the beginning of all things what is first among them. We do not speak of something second as being the beginning. For, if it comes after another, it is not the first; and, if it is not first, how much more is it not the beginning? If someone wants to examine this exactly, he will discover that the word "beginning" signifies something more than being the first. For something may be first without it being called "the

beginning." For it cannot be accurately designated by this term. To be sure, [the notion of] "first" is also connected to [the idea of] "a beginning" in every case. But, if someone called something that is first likewise the beginning, he would be using this term in an improper way. But [the idea of] "beginning" is also known [to be connected] with the notion of "first." It is clear that what is first is also connected in every way to [the notion of] "beginning." As, for example, if anyone wants to remove a pile composed of several stones one by one and then says: "Take a certain stone first from among these." He is thereby indicating what is [to be] the first, but in no way showing what is indeed the first one [that began the pile]. For the fact that the gathered stones are alike does not permit this, unless someone says in addition: "Such a stone was the one that is to begin their removal." For then adding "Take away such a stone" specifies what was [the stone] that began this, but it is called not the first one that began [the pile of] stones but the first one removed.

What then? I have shown through this examination that the word "beginning" is broader (14) than "first," [that is] if we have inquired exactly. For when we consider "first" [we mean] that something is said to follow after it. But [the term] "beginning" is the beginning of something. For it is clear that it does not receive its [notion of] beginning because something follows after it, but that it is the beginning even when there are none following it that call it their beginning. Rather something is rightly the first when it is connected to what follows after. The first is then called the beginning but not because it has been such. Rather it is called the beginning of those things that did not exist [originally with it] but later follow after it. For this reason, it is an accurate statement. The blessed Moses meant this when he said not, "It was evening and then there was morning, the first day," but rather "It was evening and then there was morning, day one." He called it [day] "one" because it was before another day. But he did not think that it could be accurately asserted to be the first, as there was not up to then another day after it, so that it could be called the "first day," although there was, in fact, a second created after it.

(21/14) Briefly, therefore, they also say to those who ask, "Why does [John] call this One the 'Word'?": we respond that in no other instance does the Scripture employ this term "word" in the sense of a *gnōmā* (*hypostasis*/"person"). But here he names the Son as the Word in [the sense of being] a *qnōmā* when he designates Him in a singular and absolute sense without [any] addition or definition. For the Word has been affirmed as if in a literal sense. These [adversaries] also confess this when they strive to explain the reason why he was called thus. But he was not called thus in the sense that they want to explain it. With God's assistance, we have clearly shown above that He was designated in our way [of interpreting it]. What, therefore, do we say? We [understand] the [term] "word" in a twofold sense. One is what is uttered as a sound by our tongue, and the other that which is present in a hidden way in our mind – which we say is found in our rational soul and is innate to it. Our focus, however, is not centered on how this term, namely, the "word," is so designated. It comes from the soul and is known to be always within it.

We clarify our interpretation through an example. Just as we see that this word [issuing] from our soul is not separated or divided from it, not even when it is for a time distant from it but always existing with it and recognized as being in it, how much more ought we not to doubt that the Son is from the Father without division or separation. Nor has He received in time His coming to be from the [Father's] nature, but He is always with Him and in association with Him. Nothing exists between them as He is with Him in a divine way and has only the Father as his beginning. The Son is with Him in substance and is united to Him.

(28/19) We do not proceed [by relying] on many words in an unmeasured, discursive way. For we have spoken, O Porphyry,[2] [most] noble of all the bishops, about these things in a lengthy way above, where we assert that we find these contrived protestations of the heretics to be very perverse. For we maintain that it is the task of the interpreter to clarify the true sense of a statement not only by what he has said but also by rejecting what are the contrary opinions. We respond at length to those genuinely seeking by their questioning to obtain an understanding of words needing explanation, seeing as these are the words encountered in [the Scripture]. Know, therefore, my Lord, that we can say many other things, with God's grace, to confirm what you have sought. But we refrain from doing this, intent on speaking only about those points that are opposed, in our opinion, to the clear meaning of the [written] words.

(33/23) "And the Word was made flesh." [John] uses this [term] "Word" in a very clear way [to mean] "Behold, He came to this one as though He was made flesh." For this is how those who witnessed His "becoming" taking place would have thought, seeing that He was in this man in such a humble way that He was believed by many to be only as he appeared. Then, to explain "he was made," John affirmed, "He made his tabernacle among us," that is, He was made flesh in the sense that He dwelt in our nature. For [the words] "He made his tabernacle with us" clearly means that "He has dwelt in us," as the Apostle said of us human beings, "We groan while we are in this tabernacle" (2 Cor. 5:4), calling our body a dwelling place; and again, "We know that if our terrestrial dwelling place is dissolved" (2 Cor. 5:1). It is acknowledged that it was customary for Scripture to designate the whole human being by [the term] "flesh," as for example, "All flesh will come to you" (Ps. 64:2). And so likewise [John] evidently (34) means "He was made flesh" in the sense that "[the Word] was in a man." But, because He has not changed, he said "He was made," but in the sense that He was presumed to have been because of his appearance. [John] said this, therefore, to expand upon what has been declared regarding His kindness and the accusation of those who do not believe. Indeed he has rightly said "He was made flesh," in order to magnify by inferior [flesh] both their accusation and the manifestation of His kindness.

this man in such a humble way that He was believed by many to be only as he appeared. Then, to explain "he was made," John affirmed, "He made his tabernacle among us," that is, He was made flesh in the sense that He dwelt in our nature. For [the words] "He made his tabernacle with us" clearly means that "He has dwelt in us," as the Apostle said of us human beings, "We groan while we are in this tabernacle" (2 Cor. 5:4), calling our body a dwelling place; and again, "We know that if our terrestrial dwelling place is dissolved" (2 Cor. 5:1). It is acknowledged that it was customary for Scripture to designate the whole human being by [the term] "flesh," as for example, "All flesh will come to you" (Ps. 64:2). And so likewise [John] evidently (34) means "He was made flesh" in the sense that "[the Word] was in a man." But, because He has not changed, he said "He was made," but in the sense that He was presumed to have been because of his appearance. [John] said this, therefore, to expand upon what has been declared regarding His kindness and the accusation of those who do not believe. Indeed he has rightly said "He was made flesh," in order to magnify by inferior [flesh] both their accusation and the manifestation of His kindness.

We think, therefore, that these [remarks] are now sufficient to explain the text. Nor [is there a need] for us to speak at greater length than this, since there seems to be no time. Yet I do think that a brief response [ought to be] made against my adversaries. For they say that "He was made" [ought to be interpreted] as "He was changed" – a stated position I believe they do not modify, at least so it seems to many. But the evangelist has deftly interpreted this when he added to "He was made" [the words] "He dwelt among us." But if you are anxious in your desire to learn more about this, you can obtain the book we wrote on our Lord's human nature.[3] (24) You can accurately learn there about this [verse] as well as about his entire life.

(34/24) Then the evangelist returned to following the order of his text, lest [his statements] that "He was made flesh" and "he appeared" block [Christ's] majesty from being seen. So he adds: "And we have seen his glory, the glory as of the Only Begotten of the Father, full of grace and truth." For [it is] not because of [Christ's] many deeds that I make known who he is. Nor do we rashly consent to believe in him. But because of what we have seen, we have truly accepted him as the Only Begotten Son. For what we have seen amply demonstrates the majesty of the one who has appeared. (35) Because of what came to be, he can be none other than the Only Begotten who perfectly possesses the image of his Father. For what was accomplished by his means was full of true grace. [John] has called "truth" to be "grace" in a way similar to the Jews. For [John] seeks to show by this comparison [Christ's] majesty, in order to accuse those who do not believe his words that clearly manifest his intent.

Therefore, [John] calls "grace" by the name of "truth" (that is, true grace) because Christ has pardoned former transgressions and has provided salvation for the remission of sins. Moreover He has also destroyed death, which has ruled because of our sin, and given us a firm hope of resurrection as his adopted children. [This is done] not by word alone as the Jews do, but by what has been achieved through the power of the Spirit, who has regenerated us in the hope of the resurrection, of which baptism is a type and which death will not void. Moreover [Christ] has prepared for us the delights of the celestial kingdom, if we but keep unimpaired by our upright way of living the honor of the adoptive filiation conferred upon us through baptism.

But because [my adversaries'] stupidity surpasses all [bounds], we ought not to make light of the fact that some have dared to raise the objection that [the evangelist] says "the glory as of the Only Begotten" (John 1:14) and not [simply] "of the Only Begotten." But who does not know that "as," if it is asserted in an illustrative way, compares one thing to another, [presuming] that what is stated is affirming the full reality of what is known? Such usage is often discovered in the Scriptures. If, therefore, "as of the Only Begotten" is being affirmed in a comparative way, the Scriptures are then showing us to whom the evangelist is referring [when] he says that he saw the glory as of the Only Begotten. But because the [comparison] is not [being made], the [evangelist] is seeking to highlight the majesty and reality that is known about the one whom he is affirming. For truly his aim from the first line, throughout all these verses, is to extol [Christ's] praises by asserting a truth [untouched] by [any] falsehood. The evangelist wants to say from experience [that] we acquire evidence of what is said. For he is demonstrating His majesty by means of what He has accomplished, thereby indicating that He is the Only Begotten Son who has a likeness to His Father.

(78/55) Even if human beings are thought to differ in this life from one another by a distinction of persons (Syriac *prṣwpe*), we are all nevertheless one human being by the bond of [our] nature, insofar as each is known to constitute one [common] body, with each one of us being seen in every way as members of the whole but with all of us being this mortal and corruptible human being. For all of us together are

included among those condemned to death. But our Lord has wanted
by his overflowing grace to recreate, and lead us to a better state in the
life to come in which all of us will rise after our death. We will not only
receive a new existence and life but also remain incorruptible. Then,
as soon as we have received this transformation, we remain in the
incorruptible state in which our body has been fashioned. Adam was
the first one fashioned for our life here and now, and Christ our Lord
for the one to come. For just as Adam, the first among human beings,
was mortal, and so too every one of his offspring, so also is Christ the
first one [to rise] after dying. He has also granted his followers a reason
[to expect] their resurrection. We come forth into our present, visible
life through a physical birth and are all thereby corruptible. But then
we are all of us changed into this future life by the power of the Spirit,
and we also rise incorrupt for this reason. Therefore because what has
occurred at that time [that of baptism], Christ our Lord wanted us to
change from that [state of mortality] to this [new life] in a typical way
and so gave us baptismal rebirth (79) in him. For the birth that takes
place here is a type of the resurrection or a rebirth, which will be then
completed for us when we will be changed into this [new] life. Because
of this, he called baptism a "rebirth."

(83/59) After speaking about the divine nature in the previous passages,
[John] turned then to the man [Jesus], saying: "For the one whom God
sent speaks the words of God" (John 3:34). This one has not acquired
this honor by his nature, as [John] indicates by adding: "For God did
not give him the Spirit in a measured way. The Father loves His Son
and distributes everything through him." He gave him not merely a
small portion of the Spirit's grace, as He does all other humans, but its
fullness, because of His love for him. And for this reason He bestowed
on [Christ's humanity] universal domination over all. For He knew
that these [honors] were in harmony with his human nature. Because
of its union with God the Word, [Christ's humanity] has received
universal rule. For this reason, [John] rightly mentioned, first of all,
the Spirit through whose mediation [Christ's humanity] received his
union [with the Word], a rebirth and a universal rule. Then [John]
said that [the Word] always acted through the mediation [of Christ's
humanity] because [John] thought otherwise this would not be seen
as belonging to our Lord's humanity – that is, that [his humanity] had
received universal domination – unless the power of the Spirit verified
in a truly undeniable way that this statement was trustworthy.

(103/73) But what did [John] mean [by saying]: "My Father is working up to now, and I myself am also working"? He did not want to make mention of these [activities] because every one of them is moved by God's decree. But he mentions his Father who always provides by a powerful, rationally guided will. So [Christ in the flesh] does not cease on the Sabbath from doing what is beneficial for us, seeking at every moment what is suitable for our reformation, with knowledge that [Christ] possesses the same power as [his Father] has. Even though [the Father] has established the Law for others to cease working on the Sabbath, [Christ] possesses the power to always act, because he is not subject to the Law as he also possesses equal power. Moreover there is no lawful decree preventing him from doing whatever he intends. When [the Jews] complained, therefore, to [Christ] about his disciples plucking the ears of corn and then rubbing and eating these with their hands on the Sabbath, he reminded [them] about the example of David and the priests and what the Law states in writing. He makes known from this [example] that it was licit for them to do so in a time of need, even though it appeared contrary to the Law. When then [Christ] was accused of this, he did not (74) refer to himself as one under the Law, seeing that the reason why they acted [as they did] clearly [applied] to another. [Christ] then mentioned the activity of His Father, saying (104): "My Father is working up to now, and I am also working." Neither does my Father cease working, nor do I. [The Father's] providence is [working] for humans just as it does for His handiwork. There is no law preventing (the Father) from this, nor is there a limitation prohibiting Him from doing this. Likewise I also act whenever I want, since there is no set time for me to act for the sake of human salvation. So, just as [the Father] has the power to act, so also do I. If, therefore, you find fault with me because I work on the day of the Sabbath, you ought also to reprehend the Father for acting. If no one finds fault with Him, because His Lordship gives Him that power, then no one ought to fault me. For I also have equal power to act.

(162/115) "These Scriptures give testimony of me" (John 5:39). [Christ] is endeavoring to say that everyone who follows the Scriptures and believes in me will be filled with grace, like a spring which not only is not dried up, but is bubbling up, so that it suffices to serve him and many others. So also the Apostles, after they received the Spirit, were the reason why so much of their received wealth was bestowed on many others. We also understand by this that "the Holy Spirit" does not often designate the Holy Spirit's Person (qnōmā) and nature but His operation and His grace. Here [Christ] is evidently speaking about the grace that the Apostles were about to receive and which was to be transmitted by their means to others. This [bestowal of grace] was not yet done, as it will begin [only] in those who receive it and in whom it will grow. But [this grace] will also diminish as often as those obtaining it [fail] on account of their worthlessness. Therefore Paul has said: "Do not extinguish the Spirit" (1 Thess. 5:19).

(167/119) When the Apostle speaks concerning our soul and our body in his Epistle to the Romans, he is teaching us how the soul can be inclined to virtuous conduct and how the body, because of its natural mortality, is also easily inclined by its natural passion for sinning, saying: "Therefore I discover a law within me that wants to do good, yet because evil is close at hand to me" (Rom. 7:21). But he is not affirming "me" in the same way in both instances: "To me wanting to do good" and "evil is close to me." Therefore, this ought not to be taken as an incongruity, even though the apostle used "me" equally in both of these [statements]. For he said "to me who wants to do good" as it pertains to the soul, and "yet evil is close at hand to me" to the body. Because he was speaking of two natures, he used "me" in both of these statements as [referring] to two distinct realities aptly distinguished by their natures, yet being one; that is, he is speaking of these two as being one person (*prṣwpā*) because of the body's bonding[4] to the soul. So also when our Lord (168) speaks of his humanity and his divinity, he uses this "I" as referring to the (120) common person (*gwa prṣwpā*); and, in order to let us know by all these [remarks] that he is not speaking about the one and same nature, he indicates this by making distinctions when he says "I myself do not judge" and says in another place "If I judge." He thus intends the former [statement] in the sense that we have explained it above. For, after he said to them "You judge in a carnal way," he let them know that they should in no way doubt this, by adding "I myself do not judge anyone; and if I do, my judgment is true." This is similar in meaning to "The Father does not judge anyone but has entrusted the entire judgment to His Son" (John 5:22). For He is also saying here that you are rightly confused over what was said about his human nature, just as you also do not understand [the saying] "I myself do not judge anyone," for he is saying this in regards to his divinity. For [the Father] who will judge will be the One carrying out the actual judgment by means of [Christ's humanity] who will be seen by those to be judged. And the judgment he will make will be true and also just. Because he shares in [God's] majesty, he [can] rightly judge everyone. For he is not alone and does not make these [kinds of judgments] by himself. For in no way do we believe that he could accomplish such works as these because of his nature's power, but [it is because] of [the promise] "I am with him"; that is, because of the divine nature, the Father is also with him. This is necessarily so. For, because [the Word] is united to me, I am also [united] with the Father.

(213/152) After [Christ] said that no one can snatch these [sheep] from my hands nor from the hands of my Father because He is greater than all, he adds opportunely: "We are one, the Father and I" (John 10:3). Because, Christ says, just like Him, I am greater than all [others] in this that I am also, just as He is, the cause of creatures, and have created them with Him; and I am equal with Him in power. We are one "ego" (214) in majesty and in potential power.[5] For this reason, no one can snatch these [believers] away from my hands nor from my Father.

(Verse 31) "The Jews, therefore," because they cannot bear with what Christ has said, "picked up stones, to stone him." The heretics, however, because of their evil [nature], wanted to do [more] than this and sought to corrupt the manifest sense of what he said by asserting: "Behold, he says in another place, 'I do not ask only for them, but for [all] those who believe in me through their word, in order that all may be one, just as you my Father are in me, and I in you'" (John 17:20–21). Nor do we believe because of this that [those believing in Christ] are like God in power or nature. We will clearly show, with God's help, the meaning of this statement when we come to [that point] where the equality of the Son with the Father is shown in nature. However, I will [simply] mention this [equality] now, lest I introduce a multitude of superfluous comments [upsetting] the [right] ordering of my commentary. For these comments are going to be explained in their own place.

For instance, the word "one" signifies at one time a "consensus" and then, at another time, a "likeness," and, in fact, many other [meanings]. When one says: "There was one soul and one mind for the multitude of believers" (Acts 4:32), it is evident that [the sacred writer] means "one" in the sense of a consensus. But then when [Paul] states, "We have also all been baptized in one Spirit into one body" (1 Cor. 12:13), (153) he is clearly designating a likeness of nature, because all of us have become [transformed] by this one spiritual regeneration from one state into another.[6] So all of us are gathered into the one Body of Christ. For just as we are all one body by our nature, and Adam is the head for all of us, because he was the beginning of our nature, so also we are called the one Body of Christ, because (215) we are born by his Spirit into incorruptibility and confess that Christ is our head in [the sense that he is] a type of our resurrection because he was the first to rise from the dead. For it is clear that baptism is a type [signifying] his death and resurrection, as the blessed Paul clearly says: "We have been buried with him by being baptized into his death, so that, as Christ rose from the dead into the glory of his Father, so also we will walk in a new life" (Rom. 6:4). Since the term "one" is clearly used then in diverse ways, being used at one time as a likeness and at another as a consensus – this in no way means that we should not inquire whether it is said somewhere else in a different way – rather we should examine how and in what sense this [word] is meant here: whether as an equality or in some other way. The contextual setting – which one ought to trust above all else when interpreting the meaning of a verse – indicates the latter [sense]; that is, [one] in power. For [Christ's humanity] can be said to be "one" [with his Father] because he is the chief of all and surpassing all [others]. And this appears from the explanation of [Christ's] words. Although the Jews took up stones, they did not use them. It is evident that after they took up stones, our Lord calmed their rage by his hidden power.

(Verse 32) "Jesus said to them. I have shown you many good signs from my Father. For which of these signs do you stone me?" He said it well: "Is it because [I spoke] of being [one] with my Father." For his miracles caused them extreme embarrassment, seeing that they were reckoned to be the Father's [miracles], so that they would have no excuse for accusing him of iniquity. (v. 33) Indeed they said to him: "It is not because of your good works that we stone you, but because you blaspheme and, although you are a man, you are making yourself God." But since they could not deny the works, (216) because they were clearly seen to be miraculous and salutary, they charged him under the pretext of blasphemy, [saying]: "Although you are a man, you make yourself God." And they were right to say this. For he said: "We are one, my Father and I," (154) making himself to be the Father. What, therefore, does our Lord mean? He accomplishes two things at the same time: he has rebutted their statement and, by making a comparison with inferior things, he shows that the accusation of the Jews is empty. For customarily, by comparing something with lesser things, one highlights it even more. What, therefore, did [the Lord] say? "Is it not written in your Law: 'I have said you are gods'?" If he has called them gods, seeing that this was said of them – and Scripture cannot be voided – then you are saying to the one whom the Father has sanctified and sent into the world "You blaspheme" because I said to you: "I am God's Son." But behold, in your Law it is also affirmed of humans that "You are gods." Although this was spoken of them simply [as humans], yet they were not changed into the divine nature. Rather it is by the grace of God that they received this designation. Although this statement is confirmed, I nevertheless appear to you to be blaspheming because I have said of myself: "I am God's Son." But, according to this context, [our Lord] ought to have said: "You say: 'You blaspheme,' because I said: 'I am God.'" They also objected to this, but the words of our Lord require this. For he says: "If [the Law] said they are gods," he ought then not to have added in a corrective way: "You say: 'You blaspheme,' because I said: 'I am God.'" But, because his statement was spoken only to them, he said: (317) "We are one, the Father and I." There is a great difference between his statement and theirs. He sought to show this by pointing out that it is a blasphemy for someone to be called by the name of "God." But this differs greatly when compared with "We are one." So that they would not believe that he said "one" [in the sense] that he is like the Father, the cause [of all things], he rightly adds that "I am the Son of God," so that it is evident that, even if he said of himself that he is one with the Father, nevertheless he did not say that he has no beginning together with the One who is without a beginning, being rather like the Son in relationship to his Father who possesses a perfect likeness to him at his generation.

(269/192) "The words that I speak I do not speak on my own" (John 10:10). If you [Thomas] do not believe these, know that we [the Father and I] are wholly united by nature, will, and power and that our words are not to be distinguished. Everything I say belongs to the common "ego." For I do not speak solely on my own. It is my Father who dwells in me who does these works. And he rightly states after this that he connects [the words] "I do not speak" with "My Father speaks." For [Christ] said above that "These are the words I speak" and then that "My Father acts," to highlight the common nature, common words, and even common works. But clearly I am not speaking here of my own accord, as I am not speaking according to my inferior [human nature], but by my perfect participation and our inseparable bond. This is especially evident from the passage's context. Yet no one [should] be surprised that, although [Christ] was found to be [subject] to suffering and spoke many times as a man, he switched over to words befitting his divinity. For these words needed to be said for [the benefit of] his disciples, so that [later on] when they recalled the words spoken to them, and having finally grasped their meaning, they would perfectly understand in a rational way, as [for example] when they failed to grasp the meaning of the resurrection after they first heard [about it]. Afterwards they understood. But then these words needed to be spoken once again. For he wanted to show his disciples how they are totally lacking in an understanding of what is hidden. For they did not even know the one whom they thought they knew. He [could] not [achieve this] in any other way except by making use of words that revealed his divinity.

(314/224) What, therefore, happened? Because Christ in the flesh received his resurrection through the Spirit, we also necessarily (225) receive the same through the providential action of the Spirit. The Apostle teaches this, when he clearly says: "If the Spirit of that One who raised Jesus from the dead dwells in you, the One who raised him from the dead will also give life to your dead bodies because of the Spirit's dwelling within you" (Rom. 8:11). But [the Father] would not have resurrected him in the name of the Spirit, unless [the Spirit] were in some way helping in resurrecting our Savior. [John] especially reveals this by saying not the "Spirit of God," but "the Spirit of that One who raised Jesus." For just as he showed His power above, so He rightly establishes it [here] again.

(315/225) God the Word is naturally bonded to the Father. Through (226) the assumed man's bonding with [the Word], he has also received a union with the Father. We too possess, insofar as this is possible for us, a natural union with Christ in the flesh and have thereby received a spiritual participation with him and have become in this way his universal Body, [with] each one of us being a member. We, therefore, are expecting both to rise at the end [times] as he has done and, by our approaching God the Word in this way, to be born into an eternal life.

14

COMMENTARY ON PHILIPPIANS 2:5–11

[The present selections are taken from Swete's Latin text (1880: 215–18) and the Syriac extract on this subject found in Sachau (1869: Fol. 12a–13b/45–9). This passage from Philippians is one of the most commented upon in all of Scripture because of its implications for christology. It is especially valuable for understanding Theodore's way of applying attributes to the human and divine natures and to their unity in one common *prosōpon*.]

(Verse 6) (215) "Who, although he was in the form of God, did not think that being equal to God was a prize to be grasped." Humans usually seek what they think they can acquire. For we frequently say that (216) faith ought to be an act whereby one quickly takes hold of what can be greatly beneficial for oneself. Therefore [Paul] says of Christ "that he did not consider being equal to God to be a prize to be grasped"; that is, he did not reckon his equality with God to be a great [prize] and wanted to continue to enjoy this dignity. But, to benefit others, he preferred to undertake tasks more humble in themselves, even though he existed in the form of God – who is, as they say, the living God, the Lord, Ruler, and Author of the universe. For everything that is said is truly being affirmed as flowing from the name of God. What then did the One [being the form of God] do?

(Verse 7) "But he emptied himself, taking on the form of a slave." The divine Scripture uses the expression "the One who emptied himself" as being equivalent to being non-existent; as it is written in another place, "Faith has been emptied," that is, it has been seen to no longer exist; and also [in another place] (217) "Our preaching, therefore, has become empty," that is, it is void and futile. [Thus the statement that] "he emptied himself" signifies that he did not reveal himself. For, when he takes on the form of slave, he hides his dignity.

109

Not only did those meeting him consider him to be who he appeared to be – since his divine nature was hidden to all – but [Paul] calls his human nature "the form of a slave," that is to say, the nature of a slave, for human nature is servile. So, just as what he says about being in the form of God is being said of the divine nature, so too when he speaks about "the form of a slave," [he is speaking about what] was common to human beings, beasts of burden and angels, for they are forms of "slaves," seeing that they have been created. [Paul] also adds, (218) "made in the likeness of a man," intending thereby to make known that, when he speaks of "the form of a slave," he is referring to what is proper to [Christ's human] nature. [Paul] chose [the term] "made" to indicate how [Christ] was being considered when he said "in the likeness of a human being," meaning by this [that he is] "in a human state." For [to be in] the likeness of a human being is to be a human being. Then [Paul] combines all these together, affirming of the Word of God that "He was regarded in his outward appearance or looks as a human being," employing [the terms] an "outward appearance" and "looks," since they convey [the idea] that [the divine] nature cannot be regarded as having any outward looks and appearance. He chose [the words] "outward appearance" and "looks" to assert that the invisible [Word], who lacks all visual aspects, wanted to be seen as being present in the human being.

(Verse 8) "He humbled himself." Up to this point, [Paul] is seen to have been speaking about matters proper to the divine nature. (219) In the subsequent verses, he moves on to what can be applied to the human nature: "having been made obedient unto death, a death on the cross." [Such words] are properly said of a human being. They can never be applied to the divine nature. For the [divine] nature that promised to raise [Christ] when he dies cannot suffer death, as the Lord Himself has clearly said: "Destroy this temple, and in three days I will raise it up" (John 2:19). So [Christ] relates the temple's destruction to what will take place at his resurrection. [Paul] immediately adds: "in Christ Jesus" (Phil. 2:14), thus speaking, as he customarily does, about one *persona* in a singular sense. He makes mention of two relations and natures, maintaining that "the one who is existing in the form of God . . . accepted the form of a slave," clearly stating that the form of God is one, and that of the slave another, meaning that one is assumed and the other, the assuming One. To make this verbal distinction entirely clear [as referring] to no other but Christ, [Paul] (220) affirms that "the one who exists in the form" etc. is to be wholly understood [as referring] to Christ's *persona*. So there is no consideration being given [to the possibility] that "the form of a slave" can be thought to be referring to any other than Christ, because [Christ] received this [designation]. When [Paul] speaks, therefore, about what ought to be said of the divine nature, he has joined together in one and the same *persona* what properly belongs also to [Christ's] humanity in order to enhance his humility. Yet, when he speaks of the honor [Christ's humanity] obtained after his passion, [Paul] added: "Jesus Christ is the Lord." Clearly [Paul] is showing that he considers the assumed man to be none other than Christ. He shows too how the natures differ by reason of what is said. For, by having every statement asserted of one *persona*, he shows the union in an ample way. So, wherever there is a dispute about Christ, [Paul] generally says everything as [being asserted] of one *persona*. He thus unites within one [subject] all the practical differences due to the different natures, in order thereby to keep their prosopic unity undivided.

In this case, [Paul] seems to have acted prudently, and at the same time out of necessity. This manner of writing was very appropriate, not only because of his habitual desire to employ precise teaching regarding dogma, but also because of how much it [was needed] for his actual argument. This was his intent: to teach the Philippians that humility is good, with the potential to reward (221) one who so acts. He confirms this [by appealing] to the example of Christ. He then expands upon it in a fuller way that rightly [imparts] more knowledge. How? Had the apostle spoken only of the Deity, he would have sufficiently shown how very fitting it was to appreciate humble things. But he would also be showing the divine nature acting in such an incredibly humble way that it would far exceed what accords with His dignity. Since this is so, he could not show how one can profit from acting in this way, because he would be unable to prove how one could acquire such a nature. If, however, he were speaking only about his human nature, he would then be showing how one could profit from what [his nature] had attained. Yet [Paul] would be unable to prove that humility is fitting for a human being, unless the divine nature that cannot be subject to death were shown to be present in [Christ]. Moreover, if [the Word] succumbed to death, He would not accomplish what obedience required of Him. For, by undergoing death, He would be denying the natural limitation up to now required of Him. Prudently, therefore, as I said, [Paul] links all [that is said] to one *persona*. He does this by gathering into one those [statements] that seem to differ practically because their natures differ, in order to make use of both, so as to further (222) his exhortation [on the need for humility. By employing words that

111

pertain to the Deity, he persuades us that we must show humility] in our way of thinking – seeing that this is what God the Word has said of His own accord – because He considers that we all must honor humility [as a way] to promote the salvation of others. Then as regards what [Christ] has accomplished in regards to his humanity, [Paul] has shown that [humility] is important for anyone who seeks to achieve as much glory as [Christ] has attained after his passion. Then [Paul] says: "He was made obedient unto death, a death, however, on the cross." It belongs to human nature to undergo suffering. Yet [Paul] has made it clear through what has been said that it was the divinity that spoke out in extolling humility, even though It could not suffer if It wanted [to do] so.

(Verse 9) "Therefore God highly exalted him." I do not know if anyone can be found so stupid to think that the Word of God was exalted after His passion. But what is this "exaltation," when [Paul said] "He gave him a name above every name"? It is clear that [the term] "name" is referring not to [the primary meaning of] the word [itself] but to some reality acquired by him, as it is written: "They know your name is Lord"; that is, that you are the Lord. Indeed, [Paul] interprets [the significance of] this name: "that at the name of Jesus every knee should bend in heaven and on earth and under the earth, and every tongue should confess that Jesus Christ is Lord to the glory of God the Father." For [God] has granted him this [honor] that all will adore him and that all (223) will confess that Jesus Christ is God, having been made in the glory of God the Father; that is, he possesses as much glory as can be divinely allowed for one possessing God as his Father because of his union with the Only Begotten. There is no one who does not know that the assumed one acquired after his passion these honors that belong to God the Word from the beginning, as the Creator of all things.[1] I do not believe that anyone can contradict this, unless perhaps one is wholly inclined to madness! [Paul] calls the invisible powers heavenly beings; living human beings, terrestrials; and the dead, those under the earth, for these confess that the Lord is the source of their resurrection through his own resurrection.

Among other things, this point ought to be explained to the heretics who want to undermine the [scriptural] witness that "He did not think that being equal to God was a prize to be grasped," because they understand this [to mean] that Christ thought that it was not fitting for him to possess the equality that God clearly has. This position (224) reveals enormous stupidity, for Christ could figure out that, if he is, in their [heretical] view, a creature of that One who is made from nothing, he would know that this One who is the source [of his humanity] would be his Maker and His Creator. If the heretics perchance do not hold this, seeing that [Christ in the flesh] has not claimed to be equal to God as attested by the demons,[2] yet they should be aware of this fact when they are constantly asserting their utterly insane statements! Their sayings are only minimally suited to say much about Christ! But even granting that they do so, who says such things about the Son as they do? They do not appear to have examined what the Apostle means when he says: "Humble yourselves by thinking of one another as better than yourself" (Phil. 2:3). For by these words he is clearly teaching that those inferior should show the honor due to their superiors. He is thus admonishing those equal in honor to think humbly of how another surpasses oneself. Therefore he posited this [term] "another," so that these [superiors] might realize their parity with those [inferiors] and vice versa. A fitting example of this is that, when Christ laid claim to being equal with the Father according to His divine nature, he had acquired this [equality] when [God] dwelt in him as a man, thereby acquiring such a lowly opinion among human beings that they considered him to be no other than what he seemed to be: merely a man. But if it should be proper for him to have no equality with the Father, then the only way for him to fulfill the declaration [made above] is because the [divine] nature has brought about the required conformity with him. Therefore, [wholly] in line with the Apostle's intent, it is ridiculous to assert that, since Christ did not rise up against the Father, he would not have attempted to lay hold of the equality he had with the Father (225) who was advising him, so that those who might think that they were equal to him by cooperating [with him] in good works might think that they surpass him by their humility.

(Sachau 1880: Fol. 12a–13b/45–9). Is the one who has been assumed the form of an assuming God or the assumed form of a slave?[3] You[4] assert that the form of the assuming God is the form of the assumed slave. Why do you resort to such clever questions and why do you not distinguish these [natures] as do the divine Scriptures and not seek to introduce into your life a completely reasonable understanding of how to worship God? For how is the assuming One like the one assumed, or in what way are God and a human being, the slave and the master, the form of God and the form of the slave, equal? For you see how [the Scripture] clarifies in a thorough way the distinction of the natures, and calls the former the form of a slave and the latter the form of God;

the Assumer and the one assumed. [The sacred writer] compiles these distinctions to teach us about the one "person" (*prçwpa*). For [Paul] says: "But He emptied himself and assumed the form of a slave and came to be in a human form, and by his outward appearance he was found to be as a man." Then, after [Paul] testifies about [Christ's] bodily nature, he proceeds to [discuss] his human qualities, indicating by this revelation [the humanity's] union with God the Word. For [Paul] says: "He humbled himself and became obedient unto death, a death on the cross." Clearly these actions are in agreement with [Christ's] human nature, namely [that] of the one who was crucified and died in accordance with his nature. The fact, however, that He humbled Himself is a sign of the union. For was it not a human being who humbled himself and obeyed unto death, all the way to the cross, by bringing death upon himself, a death that God imposed upon our nature as a punishment from the beginning? The one assumed by God the Word was able to overcome death because of his union, and was willing to endure his passion for our salvation.

[Paul] then proceeds further, saying what befits and coheres with human nature, by adding: "For this reason, God also exalted and raised him up and gave him a name surpassing all other names." Who then do we say is the one exalted? God the Word? How can this be [said] of the One who is the form of God and equal to God? For this One cannot undergo death as something proper to His nature. Paul has said about Him that, (Fol. 12b) even though He is truly equal to His Father, He has willingly consented to conceal his glory and to appear in the form of a slave for our salvation. He also accepted being exalted on high. Why then did he accept being exalted in a superior way beyond what has been [just] affirmed? How did God exalt His equal and how does He now magnify him above [all] His creation? It is absurd to say this! For, if one of those who are equal remains on [the same] level, then another who rises above that level of equality is necessarily transcending this equality. Then the one who is exactly equal from the beginning is seen from now on to be the eminent one. And again how can one among equals give, and another need, grace? And what now is given? As we have seen, it is [Jesus'] "name." But what is [meant by] saying: "In the name of Jesus every knee is bent in heaven and earth and under the earth, and every tongue will confess that Jesus Christ is the Lord to the glory of God his Father?" After his death, the Creator of the universe received this hymn of praise. For he is the One by whom all things are made and without whom nothing comes to be from what exists at present. If then anyone maintains that this praise has been given to God the Word – which many have wickedly asserted previously but have finally reverted to the knowledge of the truth – and has adored him, then one ought not to think it to be beneath the Father to have received this praise. For many have perversely asserted this but, after the coming of Christ, have returned to knowing [the truth]. If then we can rightly affirm that the Father has more and more accepted this praise, as these [converts] are maintaining, then our Lord by his coming and by his passion enabled every one to come to the knowledge of his Father. He then says to his Father: "I have made your name known to humans." Indeed it is clear that these things are said of the assumed one. All of creation glorifies him and confesses that he is the Lord, to be worshiped by all in heaven and on earth and under the earth. The assumed one accepted this grace, since he is not simply a mere man but one in union with God the Word. (Fol. 13a) For since all glory is owed the Only Begotten God the Word from His creation, and since everything has come to be through Him, those [in heaven and on the earth] adore Him, knowing that the form of the assumed slave is one with Him. Thus, when they honor Him, they also worship the form of the assumed slave, since they acknowledge the union between the form of the slave and that of God the Word.

If someone wants to say that "God exalted him" also [applies] to God the Word, he seems to me to be speaking rightly. This likewise agrees well with how [my adversaries] think about the Word. For He assumed the form of a slave and, because of His union with [the assumed man], He exalted him and raised him up and allowed him to be adored by all creation. What is meant here then, that the one being raised is the one raising? Did the assumed one assume the form of God or that of the slave? Is he the Creator of the universe or did he rise and receive worship because [he was] graced? Let every tongue stop such blaspheming! For the blessed apostle clearly teaches how the natures differ; what is the glory belonging to the assuming nature and who is this one who has been assumed. The former is the form of God, and the latter the form of the slave. And this latter consented to [his being assumed] by the mercy of that One who emptied Himself of his glory. This [man] was then assumed by Him in grace, and is adored by all creation because of this grace. In addition to this, [Paul] teaches us about the unity. He accomplishes this by combining both [statements] into one when he says of God the Word that He is the form of God etc. and in the form of a man. For [the assumed one] is considered by his outward appearance to be like a man. So [Paul] adds that he humbled Himself and surrendered to death, a death upon a cross –

which indicates his human condition. [Paul] repeats that [his human condition] was then assumed by the Word in grace and is adored by all creation because of this grace. For this reason, God also exalted [his humanity] and exalted those who are blessed, when [Paul] says: "He exalted all these." These [statements] seem opposed. But I am especially amazed at how accurate the Apostle's words are when he wants to speak first of all about the One who he said is the Assumer and then about the one assumed. He calls the former the form of God and the latter the form of a slave. Then, after he has accurately distinguished the natures, [Paul] also recalls [Christ's] corporeal nature and (Fol. 13b) his death on the cross and what happened to him after his death and, if I may say so, the glorification [his humanity] received from all creation. [Paul] indicates by these statements the unity [of the natures]. For it is because they both have a role to play in the assumption that we distinguish the natures: between the One who assumes and the one who is assumed, and between the One who is the form of God and the other the form of a slave. We recognize the prosopic (*prçwpa*) union by the glory that the latter imparts to God the Word by his death on the cross.

These [opponents], however, do not want to consider what has been said and, scorning to learn the truth from the Scriptures, they inquire at times into whether the "one" is the "other"[5] or is the same, and also whether the one who has found mercy is the one showing mercy, and whether the one who is helped is the one who helps. What we have said sufficiently answers these questions by showing that the natures are distinct and are united in the person (*prçwpa*). [The assumed man] is helped because of his nature; the Other then is seen to be the one helping. Because the unity of both is recognized, we have thus accurately shown in multiple ways, from the words of the blessed David, who is the one who is receiving worship from all creation, when [David] witnesses to and explains his statements and how [these statements] are understood by our Lord and by the Apostles, that is, by our Lord, in the sense that [our Lord] also speaks through his Apostles. The blessed David foresaw by the grace of the Holy Spirit the whole future divine plan [for salvation], that God the Creator of all was going to take delight in dwelling within a man for our salvation, that He was going to assume him in the form of a slave and was going to make him to be one with Him and, by His unity with him, His [form] was going to rule over the universe. [David] is amazed at His mercy and dumbfounded at how great an honor was [bestowed] on human beings who were deemed worthy to have God dwelling within our nature.

[David] even foresaw by a revelation of the Spirit that [Christ] will be known to everyone as God and Creator of the universe, that his name will be praised in creation, and that everyone will know the Creator whom they did not know beforehand. But [David] was struck by two things in his vision: [first] that [Christ] wins back to a virtuous [life] those who have been inclined to evil, and second that [God] actively employs this "man" as [His] instrument because He has assumed him to be the head of our whole race and is prepared to [accomplish] in him everything [needed] for the salvation of our life.

15

SELECTIONS FROM THEODORE'S COMMENTARIES ON THE EPISTLES TO THE GALATIANS, EPHESIANS, AND COLOSSIANS

[The present selections have been taken from Swete (1880). The passages have been preserved in Latin. I have indicated in the text when I have also chosen to follow a Greek excerpt that Swete has included within a footnote. The focus has been to highlight Theodore's understanding of the revelatory and unitive roles that Christ's humanity plays in salvation as the head of his Body, the church; the bond recapitulating the universe; and the perfect visible image of God.]

(Gal. 2:15–16) (Swete 1880: 30) All of us who believe in Christ are living now between our present and future lives. We are accordingly mortal by nature and bear the mutable traits accompanying it. Because we possess such a nature, we usually need law, instructing us what is the right thing to do and what is to be avoided. Yet we cannot attain the virtues without labor and sweat, even when we are seemingly most strongly resolved [to do so]. But we will see that we have now been transferred by faith into a future life and have been brought all the way to baptism (which is a type[1] of Christ's death and resurrection). At the same time we also receive the Holy Spirit who is given at our baptism. [The Holy Spirit] is the first fruits of [promised] future things, because He has to be given to us for [the attainment of] our complete immortality. We thus speak of the Spirit as One who regenerates, because His operating mode is to regenerate us in our second life. For this reason, we live without the need for precepts that regulate our body and those that properly pertain to ritual, such as circumcision, sacrifices, daily observance, etc.

(Gal. 3:27–28) (Swete 1:57/Greek) [This text is valuable for indicating how the Latin translator of the following passage has rendered what appears here to be Theodore's original.] Adam is the one who has begun the present life for all. We all are one human being by reason of our nature. For each one of us holds a membership role for the common good [in common]. So also Christ is the one who has begun the future life, with all sharing in a common way in his resurrection and, after his ascension, in his immortality, seeing as we have become one with him. For each one of us has a communal membership role with him due to our actual resemblance [by nature to him]. For there is no longer thought to be male or female. Nor is there marrying or being given in marriage. Neither is there Jew nor Greek. Nor does circumcision have a place within an immortal nature, so that the uncircumcised is separated from the circumcised. Neither is there a slave nor a freeman. For all diversity has in fact been taken away!

(57/Latin) Adam exists as the one beginning the present life for all. We are all one human being by reason of our nature. For all other humans who are known to have been born in the present life possess a common essence with him. Thus, on the level of nature, we are all one human being. Yet, as regards our common humanity, each of us also fills a membership role. In a similar way, the beginning of that immortal future life that is to take place after the resurrection has started in Christ. For all of us who participate both in his resurrection and in that immortality that is to be experienced after the resurrection are now one with him, provided that each of us likewise fulfills our membership role in communion with him. For then there will be "neither male nor female" . . . (59) A little later he confirmed that [the baptized] have become, on the basis of their nature, sons [and daughters] of Abraham. (Greek) For, if you are the body of Christ because you have been regenerated in a typical way at baptism, then, since Christ is [from] the seed of Abraham, you will also possess a similar relationship to [Abraham]. For, since you are [Christ's] Body, you are by necessity Abraham's seed just as Christ is, and are thereby, in a logical way, also heirs of his promise. (Latin) Otherwise it is impossible for us to think that we [can] be one in a bodily sense, when our head belongs to one [body] and the rest of our body to another. So you have been rightly made heirs of the promise. For, just as you have accepted being united to [Christ], so also you are necessarily reckoned to be [bonded] with him and will be heirs of these [promises]. For you are sharing in those promises that God made him, when you consider that you have the same Father and have rightly accepted God's blessing that flows from the promises made to him.

(Gal. 4:24) (73) "These things are said by way of allegory." These [interpreters] are very eager to reverse the senses of the divine Scriptures by misappropriating everything posited there and then creating some silly fables on their own – which foolishness they call an "allegory." They thereby twist the apostle's [understanding of the] term, as though they were empowered to set aside the whole understanding of the divine Scripture, on the grounds that the apostle affirms that [these things are asserted] "by way of an allegory." But they do not understand how they differ from what the apostle is saying here. For the apostle does not eliminate the historical [element in a] narrative. Nor has he detached the factual elements from the past, but has proposed them as happening at that time. He has made use of the historical [element in the] narrative to [express] his own understanding of an event, as when he says that "[Hagar] [as Mount Sinai] corresponds to what is now Jerusalem," and so too when he says "just as the one born according to the flesh persecuted the one born according to the Spirit." So he cites the historical element in all these instances. Otherwise he would not have related [his statement] "who is now Jerusalem" – which he cites as now existing – to his remarks about Hagar. Nor would he have employed "just as" for something he did not think existed. For, by [choosing to] say "just as," he certainly expresses a likeness. But a likeness cannot be asserted, if the [compared] things do not exist. So, when [Paul] adds "then," he is saying that, because he considers the time to be indefinite, he mentions a great deal of time. But such an emphasis on time will be superfluous, unless [the event] has factually taken place as the apostle says it has. But [my adversaries] are acting in a totally contrary way in their desire to make every historical element in the divine Scripture to be in no way different from nocturnal dreams. For they say Adam was not Adam, especially in those instances when they come to explain [the creation story] within the divine Scripture "in a spiritual way." When they state that paradise is not paradise, and the serpent is not a serpent, they are willing to have their spiritual interpretation called (75) foolishness!

I do not intend to make any response [to this example]. For, by so entangling the historical narrative [with extraneous material], they no longer have a historical narrative. Since this is a fact, let them say what their source is for declaring who the first man was to be fashioned, in what way the disobedient one exists, and how the sentence of death has been introduced. If they have indeed learned these things from the Scriptures, then what they call an "allegory" is evidently manifest foolishness. For [their allegorical interpretation] is proven to be superfluous in every regard. If, however, it be true that the text does not relate what has actually happened, this indicates something that above all needs to be understood: does what they have seized upon in their way of speaking as being "spiritual," truly exist as spiritual [possibilities]? Where, therefore, have they derived this knowledge that they have accepted? How can they say that they have learnt to speak thus from the divine Scripture? At any rate, I keep silent, seeing that such is the situation. [. . .] (79) Therefore this is [what] [Paul] means by "what is said by way of an allegory." He calls an allegory the comparison that can be made between what happened long ago and what exists at present.

(Ephesians 1:9) (Swete 1880: 127/Latin) "With all wisdom and prudence He has made known to us the mystery of His will, according to the good pleasure that He bestowed upon Christ." (Greek) [The sacred writer] speaks of "the mystery of God's will" as being His hidden and obscure will, calling this a "mystery" for all. Therefore, [God] has made known to us, with great wisdom and prudence, what was foreordained in the past and seemed good to Him. [The writer] affirms it thus: "[God] shows this by the deeds themselves." (Latin) "[God] has manifested this through the divine plan that He has accomplished through Christ."

(Ephesians 1:10) (Swete 1880: 128) "To restore (or rather recapitulate) in Christ all that is in heaven and on the earth." (Greek) "Recapitulation" is clearly meant to be a concise summing up of many meanings. (Latin) For [the author] wants to state specifically that the God of the universe made all creation one body (129), composed of many members from rational as well as sensible orders [of existence]. He fashioned, however, one living being, who is related, as a human being, to the invisible natures by his soul and joined to the visible natures by his body. For God fashioned our body from the four fundamental elements of earth, air, water, and fire and constituted a human being to be His pledge of friendship for all of creation, because all have been united in him . . . But after death was introduced because of our sinning, there occurred a dissolution of both elements; for the soul was separated from the body, and (130) the body, when detached, underwent a total disintegration. The bond of creation was thereby dissolved.

[God] then "restored" (or rather "recapitulated") in Christ everything in the heavens as well as on earth, by effecting a renovation and reintegration of the entire creation bonded to him. For by making his body incorruptible and impassible by his resurrection and returning [his body] to its soul in its immortal state, so that it can never again revert to a corrupt state, [God] was seen to have restored His bond of friendship with all creation. This was much more fully achieved in Christ, with every creature regarding us in relation to him. For God the Word was dwelling [in his nature], with all convinced that the divine nature manifests itself through him because of this inhabitation. Therefore He termed this a "restoration of all" because all things are gathered into one and seek out this oneness by [achieving] a harmony with one another. For the Maker intended [this to be so] from of old, and so from the beginning fashioned everything for this end that He might now bring [His plan] to pass with the greatest of ease through Christ. This [coming] will happen in the future age when all humans and spiritual powers will look to him in the way God intends and acquire a firm, harmonious peace among themselves.

(Ephesians 1:23) (Swete 1880: 140) The church is the body "and the fullness of that one who is fulfilled wholly in all." (141/Greek) He has not said that he fills all things, but that he himself is fulfilled in all; that is, he is fully in all things, being totally in each because of his unlimited nature since he is not divisible into parts. The addition of "all in all" is also necessary, showing that [Christ] is wholly in all, being in each as far as one [can] imagine, whether by essence, or operation, or power, or authority, or by any other way, seeing as how his unlimited nature relates to everything. [It is] in this way [that] [Christ] is seen to be wholly, in every way, in each (142) because he is all in all and is logically able to be wholly in each. (142/Latin) Therefore [the sacred writer] amply reveals the honor that [is coming] to us, when he tells us that the Body is Christ's and is "the fullness of [Christ] who is fulfilled in every way in everything," asserting that because of our faith we are truly the Body of Christ. Unlike others, we possess within us that one who is unlimited (who is wholly, in every way, in all things), because we have received a benevolent, intimate relationship with him. If we are indeed the Body of Christ, then we are deemed worthy to possess more than other [creatures] a greater union with him. For he is our head in whom the divine nature dwells by a benevolent disposition.

(Ephesians 4:16) (Swete 1880: 170) "From whom the whole body, fitted and knitted together by every ligament, operating in accord with how each member functions in promoting the growth of the body, so as to build it up in love." For, just as all vital power flows from the head to the rest of the body [enabling] each member to live and move and be attached to the rest of the body, so also spiritual grace flows to us from Christ our head, through whose regenerating grace we achieve communion with him in one Body. He shows how the members differ by the way that their graces differ. For he says that the new Body of the church is bound to and embodied in Christ as our head, to the point that there is operating in each one of us a spiritual power that each of us receives for some unexplainable reason [and is enabled to] perform his own ministry in the community. For when [the sacred writer] says "in the building up of [his body] in love," he is speaking of Christ, indicating [thereby] that it is Christ who acts in this way to build up his own Body because of the love that he has for us. [The writer] is thus showing that he is making a distinction [about the number] of graces [each receives], not that there must necessarily be a division [of ranks]. For not only is Christ one and distributing these [graces] to us as one [head], but we have all also become one body by means of a spiritual regeneration. Since all necessarily [share in] a common [body], (171) with each contributing what they can for the common good, then the one who has seemingly [received] an insignificant grace is not to be thought of as being of less worth for the common good. For it has been established that the members of the Body possess one nature. As such, we [ought] also have a communal solicitude for all the members, striving, thereby, to perform all things for the stability of our communal body.

(Colossians 1:15) (Swete 1880: 261). "Who is the image of the invisible God." Well does [the sacred writer] add "invisible" [to God], not that He may also [actually] be a visible God but in order that he might reveal His grandeur. Yet we see that his invisible nature [is present] in [Christ] *qua* [God's] image in that he is united to God the Word. [Christ] will also judge all the earth when he appears in the future age, in a way rightly befitting his nature, by coming from heaven in great glory. [Christ] will clearly fulfill the role of image for us, (262) because we all believe that the divine nature in whom the fullness of creation is restored [dwells] in him as an image, though we do not think that his authority to judge belongs to his visible nature. I am amazed, however, by those who have accepted this [role as image as referring] to the divine nature. First of all, they do not pay attention to the fact that the blessed Moses is speaking about a human being when he states, "God made him to His image"; the blessed Paul also does [the same]: "A man ought not to veil his head, seeing that he is the image and glory of God." This [affirmation] would never have been asserted of human beings, if this were peculiar to God. Moreover they have not realized that every image, as long as it is seen, reveals what is not seen. Therefore it cannot be that there ever exists an image that is not seen. For, generally speaking, images are clearly made by those who are motivated to [manifest] either honor or (263) affection, with this purpose [in mind], that they may provide a memento of those no longer seen for those who can still see.

Then he adds: "the firstborn of all creation." Some very learned [interpreters] have added that [the phrase] "the invisible image of God" is affirmed of the divine nature, since one "firstborn" can be neither viewed nor accepted as applying to humanity. But they ought rightly to discern that this [title] cannot be applied to the divine nature. For, if the "firstborn" were merely a creature, he ought then to be correctly called the "first-created." But, if they maintain that he is "begotten," there will apparently be great confusion over this. For the uncreated One is also said to be the firstborn of creatures. The one who is said to be the firstborn can certainly be spoken of as being the firstborn for those who essentially preserve their likeness to him. The apostle clearly reveals this, when he says to the Romans: "He predestined those He foreknew (264) to become conformed to the image of His Son, so that he might be the firstborn among his many brothers." He clearly affirms that he is their firstborn brother. And those conformed to him, in accordance with the likeness they possess with him from God, rightly consider him to be their firstborn, as he is pre-eminent in this regard. Yet he did not say that they are "conformed sons," but "sons of the image," [thus] clearly speaking about the son's image as it refers to his visible nature. Those [who assign image to the divine nature] question too how the assumed man can be regarded as the "firstborn of all creation," because he does not exist before all creation, but has received his existence in these final days. But they do not realize that "firstborn" is affirmed not only in a temporal sense but also frequently in the sense of being specially honored. For [the term] "firstborn" is also said of those born afterwards. One born prior to [an individual] who has been specially honored certainly [can be said to] come after him. This is both verified by natural reason and (265) approved by the divine Scripture.

(Col. 1:16) (Swete 1880: 269) The first fruits, therefore, of our renovation, in whom all things are bonded and reintegrated, is Christ according to the flesh. [It is he] who has brought about the most excellent and, as has been said, the desired recreation of all things, as the blessed Paul says: "If anyone is in Christ, he will be a new creation. For the former things have passed away. Behold, all things have been made new" (2 Cor. 5:17). Thus there will be preserved from this time on a harmonious, peaceful, and universal binding of all those living who are in [search of] incorruptibility. And from now on, the invisible powers will love us as intimates of God. [The sacred author] has spoken well, "In him all things have been created," not only because we have acquired the promise of the future things [that Christ in the flesh has achieved] through his accomplishments, but also because he will preserve the perfect bonding of all things. Since the divine nature dwells [within him], there can be [in the future] no further dissolution of [the unity] that we possess in a communal way. On the one hand, all love him because of the intimate relationship that they are able to have with him as a man who possesses a visible as well as an invisible nature. On the other hand, they turn to him with great [reverential] fear because God the Word is presently united to him in an inseparable way.

(Col. 1:19) (Swete 1880: 275) "For in him all fullness was pleased to dwell." [Paul] also calls the "fullness (plērōma) of God" the church, and indeed all things, seeing that he is also in all things and fills all. This is clearly known from what he said when writing to the Ephesians: "And He gave him to be the head over the whole church which is his Body, (276) the fullness of him who fills all in all." He says this because God took pleasure in him, that is, all fullness is dwelling in Christ, when he affirms: "(God) has agreed to reconcile to Himself all creation that is filled by him."

(Col. 2:9) (Swete 1880: 286) "Because the entire fullness of the divinity dwells in him in a bodily way." He again states here "The entire fullness (plērōma) of the divinity," [affirming thereby] that all creation has been filled by him. For he reaffirms what has been said above that the whole of creation dwells in him; that is, that creation has been conjoined to him and that he constitutes in his own self a body to which [all creation] has been attached because of its union to him. It is not right then for a teacher to intend anything other that what [Paul] has taught about the one to whom all things have been fitted and bonded. For by common consent he has made himself to be anathema.

16

ON THE INCARNATION

[The following are most of the passages that have been preserved from Theodore's major work *On the Incarnation*. I have translated the texts provided by Migne in PG 66, by Swete in the appendix section of his second volume, and by Sachau in his collection of Syriac excerpts. All these may have survived because his adversaries chose them, to highlight what they considered to be his heretical views or tendencies regarding the unity of Christ's divine and human nature. This work seems to have been written in the middle or late 380s in opposition to Apollinaris' christological position that stressed the Word's assumption of Christ's human rational soul as best explaining how the Word and Jesus can be truly considered as a singular substantial unity.]

(Book 1) (*PG* 66: 969/Latin) If, therefore, Nathanael is shown by his confession not to have acknowledged [Christ's] Deity – [for even though] the Jews and Samaritans were awaiting this – they were far from knowing God the Word. So too one [can] show that Martha, when she made her confession, did not have knowledge of [Christ's] Deity. Neither, clearly, did the blessed Peter. Yet they still had received sufficient revelation to [be able to] accept some essential points that would have had them looking upon him as greatly exceeding all other possible human beings. When the Spirit led them to [full] knowledge after the resurrection, they then accepted the full knowledge of what had been revealed: that [Christ] reached his pre-eminent state, surpassing all others, because he had received it not as some pure honor from God, as do the rest of humans, but because of his unity with God the Word, whereby he shares in all His honors after he has ascended into heaven.

(Book 2) (Swete 1882: 291–2/Latin) Jesus the Man. For "What is a human being that You are mindful of him?" (Ps. 8:5). The apostle affirms that this has been said of Jesus. For he says that "The one whom we see who has been made a little less than the angels [is] Jesus" (Heb. 2:9). How is this so? For Jesus is a human being like all human beings, differing in no way from those sharing his nature, other than that [God] has graced him. But the grace given to him does not change his nature. Then, after incurring death, "God gave him a name above every name" (Phil. 2:9). God is the One giving, and the one given [this grace] is Jesus Christ, the first fruits of those who will rise. For he is "the firstborn of the dead" (Col. 1:18). He has ascended, sits at the right hand of God, and is over all. What an all-surpassing grace has been given to Jesus – a grace that transcends every nature! Although he has the same nature as my own, he has been shown to be above the heavens, sitting at the right hand of the Father. I say to him: "Your nature and mine are not one. For you are in heaven, while I am [burdened] with passions. You are over every principle and power, while I exist in filth." But I hear [in response] that "The Father has been well pleased with me. Will the one who has been fashioned say to the One fashioning him, why did you make me this way? I have nothing at all to say to this. For my brethren, sons [and daughters] of mothers similar to my own, say to me: "Do not separate God and humans, but affirm them to be one and the same by stating that being human and God are [states] connatural to me."[1] If I say that God is connatural [to me], state then how a man and God are one. Is there one nature for man and God, for the Master and the servant, for the Maker and [His] handiwork? A human being is connatural with [another] human being. How then can man and God be one in a unified way, the One saving and the one saved, the One who is before the ages and the one born of Mary? Therefore, I am deeply grieved that my colleagues say to me that I am proclaiming in the church what a truly wise man ought not to say.

(Book 2) (*PG* 66: 969/Latin) [This is clearly a partial version of the previous selection, indicating how the Latin translators can vary.] But you say to me as brothers who are sons of the same mother: "Do not separate the man from God but affirm that the man is one and the same [with Him]." I say that the one who is connatural to me I call God. If I say that the One who is connatural to God is the one I call a man, how is it that God and man are one? Is there one nature for the man and God, for the Lord and the servant, the Creator and the one created? Is the man consubstantial with [other] humans, and God consubstantial with God? How, therefore, can the man and God be one through a [true] unity – the One who saves and is saved, the one who is before the ages and who appeared from Mary?

(Book 5) (*PG* 66: 969–70/Latin) When anyone considers the natures, he necessarily discovers [that they are different from] one another. Nor do I think that there is any controversy here, since God the Word is one by nature and the other is admitted to have been assumed (whatever this may mean).[2] Yet this latter is said to be simultaneously the same person (*persona*) whose [two] natures are in no way confused, but [are one] because of the assumed one's union with the assuming One. For, if one willingly grants that the latter is other than the former by nature, it is evident that the one assumed is not equal to the One assuming. However each will be clearly found to be the same one in a prosopic union. Therefore, one has to make distinctions in regard to Christ without there being any contradiction here. For these [distinctions] closely conform to what the divine Scriptures [state]. So the natures are not to be confused, nor the person to be perversely divided. Both the way the natures relate to one another must stay unconfused and the person must be acknowledged as undivided. On one hand, the natures exist by what is proper to [each], with the assumed one being distinguished from [his] Assumer. Yet on the other hand, [they are undivided] in their prosopic union. For they are said to be as one because the natures of the Assumer and the assumed are [each] considered as belonging to their [natures'] whole [unity]. And, if I may say so, we call God the Word by the name of Son and at the same time also affirm [the same] of the assumed nature on account of his union to the [Word].

(Book 6) (*PG* 66: 970–2/Latin) If, therefore, we appear to them to be rightly characterized [as one of] the *hominicolae* (those who are overly obsessed with [Christ's] humanity) when we state that Christ is human, Scripture has taught all this – [even] before we asserted it – in those [passages] where it does not hesitate to call him a man, as we have shown above in very many places where Christ is referred to in this way. They say: "Those asserting Christ to be a pure man ought to be called *hominicolae*." This is an open lie on the part of those who would want to say this. For no one has ever heard us say these things. I think that such an open lie cannot be [seriously] maintained, not because these [enemies] are not knowingly given to lying, but because they can be easily refuted. However, if one pays little attention to what is said, this [charge] may perhaps be taken [seriously]. For us to say this, namely to deny the divinity of the Only Begotten, would be, in our opinion, utmost madness.

Why then is it that the heretics are now distancing themselves from us? For what reason do we suffer such and so many kinds of persecutions? Who is ignorant of the opposition that the heretics are always waging against us? Every mine and every deserted location [where prisoners are sent in exile] are overflowing with our brethren because of our devotion to [the true] doctrine [lacuna]. The blessed Miletus[3] was the first subjected to all these [attacks] by the heretics and then, after him, many others throughout our provinces, cities, and neighborhoods, what was the reason? Is it not because they were preaching that the true Son of God was begotten from the Father's essence, always existing at the same time with [His] generating Father, together with a fervent confession of the Holy Spirit? Can we, therefore, who have suffered as much [as these have] in making this confession, suffer those [now] calumniating us [with the charge] that we are affirming [Christ] to be a "pure man" – though the facts clearly contradict this calumny?

(Book 7) (*PG* 66: 972/Greek) For, if we learn how the indwelling takes place, we will know both its mode and its modal difference.[4] Some declare that the indwelling has occurred in a substantial way and others [that it has occurred] in an operational way. Let there be, therefore, a careful examination [to learn] if there is any truth to these [statements]. First of all, let us agree: does [the Word] dwell in all or not? But it is evident: not in all. For God has promised that His [indwelling] comes as a special relationship to the saints or, generally speaking, to those whom He wants set apart for Himself. But, if this is so, what was [God] promising when He says: "I will dwell and walk among these [faithful ones] and be their God, and they will be my people" (Lev. 26:12), showing them thereby some special favor? But [how] do those human beings who disobey [God] publicly share this [favor]? For if He does not dwell in all – and clearly I am speaking here not only of things but also of human beings – there needs to be some special reason for His indwelling, whereby He is present only to those in whom He said He would dwell.

To say, therefore, that God dwells [in Christ's humanity] in a substantial way is wrong. For then one would have to restrict His substance to only those in whom He said He would dwell, thereby being distant from all others – which is absurd to say about an infinite nature that is present everywhere and limited by nothing. So if someone states that God is present everywhere, by reason of His substance, he [must] also attribute His indwelling to all, not merely to humans but also to irrational and inanimate beings, [that is] if we maintain that He dwells by means of His substance. Both of these [statements] are clearly false. For to say that God dwells in all is to state an outright absurdity, and to equate this [universal] substance to Him is unbecoming. Therefore to say that the indwelling occurs by reason of substance should be [considered] utmost folly.[5]

Someone can also say the same about [God being present] by means of His activity. For His operational presence ought again to be limited to those alone [experiencing His power]. (974) How then will we account for the fact that God foresees all things and governs all things and acts upon everything in an appropriate and correct way that accords in a consistent way with [each nature] by means of those serving as His agents in the universe? For, since He endows all things with the power for each to be its self and to work according to its own nature, we [can] say that He does dwell in all things. Thus [we can] clearly state that it is in neither a substantial nor operational way that God has effected these kinds of indwelling. What then is left? What reason can we offer that seems to preserve what is special about these [indwellings]? Clearly, it is fair to state that [God's] indwelling has taken place by good pleasure.[6] Good pleasure is said to be God's most excellent and noblest desire to benefit those who are pleasing to Him because of their effort to be devoted to Him. For those deeds that are [done] well in a noble way are seen to be pleasing to Him, [a view] usually taken for granted by the Scriptures and found in them, as the blessed David says: "His will does not [rely] on the strength of a horse, nor is He well pleased about a man's speed. The Lord takes pleasure in those who fear Him and hope in His mercy" (Ps. 147:10–11). Although [God] affirms His refusal to cooperate with some and His unwillingness to work with others, yet [God] says to those [reverentially] fearing Him that He esteems them greatly and is pleased to work with them and aid them. In this way then, it is fitting to speak of an indwelling. For, being infinite and unlimited in His nature, [God] is present to all. But by His good pleasure He is thus distant from some and near to others. [The Scripture] agrees with this viewpoint: "The Lord is near to the broken hearted and will save the humble in spirit" (Ps. 34:18); and elsewhere: "Do not cast me away

from your presence and do not take away your holy Spirit from me"
(Ps. 51:11). Thus He is near because He is [fondly] disposed toward
those worthy of His nearness, and again far from sinners, although He
is neither separated [from them] nor found to be closer by reason of
His nature. He responds to both in light of how His will is disposed
[toward them]. So He is near and distant by His good pleasure, as is
evident from what we have said when we spoke about [God's] good
pleasure.

Therefore, we have discussed in precise ways what is meant by
the assertion that [God] effects [His] indwelling by good pleasure.
He is not limiting His substance or operation in these instances,
because He exists apart from all others. Rather He is present to all in
a substantial way, but separated from the unworthy by how He is now
disposed [towards them]. For in this way His unlimited [existence]
is better preserved, since His unlimited nature appears here not to be
essentially restrained. If He were indeed present everywhere by [His]
good pleasure, then He would once again be found to be necessarily
constrained to be there. He would then not be present in a voluntary
way but by means of His infinite nature, with His will being [by
necessity] in agreement with this. Since He is both present to all by
[His] nature, and separated from those from whom He voluntarily
wants to be, then in no way do the unworthy profit from the presence
of God. In this way, His infinite nature is preserved, and is true and
complete.

(976) So, therefore, (God) is present to some and separated from
others by [His] good pleasure, to the extent that, even though
separated from all the rest, He is [nevertheless] with all these by [His]
substance. In the same way that the indwelling occurs according to
[God's] good pleasure, so too does [His] good pleasure vary its mode
of indwelling. For what prompts God to dwell in some, and to reveal
to them that He is present everywhere by reason of [His] substance,
and dwells in even the most unlikely beings – I am speaking here about
[His] good pleasure – [this is what] conditions the mode of [God's]
indwelling in all cases. For just as He is said to be dwelling not in
all when He is present to all by His substance, but only to those in
whom He is present by His good pleasure, so [in this sense] He can be
said to dwell. But this [mode] of indwelling is not found to be equally
everywhere, but is dependent upon the extent to which God dwells by
His good pleasure. Therefore, when He is said to dwell either in the
apostles or generally in the just, then He dwells there insofar as He is

pleased with these upright individuals, just as [He does] when pleased with the virtuous. However, we do not maintain that the indwelling took place in [Christ] in this way – for we would never be so mad, but as in [His] Son. For since [God] was well pleased [with him] He dwelt [within him] in this way. What then is [meant by] "as in [His] Son"? [It should be understood] in the sense that, when [the Word] dwells [within his humanity], He has united Himself wholly to the assumed one and made him share in every honor that [the Son] shares, because he is the one in whom [God's] Son dwells by nature, to such an extent that He is accounted to be one person (*prosōpon*) because of his union with him. [God], therefore, shares all His power with [his humanity], so that all things will be accomplished by means of him and that [the Father] will pass judgment on all, by examining through him when [Christ] will come [at the end of time], but with the clear understanding that [the Father and Jesus] differ [from each other] in accordance with what correctly pertains to their natures.

(Book 7) (*PG* 66: 976–7/Greek) Although we will in the future be wholly guided by the Spirit in what pertains to our body and soul, nevertheless we now possess a small portion [of His grace] as our first fruits. Because we are now being aided by the Spirit, we are not impelled to follow the evil thoughts [that arise] out of our soul. [This would also be true in the case of] our Lord, even though he would later most certainly have God the Word completely acting in him, with his every action being inseparable from Him. But, prior to this, [God] would be implementing in him, as much as possible, most of what he needed. Up to the time of his crucifixion he was allowed to excel in virtue for our sake, by relying on his own resolve, but with God urging him on in these efforts and aiding him to completely fulfill what was at hand. For [Christ's humanity] was united to [the Word] right from the beginning of its fashioning within the womb. So, when he reached the age when human beings acquire the power to discern between good and evil, he had already earlier acquired this critical power to discern such differences much faster than all others who attain it, but they generally do not do so all at the same time. For some more quickly devote themselves to the [attainment of] greater practical wisdom about what needs [to be done], whereas others acquire this over a longer period of time by means of training. What stands out in [Christ's] relationship, in comparison to all others, is that his [growth] occurred more swiftly for him than it is customary for others of [his] age, yet in a way fully appropriate [to his state]. But he also possessed something more in his relationship to others: he was not born as humans regularly are in a natural way through the union of a man and a woman, but rather he was formed by the activity of the divine Spirit.

(Book 7) (*PG* 66: 977/Greek) [Christ in the flesh] was also inclined not [to seek out] what is better in a haphazard way because of his union with God the Word. He was deemed worthy of this because God the Word foreknew that He would unite him to Himself from the beginning. Because of all this, he possessed from the very beginning a deep hatred for evil. Since [Christ in the flesh] joined himself [to God's will] with an irrepressible love for the good, God the Word actively assisted his resolve. He then persevered, not yielding to [any] inferior tendency. With this [kind] of purposeful thinking, which God the Word actively provided for him, he then pursued with exceptional ease the most perfect [life of] virtue, both by keeping the law before baptism, and after baptism by pursuing his public life, [aided] by grace. He submitted his [life] as a type for us, since it establishes for us the way to [achieve fulfillment]. Then later, after rising and ascending into heaven, he revealed that he himself was personally worthy of the union that had taken place earlier, at his fashioning, because of our Lord's good pleasure.

[Christ in the flesh] truly reveals that in his union he has no separate operation apart from God the Word, because he has God the Word accomplishing all in him because of [His] union with him. So, therefore, before [Christ's death on] the cross, we see him hungry, observe that he is thirsty, learn that he is fearful, and discover that he does not know [fully his motivation] when he reflects on his reason [for acting] in a virtuous way. The prophet Isaiah witnesses to all this when he affirms: "Before the child knew good and evil, he was set free from evil, to choose the good" (Isaiah 7:16); that is, by [his ability to] be aware of why he hates the former and loves the latter. For every act of choosing always involves an act of discerning what is inferior. How, therefore, was this accomplished that "Before the child knew" – that is, before he came of that age when all other human beings ordinarily discern what is to be done – he was more exceptionally gifted than the rest of humanity? Since we frequently find among us an infant wise for his years, who offers such signs of advanced knowledge that onlookers become wonderstruck at how such a one manifests more knowledge than [one expects at their] age, I presume, therefore, that [Christ] must have far surpassed all those of the same age as himself.

(Book 7) (*PG* 66: 980/Greek) "Jesus advanced by age and wisdom and grace before God and human beings" (Luke 2:52). For he advances "by age" with the passage of time; "by wisdom," by acquiring knowledge over time; and "by grace," by pursuing virtue in ways consistent with practical and theoretical knowledge. God's grace increased his virtue, and he was thus [able to] progress "before God and human beings," [at least] before those who see his progress. For [God] not only observes this but also testifies [to it] and works with him in what he does. Clearly [Jesus] has completed a virtuous life in a more perfect way and with greater ease than it was possible for all other human beings. Seeing how fully God the Word foreknew what sort of person [Christ in the flesh] would be when He united him to Himself from the very moment of his fashioning, [God] has enabled him to cooperate with Him in a far greater way for the successful accomplishment of righteousness by dispensing through [Christ's humanity] what [is necessary] for the salvation of all, by urging [Jesus] on to more perfect [undertakings], and by diminishing those struggles [affecting his] soul and body, and his very self from the moment of his fashioning. [God] has thus enabled him to cooperate with Him in a far greater way to successfully achieve justification, by dispensing through [his humanity] what [is necessary] for the salvation of all; by urging [Christ in the flesh] on to more perfect [tasks], by diminishing those struggles [affecting his] soul and body and thereby equipping him fully for a greater and more rapid fulfillment of virtue.

(Book 7) (*PG* 66: 980/Greek) For the assumed one became united to God from the beginning [of his earthly existence] in accordance with [His] foreknowledge. This union started from the moment he was fashioned in [his] mother's womb. Since he was deemed worthy of [this] union, he received everything that was humanly possible for one united to the Only Begotten Lord of all. For he was judged to be worthy of obtaining greater [gifts] than all others, seeing how utterly exceptional was his union. He was furthermore thought worthy of becoming first among all other humans [to experience] the Spirit's indwelling. He was deemed worthy of this [but] not in the same way as all others. For he received within himself every grace [belonging] to the Spirit and has passed on to others a partial sharing in the Spirit's fullness. The Spirit has agreed to accomplish everything in him when He spoke in a loud, clear voice, affirming that: "He was a man." But the meaning of these words is multifaceted and ambiguous.

(Book 8) (*PG* 66: 980/Greek) "And I have given them the glory that You gave me." What kind [of glory] is this? [It is] to share in his Sonship. For he received this [honor] *qua* man when he was earlier baptized in the Jordan. In relation to his baptism, ours has become a type. The Father's voice has attested to the rebirth that is taking place [here] when He asserts: "This is my beloved Son in whom I am well pleased." Then, after the Spirit descended, He remained with him, just as we too are going to share in his baptism, although his remains far superior (981) to our own. For, through his union with God the Word, he shares in what belongs to [God's] Son by nature.

(Book 8) (*PG* 66: 981/Greek) In every way, therefore, this mixture [of natures] is clearly superfluous, foolish, and unacceptable, since each of the natures remains indissoluble in itself. A [mixed] kind of union is clearly unsuited. For, since the natures are bound in this union, they constitute one person (*prosōpon*), in a way [similar] to how our Lord speaks of [the union of] a man and a woman: "So they are no longer two but one flesh" (Matt. 19:6). We can also speak in this way about the meaning of [Christ's] union that there are no longer two *prosōpa* but one, clearly [made up] of distinct natures. For just as they can be said to be one flesh without contradicting the fact they are numerically two – of course, this is clearly dependent on how they are said to be one – so also in the present case the union in [one] *prosōpon* does not undermine the distinction between the natures. For, when we distinguish the natures, we say that the *physis* (nature) of God the Word is complete and [His] *prosōpon* is complete. Also it is not possible to say that there is a *hypostasis* without a *prosōpon*. And the *physis* of the man is complete and likewise his *prosōpon*. Whenever, however, we look to their union, we then affirm one *prosōpon*.[7]

(Book 8) (*PG* 66: 981/Greek) Likewise we say here that the substance (*ousia*) of God the Word is His very own, and the man's his own. For the natures are distinct, whereas the *prosōpon* is one because of the union. So too, whenever we attempt to distinguish the natures here, we say that the man's *prosōpon* is complete and that the divinity's is also complete (*teleion*). But, whenever we look to the union, then we assert that both natures are one *prosōpon*, with the humanity receiving at [his] creation the divinity's honor and with the divinity accomplishing everything expected of him.

(Book 8) (Swete 1882: 299/Syriac) Therefore it is like the way we distinguish human nature. We say that the nature of the soul is one and that of the body another, understanding that each of them has a *hypostasis* (*qnōmā*) and a nature (*kyānā*) and granting that, while the soul is distinguished from its body, it remains in its nature and in its *hypostasis*. Each of them has its own nature and *hypostasis*, as we have learnt from the apostle that there is an inner and outer man. We state their unity by combining both the "inner and the outer" in a common way [as one *prosōpon*], so as not to call [the two] by a single term as if they were united in the same *hypostasis*.[8] Rather we respond to [our critics] that there is one *prçwpā* (*prosōpon*) and say that these two are [united] in one [*prosōpon*].

(Book 9) (*PG* 66: 981/Greek) We have, therefore, concluded here that the [word] ἐγίνετο (was made) can in no way be said to be different from [what is meant] by τo δoxειν (to appear). For we have learnt this from what the divine Scripture states, primarily by what our Lord has more precisely [stated] in those other [passages mentioned] above. Thus "The Word was made flesh" (John 1:14) [means] "to appear." But "to appear" here [signifies] not that He did not assume true flesh but rather that He was not made [flesh]. For when He says "He assumed" he is not speaking [here] about what appears [to have happened], but about what is true. When [it is said] "He was made," this [should be understood] as "He appears." One must then agree with the evangelist that He has not been turned into flesh. It is in this sense that we understand the meaning of this word.

(Book 9) (Swete 1882: 300/Latin) So, if the statement "The Word was made flesh" is said [to connote] some change, how then is "He dwelt" (John 1:14) to be understood? For it is clear to all that "He dwells" is different from "he is dwelt in" ... For He dwelt in us by assuming our nature by dwelling [in it] and by dispensing everything [needed] for our salvation through him. How, therefore, did the indwelling Word of God become flesh? Clearly he has not been changed or transformed; for [otherwise] he would not be said to be indwelling.

(Book 9) (*PG* 66: 981 and 984/Greek) For what is being said about how we relate to a place is also applicable to how God relates according to His will. For, just as we say "I have been in this place," so also in the case of God [we can say] that He has been in this [place]. But, whereas we change [physically from one place to another], it is God's will [that changes] because He happens to be everywhere by reason of His nature.

(Book 10) (*PG* 66: 983–4/Latin) For since we are taught by means of such statements from the divine Scripture about the differences of the natures, we thus learn about the union as often as [the Scripture] joins what pertains to both natures into a unity and speaks [of them] as being one particular reality. [Scripture] is thereby simultaneously showing both the different natures and the unity of the person. The difference of natures is understood by how they are said to differ. When, however, they are combined, we infer an evident unity, as the evangelist, the blessed John, affirms: "The next day he saw Jesus coming to him and said, 'Behold the Lamb of God, behold him who takes away the sins of the world.' He is the one of whom I have spoken. For after me a man comes who was before me because he preceded me. But I did not know him" (John 1: 29–31). By stating here that "He saw Jesus coming to him and said, 'Behold the Lamb of God,'" this clearly seems to me to signify his humanity. For John the Baptist saw this one as the one who is to undergo death, because he is a "body" that has been offered for the whole world. Indeed [the words] that follows, "who takes away the sins of the world," is in no way applicable to flesh. For it was not in his power to take away the sin of the world. This is certainly the work of the divinity.

(Book 10) (*PG* 66: 984/Greek) "There appeared to him from heaven an angel strengthening him. Being in agony, he prayed more earnestly. And his sweat became like drops of blood falling to the ground" (Luke 22:43–44). Therefore we understand from this that it is clear that Christ patiently bore this extraordinary agony.

(Book 10) (*PG* 66: 984/Greek) What kind of consistency does this statement have: "The one who descended from heaven is also in heaven" (John 3:43)? For one contradicts the other. To have descended from heaven [contradicts] being in heaven. To be [there contradicts] having descended. But [God] descended in the sense that He dwelt in the man and He is in heaven in the sense that He is present to all thanks to His unlimited nature.

(Book 11) (*PG* 66: 984–85/Greek) Therefore, he did not say: "He spoke to us in the Son," but "in [no article] a son." For what is affirmed in an absolute sense [without the article] can thereby signify both in the same way, signifying in the first instance, "the true Son." I call the "true Son" that one who acquired his Sonship by a natural generation. In the second case, he is the one who has received this [Sonship] by being designated as such and who truly shares this dignity [of Sonship] because of his [humanity's] union with (the Word].

(Book 12) (*PG* 66:985/Greek) Will (my adversaries) then end [their] shameless struggle and cease any further arrogant desire to prevail, since they are clearly being embarrassed by their words? For (the sacred writer) says: "(God) was leading many children to glory." Note how in his understanding of "sonship," the apostle is seen to be including the assumed man together with most [others], not in the sense that he shares his Sonship as these do, but because of his similarity [with them], for they have received their sonship by means of grace. Only the divine Word possesses His Sonship by nature. However, his (the assumed man's) extraordinary [gift] of Sonship clearly exceeds that of all other humans because of his union with [God]. He received this when he heard that the title "Son" [of God] was given to him. But (my adversaries) have badly misrepresented us [by asserting] that since we say that there are two complete [natures], we are also certainly maintaining [the existence of] two sons. But note that [the term] "son" is also affirmed in the divine Scripture. When taken by itself the word can also be applied to other human beings, with an exception being made for the divinity. We do not say that there are two sons. We correctly confess one Son. Although their natures remain necessarily separated, their prosopic union is maintained unbroken. For after he said that God "has led many sons to glory," he adds, "to make their leader for salvation perfect through sufferings." See how clearly he says that God the Word has made the assumed man perfect through sufferings and has called him the leader of salvation, seeing that he was the first to be worthy to be designated as the cause [of salvation] for others.

(Book 12) (*PG* 66: 985/Greek) For [my adversaries] continually apply the name "son" to all these [others] as this accords with how they interpret [Scripture]. Because this way of speaking is more applicable to humans in general, they consider it right to use this term as being equivalent to how he is designated [as Son]. Because the name "Jesus" is said to be applicable to the assumed man, in the same way "Peter" and "Paul" are used for the apostles and likewise for others too, this title [of Son] was given him when he was born of Mary.

(Book 12) (*PG* 66: 985/Greek) But they respond to this [by saying] that the name "Jesus" signifies Savior. How then can they say that [this] man is a Savior? They have forgotten that Jesus (Joshua) was also said to be the son of Nave. It is worthy of note that [Joshua] was not haphazardly given this name by Moses at [his] birth. For Moses would certainly not have bestowed this [name] on him if it had in any way indicated the divine nature.[9]

(Book 12) (Swete 1882: 304–5/Greek) "Formerly in many and various ways God spoke to [our] fathers through the prophets, but in these last days He has spoken to us by [His] Son." It is clear here that, when he affirms "by [His] Son," he is referring to the man assumed. (Latin) "For to which of the angels did [God] at any time say: 'You are my son; today I have begotten you?'" He made none [of these] a partner in His Son's dignity. But when He says, "I have begotten you," He is signifying by this that this one shares in [His] Sonship. That he has no [natural] communion at all with God the Word clearly appears [from] what has been said . . . When He brings the firstborn into the world, he says: "Let God's angels adore him" (Heb. 1:6). Who, therefore, is the one who is brought into the world and begins his mastery, requiring the angels to adore him? For someone would be mad to state that God the Word, who has given existence to everything that did not exist by His ineffable power, is the one who has been brought [into the world] . . . The blessed Apostle, however, in responding to these [assertions], attempts to show how he is a participant in the divine honor – that he enjoys this, not on account of his nature but on account of the [Word's] nature dwelling within [him].

(Book 12) (*PG* 66: 988/Greek) Therefore he calls him "Son," not only after he has been distinguished from the Word of God but also because he is said to be included under the term for sonship, together with all other humans who share this sonship. Since he has also shared the grace of sonship, because he has not been naturally generated from the Father, nevertheless he enjoys pre-eminence over all others because he has acquired his Sonship from his union with the Word, who has granted him a more dominant participation in his [Sonship].

(Book 12) (Swete 1882: 306/Latin) If someone wants to ask who I finally say Jesus Christ is, I say: "God and the Son of God."

(Book 13) (Swete 1882: 306–7/Latin) The apostle, however, agrees with this when he says: "The mystery of [our] religion is clearly great: (Greek) the one revealed in the flesh is justified by the Spirit" (1 Tim. 3:16), meaning either that he kept the law before baptism with fitting exactitude or that afterwards, with the Spirit's cooperation, he exactly fulfilled his graced way of living.

(Book 13) (*PG* 66: 988/Greek) For John's statement that "I need to be baptized by you. Yet you come to me?" (Matt. 3:14) will not overturn the fact that he who is [to be] baptized is a man. So he submits to [John] as it accords with his humanity, even though he has pre-eminence over John by reason of his outstanding virtue. But, [even more] because God's nature is dwelling in him, he is also rightly acknowledged to have rank not only over John but also over all humans and even [all] creation.

(Book 13) (*PG* 66: 989–90/Latin) It is especially helpful at this point to conclude that there is some value in what has been said about [Jesus'] way of life, [his] baptism, crucifixion, death, burial and resurrection. We do not speak about these [events] as being pertinent to some mere man. But we do not delay [here] to draw out what we have explained at some length, so as not to provide any occasion for [our] calumniators to disparage [our efforts]. For [our aim is to point out that] God the Word has dwelt in him from the time he was fashioned in his mother's womb and has dwelt in him not by reason of a general [kind of] inhabitation or by that [general] grace understood to be present in many, but according to a certain excelling grace whereby we maintain that both natures are united and that there is effected one *persona* (*prosōpon*) by reason of this union.

(Book 14) (*PG* 66: 989/Greek) Hence this honor of being able to sit at the right hand of the Father and be adored by all of creation has come to this man because he was deemed worthy of the divine indwelling. For God would not simply assume and unite a man to Himself without some useful reason: [such as] preparing him to be adored by all creation. For [God] would not allow rational natures to worship [Christ's humanity], unless what has come to pass in him was to be a common benefit for all creation.

(Book 14) (*PG* 66: 989/Greek) We will rightly say the same thing about our Lord: that, because God the Word knew his virtue through

His foreknowledge, He was pleased to dwell in him immediately from the very beginning of his fashioning, and to unite him to Himself because he was well disposed toward him. He then provided him with greater grace than what will be distributed in a continuous way to all those who are related to him. From that time on, He kept pure his resolve to [do] good. We will not assert that this man had no voluntary role [to play], for he did prefer the good; in fact, he purposely desired to accomplish the greatest good and to hate evil. His pure resolve was protected by divine grace, with God perfectly knowing from the very beginning what kind of person he is and, by dwelling in him, providing him with a considerable [degree of] cooperation, in order to strengthen him [to work] for the salvation of all of us. Thus one would not be wrong to assert that, compared with all [others], the assumed man received from our Lord unique [assistance].

(Book 14) (*PG* 66: 991–2/Latin) [Christ] fulfills the role of image for two reasons. Those who love certain individuals often fashion images after their death, thinking thereby to attain ample solace [for dealing] with [their] deaths. By looking at [their] image, they think they are looking at one who is no longer either visible or present, thereby appeasing the passionate longing of [their] desire. So too those rulers who have their image [mounted] within the cities are thought, through the cultic adoration [shown them], to be honoring the images of those [leaders] who are not present but are to be treated as being present.[10] Both of these [roles] are fulfilled by Christ. For all his followers who seek after virtue and are prepared to fulfill their obligations towards God love Him and greatly honor Him. Even though His divine nature is not seen, they can fully express their love for Him by means of the one who is seen by all, with all judging that they see [God] through [his humanity] and are always [able to be] present to Him. And so [his followers] bestow every honor upon him as the imperial image, since the divine nature is in him and is seen to be in him. For, if the Son is said to dwell [in him], then the Father is also with him. For [the Father] is believed by everyone to be in every way inseparable from the Son. The Spirit is not absent, because He also came to [Christ in the flesh] at the moment when He anointed him and is always with the assumed one. This [indwelling] should not be surprising to all those pursuing virtue that the Father is said to be with the Son: "For we will come, both I and the Father, and we will make our mansion with him" (John 14:23). All are certain too that the Spirit is inseparable from [the Father and the Son].

(Book 15) (*PG* 66: 993/Latin) Both are rightly called the "Son," seeing that there is one living "person" whom the union of natures has effected.

(Book 15) (Swete 1882: 310/Greek) When, therefore, [my adversaries] ask "Is Mary the mother of the man or of God?" let it be said by us: both. For [the former] is *de facto* so by nature, the other by a relation. For [Mary] is the mother of the humanity by nature, seeing that the man has come forth from Mary's womb. But, as regards Mary being the mother of God, His nature was not enclosed there, even though God was present when the man was born. But His will was present because this was what He wanted [to do]. (Latin) Thus it is right to say "both," but not for the same reason. For, although the man has come to be in the womb, this is not true for God the Word, who exists before every creature. Therefore, it is right to assert "both," but both of them for their own reasons. The same answer ought to be given, when they raise the question: "Has God or man been crucified?" [The answer] is "both," but not for the same reason. For it is the latter who was crucified, as he is the one who underwent suffering when he hung on the cross after being arrested by the Jews; the former [is said to be crucified] in the sense that He was with him in the way we have stated above.

(Book 15) (Swete 1882: 311/Greek) For our Lord was more troubled by his struggles with the spiritual passions than with those of the body.[11] But because of his superior reasoning power [the assumed man] conquered [lustful] desires, because the divinity was clearly mediating and aiding him to succeed in these instances. (Latin) Hence our Lord is seen to be the one especially battling against these. Since he did not surrender to an avaricious longing for money, nor was tempted by a desire for glory, he provided no opening to his flesh and thus [could] not be conquered. However, if he had not received a soul, and it was the Deity who conquered, then nothing he did would benefit us. For what advantage would there be for the perfection of our way of living in having the Deity [acting] as the human soul? For then our Lord's struggles would seem to have no advantage for us, but rather to have been [done] for the sake of show. This cannot be said [of our Lord], for it is certain that he has done these things for us and that he engaged in a greater struggle against the spiritual passions and less against those of the flesh. For it was much more appropriate that he would resist the former, seeing that there was a much greater need for a more plentiful healing here than for the flesh. For, after he received both flesh and a soul, he contended with both for the sake of both by mortifying sin in his flesh, by subduing his libidinous desires, and by easily controlling them in a better, rational way, by means of his [rational] soul, by teaching and training the soul to conquer its passions and to resist its fleshy passions. For, by dwelling within [his humanity], the Deity was also engaged in these [tasks]. [It is] because of His indwelling that [the Word] assisted [him in dealing] with both of these [passions].

(Book 15) (Swete 1882: 311–12/Greek) The Word knew from his foreknowledge that a man would be born from a virgin without intercourse and that [his humanity] would be united in an inseparable way with Himself, whereby they both have an identical will. For, having been pleased with [Jesus], [the Word] had united him to Himself. [Jesus] has clearly shown that he and his activity are exactly similar to [the Word's], so that his rule and power are inseparable from [the Word's] and the adoration [shown them] does not differ because they are equal by reason of their composition.[12]

[The following excerpt is included at the end of this section in Migne. It highlights Theodore's position on how the common *prosōpon* has one will. It is not clear from which work it has been drawn.]

(*PG* 66: 1003/Greek) When our Savior said to the leper, "I will it. Be clean," he shows here that there exists one will and one operation produced according to one and the same power, [that is effected] not on the level of nature but on the level of good pleasure whereby [the assumed man] is united to God the Word. For, in accordance with what was foreknown [about his descent] from the seed of David, he became a man from his mother, besides having [at the same time] an innate familiarity[13] with [the Word].

(The Second Letter of Theodore to Artemius of Alexandria) (*PG* 66: 1011–12/Latin). They ought to know that we adore the Father, Son, and Holy Spirit when we affirm that the divine, eternal, and uncreated Trinity is perfected in them. Since each of these [Persons] belongs to the same substance (that is, of the eternal and truly divine cause of everything made), the Father is to be adored for no other [reason] than that this is owed because of His substance; so too is the Son who receives [adoration] for no other [reason] than that His substance fully corresponds to that of His Father. Likewise, because we acknowledge the Holy Spirit to be from the same substance, we also adore Him because of His own [shared] substance. So we say three Persons, each one perfect from the same eternal and divine substance because we think that [this substance] is the cause of everything created. We adore the three Persons, believing that they belong to one, truly divine nature. How, therefore, is it possible to claim that in addition to these three there is a fourth person – the form of an assumed slave – whose form we reckon not to be of the very same substance and to whom worship is not rightfully due? We do not say that he is to be adored because of his own substance. Nor do we adore him [as existing] separately in his own person, as [my adversaries] think we have made such divisions [as regards his person].

(Letter to Domnus) (*PG* 66: 1012–13/Greek). The unity[14] of natures according to good pleasure is the reason why both of these [natures] can be said to have an identical name, will, operation, authority, lordship, rule, dignity, and power undivided in every way. For their [common] *prosōpon* is said to be one for both at the same time. Why then is it necessary to say more? The reason for the union according to substance is justified in those cases where one is dealing only with the same substances, but it is false in those cases where the substances differ from one another, because there is no possibility for them to be joined together. But the kind of unity according to good pleasure keeps the natures unmixed and undivided and makes it clear that there is one person (*prosōpon*) for both, as well as one will and one operation, with one authority and rule flowing from these . . . Since [the assumed man], having been born, as we said [earlier], from the virgin's womb, was united to God the Word according to a kind of good pleasure, he remained an undivided Temple, with the same will and the same operation with Him in all things, for there is no closer unity [than this].

[The following is taken from Theodore's *Commentary on Haggai* (*PG* 66: 485A/Greek). It is helpful for explaining Theodore's understanding of *prosōpon* in relation to that of *hypostasis*.] We have learned that the Father possesses His own *prosōpon*, and the Son His *prosōpon*, and the Holy Spirit His *prosōpon*, taking into account that each of them is equally sharing in the divine and eternal *ousia* . . . The Old [Testament], as I said, did not know of the Holy Spirit [existing] in His own *prosōpon* and *hypostasis* because [the Jews thought] He was separate from God. It called the Holy Spirit [for instance] the spirit of

God, or His grace, or authority, or care, or disposition, or something like this.

(Sachau 1869: Fol. 3b [Syriac]/29 [Latin]) Therefore this [verb form] *egigneto* (he became) is affirmed in the Scriptures as having multiple meanings. We too affirm it as generally having many senses. For it is used at times in an active sense, but at other times in a passive sense; and then too at times in its actual [literal] sense, and in a hypothetical way. Today many who do not stress something as factually true understand this term [as meaning] that something is held as if it were so. [The next two verses have been so corrupted that it is difficult to know their meaning.] It is also affirmed in a substantial way – [an opinion that] many think is an accurate one. But, when [taken] in this way, it is rightly considered to be quite ambiguous. For a term is understood in a substantial sense in a twofold way: either [that a being remains] as it was from the beginning or that it has been changed into something else in an active sense, as [the psalmist] has said: "God has become my helper and refuge, and my deliverer"; and elsewhere "The Lord has become my refuge, and God my helper." But God is not a helper and deliverer because He is changed, but rather because He is acting in merciful and helpful ways [and in this sense] indicating some activity [on His part]. So too, in the Acts of the Apostles, the blessed Peter affirms: "My fellow men, does not Scripture have to fulfill what the Spirit has said by the mouth of David, regarding Judas, that he became the leader of those betraying Jesus?" This too is stated as happening in an active sense. For Judas, in fact, did become a leader. But it is also true in a passive sense, in [the sense that] "I became like a deaf man, and there is no retort in his mouth," and again, "I became an enigma to them." But here "I became" is not to be [taken in the sense that he became] deaf because of his many hardships. Rather he is said to have become like a deaf man because of his many painful adversities, in an actual or applied sense, as when it said of Christ: "He came under the law, in order to ransom those under the law." [Paul] means that [Christ] was under the law because he was ruled by it and that he fulfilled it throughout his whole life. And [the same can be said] also of "Become imitators of me." Clearly this refers to how most are to live out their lives.

(Sachau 1869: Fol. 9a–b [Syriac]/50–1 [Latin]) Our adversaries ask us: "Who is the one needing help? Is it the one who is merciful, or the one seeking mercy, or the one needing help?" They cunningly design this so that it becomes a difficult, depraved question for the upright [to answer], for they are in no way solicitous to [promote] church teachings in a suitable and fitting way. Thus it is necessary to validate these [points] from the divine Scriptures, notwithstanding the fact that they can also be justified by the way we argued above. Since the natures differ, their properties must [be said to] flow in accordance with their differences, whenever we intend to inquire about their natures. [We are prompted to do so] because of the faithlessness of those questioning [us] in this bizarre way, as this one has done, by introducing the novel term *hypostasis* [to describe Christ's unity].[15] So we have qualified his [way of speaking], to make clear that [the Word] is the one helping and [the assumed man] the one being helped. First, we have been taught by the evangelist that, after our Lord came to Jerusalem, he began to expel from the Temple those selling doves and sheep, and he said to them: "This house is for praying and not set apart for trade." They asked him for a sign indicating whose authority confirmed this and who was commanding that this long-held custom be ended. He did not say anything [directly] but replied: "Dissolve this temple, and in three days I will raise it up." The evangelist then interprets this, saying: "He is speaking here about the temple of his body." These [adversaries] thereupon approached and said to us – how enjoyable it is to use their own words against them – "The one raising is either raising the dead one who is to be raised or the one undergoing his dissolution." But these are opposites and cannot be reconciled with one another. For the one dissolved [in death] needs one who will raise him up. However, the latter transcends [such] suffering. It is by His power that the one dissolved has been raised. They tell us that we must respond to their questioning [on this point]. But we reply to this [question] without much difficulty, by saying that we have abundant knowledge of this [issue] from the Scriptures. For one is dissolved [by death], and the other is the One who raises him up. The former is the temple who is subject to dissolution, whereas the One who raises him up is God the Word, who has promised to raise up the temple that has been dissolved. How then is it that [my adversaries] do not draw from this [statement] the distinction of natures and come to know the truth, but rather they seek by these cunning questions to unsettle the upright?

(Sachau 1869: Fol. 16a [Syriac]/51 [Latin]) Humans are very often in doubt about such things because of [my opponents'] cunning. It is evident here what must appropriately be said of human nature and what distinctions [have to] be made to distinguish this [assumed man] from the divinity, since they exist together in the union. For a unity exists when all [the attributes] are referred to our Lord and Savior Jesus Christ. But whenever the natures are scrutinized separately, [to determine] what each is affirming, [one must note] how [what is stated] coheres with its nature and how this accords with the rule regarding how things are to be attributed to each nature. For, whenever they are joined together in a unity of person (*prṣwpā*), both natures are said to be [united] in a participatory way, when they are in an agreement because of the unity. For, in this situation, what is distinct by nature is also affirmed to clearly exist in a conjoined way [to the other nature], because of the unity of the person (*prṣwpā*).

17

IN OPPOSITION TO
APOLLINARIS

[The following passages have been translated from Swete's, Migne's, and Sachau's collections of excerpts from the works that Theodore wrote against Apollinaris and his followers, who were his primary theological adversaries during his lifetime. It is not clear whether these selections belong to one or possibly two or more different works Theodore wrote to refute the Apollinarian view that the Word supplanted Christ's human rational soul. Apollinaris believed on philosophical grounds that to have a true unity Christ's human nature had to be incomplete and must have been incorporated into the complete nature of the Word, in order to form a singular reality.]

(Swete 1882: 321–2/Latin) Thirty years ago we wrote our book *On the Lord's Incarnation* with its 15,000 lines. Throughout that entire work, we examined Arius' and Eunomius' errors on this topic, as well as Apollinaris' vain presumptions, in order, as I usually do, not to gloss over in any way issues that deal with our adherence to ecclesial orthodoxy and with our overcoming their impiety. For those who readily accept everything without any difficulty, and those who have been instructed by Apollinaris, the leader of this heresy, together with all those thinking as he does, have made our work well known. They seek somehow to discover successful arguments to counter what has been written here. But, since no one has come forward to refute these writings, they are like weak but cunning athletes, who are incapable of overcoming those stronger [than themselves] and try to conquer by whatever deceitful ploys they can [use] . . . For they have assembled among themselves certain indisputably weak [positions] that were never made by us. Furthermore they have to some degree interjected these into our writings and have emphasized these for their followers, even at times for our own [followers] who listen to all these [charges] with well-disposed minds because of their own good nature. They have presented these [positions] to their readers as proof of our impiety – according to their way of thinking. One such statement is that we assert two sons. They present us as having affirmed in this work that one ought to think and say [the existence of] two sons. But we vigorously defend our way of speaking, clearly affirming at the same time that two sons cannot be said to be asserted anywhere in Scripture. Therefore, those listening to these charges must view them as being not only inept but also weak. For such a [charge] cannot be substantiated as true on the basis of a strong, creditable argument. They are thus writing for those who are uninformed. For this reason, this author can very easily be proven wrong. However, one of our followers, who is of upright nature, has believed these published statements to be ours. Because of this, [our followers] have believed that this person, who has superficially read these [writings], was truly trustworthy. He reported back to us what has been written. When we learnt [of this], we blamed him because he believed what was asserted against us regarding these matters, although he often heard us discussing these [positions] in church and in private. He ought to judge our word as being more faithful in expressing what we have vowed to preserve concerning dogmatic questions.

Book 3: (Swete 2:312/Latin). How, therefore, do you [Apollinaris], so specially qualified to guide the minds of all, assert that the one born of a virgin is to be considered God from God and consubstantial with the Father, unless by chance you expect us to attribute his creation to the Holy Spirit? (Greek) O marvelous one, has the One who is God from God and consubstantial with the Father truly come to exist by the Holy Spirit and obtained his body within this woman's womb? At the very moment he was fashioned, he had already been assumed as God's temple. We cannot admit (313) that God was born from a virgin, although we do hold that God the Word is simultaneously one and same with the one born and that [the Word] is both the temple and in the temple.[1] But you ought not boldly to assert that the one born of the virgin is in every way the One who is God from God and consubstantial with His Father. For, if the assumed one, born of the virgin, is not a man, as you say, but the incarnate God, how can a God so born be said to be from God and consubstantial with the Father? For flesh cannot confirm such a statement! It is simply unthinkable to maintain that God has been born from a virgin. For this differs in no way from saying that, because He has been begotten from the virgin's substance, He belongs, therefore, to the seed of David and He has been fashioned by her. For the one who proceeds from the seed of David and the virgin's substance, who has come to be in his mother's womb, and who is the one fashioned by the power of the Holy Spirit, is the one that we say has been born of a virgin.

(Latin) Someone may respond to this, by saying that the One who is God from God and consubstantial with the Father has been born from the virgin in the sense that He has been born in a temple. But the Word of God, when He became incarnate, has not been truly born in the way that this wise man is asserting. If, therefore, one says that the one who is consubstantial with His Father is the One who has been born, then He is also flesh. But, if this is not so, then the one who is flesh is neither God nor from God nor consubstantial with the Father but is from the seed of David, and comes from the same substance of that one from whose seed he is. The one born of the virgin is not God and from God and consubstantial with the Father, unless perhaps He is [the rational] "part" (*nous*) of the one born, as [Apollinaris] calls the Deity, [regarding Him] as that "part of Christ" [when he acts] in inferior [non-divine?] ways. (Greek) But the divine nature [of the Word] is not born from a virgin. Rather it is the one composed from the substance of the virgin who is born of the virgin. In no way has God the Word been (314) born of Mary! The one who is from the seed of David is the one born of Mary. In no way is God the Word born of a woman! The one fashioned in her by the power of the Holy Spirit is the one born of a woman. That One who is consubstantial with the Father is not begotten by a mother! For, as the blessed Paul says, He is "without a mother." Rather, the one fashioned in these last times in his mother's womb by the power of the Holy Spirit is the one said to be "without a father."

(PG 66: 994/Latin) God the Word is in the one fashioned. And He was [with him] not only when he was ascending into heaven but also when he was rising from the dead in accordance with His promise to resurrect him. [The Word] was present too not merely when [the assumed man] rose from the dead but also when he was crucified, when he was baptized, and when he was accomplishing his evangelical teaching after baptism, and in fact even before his baptism, when he was fulfilling what was required, as when he was presented [in the Temple], and at his circumcision as he was required by the Law. He was even present when he had been wrapped in swaddling clothes, having been in him as he was being born from the first [moment] that he was fashioned in his mother's womb. For He was guiding him step by step to his destiny and in an orderly way to his perfection.

(*PG* 66: 994/Latin) At one moment, [the Word] led [the one assumed] to baptism, afterwards [led him] to death, and finally raised him as had been foretold. He then led him to heaven and, because of their union, set him at the right hand of God where he sits, adored by all, and where he will judge all. God the Word was involved right to the end in all these [events], since He was present in him and He completed everything in the ordered way that He thought to be rightly (994) in accord with what His will had prescribed beforehand would take place. He was also present to him by means of His benevolent will toward him from the beginning, and led him to perfection in a methodical way, according to the order that was pleasing to Him.

(*PG* 66: 995/Latin) Yet [God] cooperated with the assumed man in those tasks that were set before him. In what way does He bring this about? Does the Deity [act] in place of the assumed man's *nous*?[2] But He has not replaced the *nous* of those with whom He has cooperated. Even if He has cooperated primarily only with the assumed man, He did not accomplish this by having the Deity replace his *nous*. For, if, according to your words [Apollinaris], the Deity replaced the assumed man's *nous*, how did he then experience fear for his [impending] passion? Why did he need, as he neared death, to pray more fervently, directing his prayers, according to the blessed Paul, to God with loud cries and copious tears? How [could] he be so fearfully troubled that he experienced outpourings of sweat that the evangelist says came down like gouts of blood and with trembling that knew no bounds? Why too did he need an angel to come and visit him, in order to restore his spirit to face the evils he was encountering by strengthening his resolve, by rousing him to [come to grips with] the looming inevitability of his passion, by persuading him to bear his evils with courage, by urging him to endure his sufferings with patience, by showing that after his approaching passion [was accomplished] the outcome of his present evils would be turned into a glorious gain for him? As the evangelist states, the one comforting him, namely the angel, strengthened him by these words, emboldening him to transcend his natural infirmity and supporting him by encouraging his thoughts.

(*PG* 66: 995/Latin) For the statement "He was being led by the Spirit" clearly reveals that he was guided by Him, strengthened by Him to excel in whatever was set before [him], led by Him to [fulfill all] his duties, taught by Him what was right, empowered by Him in his thoughts, so that he would be prepared for his great struggle [in the desert]. (996) As the blessed Paul affirms: "For whoever are led by the Spirit are children of God." He is saying here that those governed by [God] are led by the Spirit, are taught by Him, are created by Him to [seek out] what is better, and receive from Him the instruction of competent teachers. Then when the evangelist said that "Jesus, full of the Holy Spirit, returned from the Jordan," he was clearly demonstrating that he received the indwelling of the Holy Spirit at his baptism for the purpose of receiving the power proposed there. He was then led by the Spirit [into the desert] to undergo the struggle that he would be undertaking for us against the devil.

(PG 66: 996/Latin) Therefore, let those who are the wisest of all tell us: if the Deity, as they affirm, has taken the place of the *nous* that belongs to Christ our Lord according to the flesh, why then did Christ need the cooperation of the Holy Spirit for these [tasks]? For the Only Begotten's own divine nature would not need the Spirit for [his] justification, nor would he need the Spirit to work miracles, nor need the Spirit to be taught what is to be rightly accomplished, nor need the Spirit for anything! Then it necessarily [follows] that, if He is accomplishing everything, the Holy Spirit's indwelling would be superfluous. But he now says that He has been anointed by the Spirit and that the Spirit has dwelt in him and aided [him] to [do] all that has been proposed. For from the time he received instruction and virtue, he has sought to do what is righteous and pure.

(Book 3) (PG 66: 996/Latin) Therefore [God the Word], as the blessed Paul says, has rightly deigned as worthy of unity with Himself that man in whom He has set the judgment of all, [making him to be] a pledge of the future things [that will occur] when He will raise him from the dead and show him to be the judge of all. Because of His union with him, [God] enabled him to share in these [tasks], so that he would be adored in common [with Himself]. All will then render the adoration due to the divine nature to this one who is inseparably conjoined to Him. It is evident, therefore why He led him to greater [heights].

(Swete 1882: 317/Greek) "I can do nothing, as you [can] see, by my own nature, since I am a man. I accomplish works, but it is the Father who resides in me" who does everything, for "I am in the Father and the Father is in me" (John 14:10–11). God's Only Begotten Word is also in me. It is clear that the Father who is with Him remains in me, and it is He who is effecting my works. One should not be amazed to think this about Christ, since it is also clearly said about all other humans: "The one who loves me will keep my word, and my Father will love him, and we will come to him and make our abode with him" (John 14:21). So, if the Father and the Son dwell within each of these [believers], why should it be so amazing [to believe] that both remain at the same time in Christ our Lord *qua* flesh? For their communion in substance also truly includes a common sharing.

(*PG* 66: 997/Latin) So even here, O most wise of all, you teach us, as those possessing the Holy Spirit, that [the Word] is the one exercising control over Christ's rational soul when He is acting prudently in [confronting] all that has to be done, as we have demonstrated in the preceding passages, that He was led by the [Spirit] into the desert to battle against the devil, and that He received by [the Spirit's] anointing wisdom and strength for [doing] what had to be done and, having been made a partner with him, He not only performed miracles but also knew how he ought to use his miracles with discrimination, in order to make religion known to the Gentiles and to bring to light the infirmities of those who are [heavily] burdened and thus bring his will to act. He was then justified and shown to be pure, both by avoiding what is wrong and by observing what is right and by progressing step by step to [do] what is better.

(*PG* 66: 998/Latin) For clearly Paul of Samosata,[3] the bishop of our Lord God's church at Antioch, has shamefully espoused the error of Theodotus[4] and Artemon,[5] who assert that our Lord Jesus Christ was a mere man. For they did not acknowledge that God the Word is the Son of God, who is from God the Father eternally existing before the ages in His own substance.

(Book 4) (*PG* 66: 997/Latin) Since we affirm that a human being is made up of a soul and a body, we maintain that the soul and the body are two natures but one human being that is composed of both. But, in order to preserve both as one, is it right to mingle the natures and invert the two, saying that the soul is flesh, and the flesh, soul? Since the latter is immortal and rational, whereas the flesh is mortal and irrational, should we say when we invert them that the mortal is

immortal, and the rational, irrational? . . . For there are some realities
that differ in one way although they assume a unity in another. They
firmly maintain their differences, while they wholly preserve their
unity unbroken. For something may be one by nature, as a father and
a son are, but yet remain [two] different individuals, even though
they cannot be [said to] differ by reason of their substance. They
each possess their own personal differences, so that neither can the
son be said to be the father, nor the father to be the son. Yet, even
though some realities do differ by nature, it happens [at times] that
they are united in another way. But they do not thereby lose their
differences as they maintain their unity in their natures. So too the
soul is united to its body, with a single human being resulting from
[the union of] both. There remains, of course, a difference of natures,
with the soul being one and the flesh another. The former is immortal;
the other, mortal; one is rational and the other irrational. Yet both are
one human being. Each by itself is never absolutely and properly said
to be a human being, though perhaps with some added notion, such
as a human being with an inner and outer [self]. But neither one is a
human in an absolute sense, but one who has an inner and an outer
[self], so that [the soul] may appear to be belonging inwardly to a
human being and the other outwardly so. We also speak in a similar
way, O illustrious [Apollinaris], about Christ our Lord: that the form
of the slave subsists in the form of God. The assuming One is not the
assumed one, nor is the assuming One the assumed one! The unity,
however, between the assumed and the Assumer cannot be separated,
seeing that this [unity] is not able to be sundered in any way.

(PG 66: 1000/Greek) Therefore by following your norms [O
Apollinaris, on how to speak about Christ] and your way of inverting
[the natures] – something that you have very cleverly established, but
which is rather a subversion – so let us set aside all these [distinctions]
about him and let there be from now on no difference between the form
of God and the form of a slave, or of the temple assumed and the One
dwelling there, or of the one freed [from death] and the One raising
him, or of the one made perfect in his sufferings and the One making
him perfect, or of the one remembered and the One remembering,
or of the one visited and the One who has visited, or of that one who
is a little less than the angels and the One who made him so, or of
the one who has been crowned with glory and honor and the One
who has crowned him, or of the one set over the works of [God's]
hands and the One who established him, or of the one receiving these

tasks as being subject to himself and the One who has given him this domination.

[The remaining selections, taken from Sachau, treat of Theodore's opposition to Apollinaris.]

(Sachau 1869: Fol. 4a/36 [Syriac]) If mortals possess natural passions when they are alive, how much more do immortals who possess an immortal life. For they possess a true, powerful *nous* (reason). But perhaps [my opponents] may say: "We have not said that the soul is irrational." Then let them tell us why there is a need for this third nature (37) that they have called *nous*. What does its makeup indicate and how does it help to complete a human being? For if the body's life is governed by the soul, and the *nous* is present there enabling it to understand [such questions as] what is the divine nature, how has all creation been fashioned, and what is [God's] plan guiding all that is and will be in the future, then one's rational nature is in possession of all these [powers]. Why then do the heretics say that there is a need for a third nature that they have invented, calling it *nous*? For the soul does not by its nature behave and act as the body does: the eye is by its nature suited to see; the ear by its nature to hear; the tongue by its nature capable of uttering words; each of the body's members naturally possesses the ability to be active. If the soul is similar to this, then it has need for another [the body] to be its vital instrument. So too do [the body's] members have need for the soul in order to subsist and move in constructive activity. Then, when the soul departs, not only do the body's members remain lifeless but they are also dissolved upon their release, because they are no longer bound to and sustained by their souls. But if the soul is not also [destroyed] – as it is not – then it is alive, subsisting in its own nature by the grace of God, and providing its body with sustaining life. For clearly it is immortal, without natural passions. Rather it is because of its *nous* that [a person] chooses what it wants to set aside. The heretics, however, dismiss all this. They do not grasp this, nor can they. For they do not examine the sacred books in a critical way. In order to prove their statement about how a human being is made up of three natures, they offer us testimony from the blessed Paul, who says (Fol. 4b) "May the God of peace sanctify you entirely and may your whole spirit, your soul, and your body be free from censure until the coming of our Lord Jesus Christ." They are aware that the testimony that they have cited to us as proof is foolish when set against this next citation, that "[Jesus] has grown in age, wisdom, and grace before God and other humans" (Luke 2:52).

The followers of Apollinaris do not deny (38) what has been affirmed about the soul's *nous*. Nor do the followers of Eunomius deny, as [the Apollinarians] do, that the Word has assumed [Christ's rational] soul. They want us to consider and understand this. For these two schismatic sects are aware that this testimony is contrary to their teaching, when the latter state that [the Word] did not assume a soul, and the former assert that He assumed a soul but not a *nous*. If there should be anyone who says that there exists a human soul without a *nous*, how then did Jesus grow in wisdom? Does he then assert that the Deity grew in wisdom? Not even these are so rash to assert this to us in their foolishness. Is it not clear that the "body"⁶ has grown in wisdom? For he has clearly assumed a rational soul, as he was able to grow in wisdom by acquiring wisdom in his *nous*. But they shamelessly assert that he seemed to grow in the opinion of others, thereby not heeding what [the Scripture] asserts, [that he grew] "in age, wisdom, and grace before God and other humans." For, if they confess that he truly grew in age and wisdom and grace, then clearly he truly grew in age – and not [merely appearing to do so] in the opinion of others – as he also truly grew in wisdom. First [it should be pointed out here that] the evangelist has cautiously worded his statement, so as not to provide an opening for their wicked guile, by adding "before God and men." Let us take into account what they have said about their view on how he grew among men, and whether in their opinion he could have grown also before God.

(Sachau 1869: Fol. 7a/38 [Syriac]) But why does [Apollinaris] not call the incomplete one "Son"? If, therefore, they call God the Word "the Son," then the one whom they call the co-equal Son of God is another outside the divine nature, being either the body alone or the body and the soul. (39) So once again the man is not complete so. Who, therefore, shall we say he is, according to you? Besides these objections, [let us ask]: is the term "co-equal" theirs or ours? But, if they say that the assumed one – it matters not whether they want to say that this is the body or the body with the soul – is joined to and has perfectly become the one Son, how do they not recognize that this term is also in harmonious agreement with our understanding, since we confess that a complete man has been assumed? For, if the Word of God is the perfect Son of God by nature, having been generated by the Father, who then is the one existing outside this nature? It is not because [the assumed man] makes Him outwardly present that he is said to be "Son." Rather it is because he is exactly united with God the Word that he is entrusted with the title "Son of God." It is evident that what is said of the "Son of God" is also understood as applicable to the one who was assumed as complete.

Nor are we forced because of this to say "two sons." For clearly the body and the soul are two natures and are not like one another. The natures themselves make this clear. For if the two natures that are assumed are not like one another, and not like God the Word who has assumed them, then there is no other "person" constituted by them, and for them, because of their union with God the Word. It is clear that the *nous* as a third nature does not, as they say, accomplish this in an additional way. For, if both the soul and the body come from God the Word who assumed them, these two [when united] together are both named and acknowledged as being truly the Son because of their exact union. This is clear even if there is a third nature. Nothing contradicts what we are affirming in this matter. For how is it (Fol. 7b) that these two natures are called, and recognized as having the name of that more excellent nature, that is, of their Assumer, because of their exact union? Even if there is a third nature, it [ought to be] designated and said to be the "Son of God" because it is not separated from God the Word. Nor do we concede that there is some other outside the divine nature, whom we understand as and call the "Son of God" by reason of his *prosōpon* (the Greek equivalent of Syriac) from it. But we too refer to the assumed one as having the title "Son of God," even though he is a complete man. But, if [the Apollinarians] assert in their madness (40) that the *nous* is more excellent than the divinity of the Only Begotten, we ought to designate this [*nous*] as being another more excellent person with a human nature. We say this because we are upset at their statement that the [Christ's] *nous* is another nature beyond the soul and body. We have shown above with God's help that this is not so.

18

CATECHETICAL HOMILIES

[The following selections have been chosen from Theodore's most important complete work. It includes homilies on the Nicene Creed, the "Our Father," baptism, the eucharist, and the Mass that were delivered to catechumens prior to their reception of baptism and the eucharist. I have translated these from Raymond Tonneau's Syriac text (Tonneau and Devreese 1949). To assist those using a different edition of these homilies, I indicate at the beginning of each selection the number of the homily and the section number where this is found within the homily, followed by the page numbers for the Syriac text and Tonneau and Devreese's French translation.]

(Hom. 1.1/1–2) What word or thought can be equal [to the task of expressing] the awe-inspiring themes that we are about to propose? Or what tongue can teach about these mysteries? It is difficult for our tongue to communicate exactly what touches our created natures, for to do so a speaker must possess extraordinary wisdom. The matters that we intend to relate to you are such that they surpass our nature, for they transcend every human thought!

(Hom. 3.6/57–8) Because [Paul] spoke thus [about God's uniqueness in 1 Cor. 8: 4–6] and revealed the divine nature and the human nature that God assumed, [the fathers at Nicaea] added: "the Only-Begotten Son, the firstborn of all." (59–60) By these two phrases, they teach us about the two natures and, by distinguishing their terms, instruct us about how their natures are distinguished. They speak to us about the unique person (*prṣwpā*) and proclaim the exact union of its two natures. They themselves wanted to use not these words, but rather the teaching of the divine Scriptures, [as when] the blessed Paul says: "From the Jews descends the Christ according to the flesh, the God of all." But the one belonging to the house of David according to the flesh is not by his nature God. For [Paul] stipulates "according to the flesh," in order to make known that his human nature was assumed. But the God of the universe – who we believe has a divine nature surpassing all – is the Lord.

(3.7/60–1) [Paul] combined these two phrases ["the Only-Begotten Son" and "the firstborn of all creatures"] about the one person (*prçwpā*), in order to teach the exact union of the two natures, so that we might know the majesty and honor of the man assumed by God who clothed him. In the same way, [the Nicene fathers] also say: "The Only Begotten Son, the firstborn of all creatures." In fact, because they must teach us regarding how the two natures exist, what is the divine nature that has humbled itself, and what is the human nature that has been assumed, they speak, first of all, about these two designations whereby they indicate the two natures. It is evident that it is not a single nature that they call "the Only Begotten and firstborn of all creatures," because one cannot assert two things of a single nature. There are, in fact, many differences between the only [Son] and the firstborn, and it is impossible that the same one be the Only Begotten and the firstborn. For the firstborn is said to be [the first] of a number of brothers, but the Only Begotten is one without any brothers. There are many differences between the Only Begotten Son and the firstborn, but it is impossible that an only begotten and a firstborn be the same. For an only begotten son is said to be one who has no brothers whatsoever, and the firstborn one who has other brothers.

(5.14/118–19) Our Lord, therefore, has necessarily received a soul, so that he might be the first to be saved from sin and, by the grace of God, to attain the [state of] immutability wherein the soul will dominate the passions of the body. When sin is, in fact, abolished and [can] no longer enter into an immutable soul, then every form of punishment and death is also necessarily abolished. The body will stay in this state. It has become a stranger to death in order to participate in immortality. This is what the blessed Paul attests to (120–1) when he asserts: "There is, therefore, no condemnation against those who no longer conduct themselves according to the flesh since they are in Christ Jesus. For the law of the Spirit of life in Christ Jesus has set you free from the law of sin and death" (Rom. 8:1–2). He is affirming, in effect, that the sentence of death for everyone has been abolished, as has all condemnation for those believing in Christ. For they have become strangers to mortal ways and received, together with the Spirit, immortality with immutability, and have been completely freed from sin and mortality.

(5.15/120–1) It is then the utmost insanity on the part of whoever does not recognize that Christ has taken a soul. He is moreover a fool who says that [Christ] has not taken a human intellect. For [Apollinaris] has affirmed that either [Christ] has not received a soul or he has received a soul but, instead of a human one, a non-intelligent one, [such as] the one that gives life to the brute animals. But the human soul differs from that of animals solely in this: that the latter does not possess its own spiritual *hypostasis*. So, when it is present in the animal's constitution, it neither subsists alone, nor is it believed [to do so] after the animal's death, because the blood of an animal is said to be its soul. So when its blood is poured out, the soul is also thought to perish in its *hypostasis*[1] and in its animal movements, where [the soul] is thought to be present before its death. But this is not true for human beings. For its soul exists in its own *hypostasis* and is far superior to its mortal body. In fact the body acquires its life from its soul and likewise dies and is dissolved whenever the soul departs. But when [the soul] leaves, it does not perish, (122–3) but remains forever in its *hypostasis*, because it is immortal, and its nature cannot be harmed by humans. "Do not fear," he said, "those who kill the body. For they cannot kill the soul" (Matt. 10:28). Certainly this clearly teaches that the former can die because it is mortal by nature, but that [the soul] remains immortal, as it cannot be subject to any harm by men.

(5.16) If there is a great difference then between a human and an animal soul, it is because the latter is without reason and does not have its own *hypostasis*, whereas that of humans is immortal. One believes that it is also necessarily intelligent. Who then will be so foolish and deprived of human intelligence as to say that the human soul is without knowledge or reason? That is, unless he wants to become [known as] promoting something novel that does not exist in this world; namely that there is a living, immortal nature that possesses an imperishable life, yet without reason. There surely cannot be such [a nature]! In fact, something immortal by its nature also possesses a life that is imperishable and is truly capable of knowing, and being endowed with, reason.

(Hom. 6.3/134–5) By briefly summarizing in their creed everything done for our salvation from the beginning [at Christ's birth] to the end [his crucifixion], our blessed fathers [at Nicaea] have handed on instruction for those who want to know the truth. Clearly, therefore, we do not think that the divine nature of the Only Begotten was born of a woman, seeing that she received her fashioning from Him. [The fathers] do not say that she [gave birth] to the One generated from His Father before all time, since [the Son] is always from Him and present with Him from all eternity. But they follow the sacred Scriptures that speak differently of the natures in different ways, while [at the same time] teaching that there is one person on account of the exact union which took place. [They do so], lest they be thought to be dividing the perfect sharing the assumed one has with his Assumer. But if this union is dissolved then the one assumed is seen to be nothing other than a mere man like us. This is why the holy books have insisted upon the two designations for the single Son, to make us know in our profession of faith the glory of the Only Begotten Son and the honor [bestowed] on the man whom He has clothed.

(7.15/184–5) And so after stating, "We are expecting the revelation of the great God," the blessed Paul added, "our Savior Jesus Christ," in order to bring out that we are expecting that the all-surpassing divine nature will be coming to reveal Himself to all human beings. But, because the divine nature is not seen in a visible way, [God] acts in a way that accords with the human capacity of those who see His revealing presence, under that form whereby they are expecting the divine nature to manifest itself. [Paul] makes this known by adding: "our Savior Jesus Christ." It is by this corporeal man that [the Word] makes Himself known and reveals Himself outwardly when this [assumed] man emerges. Through this man's outward appearance, He reveals that His divine nature has intended from the very beginning to save us through him and appear as once again bestowing ineffable benefits. Rightly, then, did the blessed fathers add "again," indicating thereby that the divine nature has bestowed on this visible one the great honor of being the one who will be the judge. For he is the one who is going to judge the whole world, as the apostle has said: "He will judge the whole world by the man Jesus." For clearly the blessed Paul is teaching that it is through this man who was assumed on our behalf, and who has risen from the dead as a sign confirming our faith, that God will judge the earth.

(8.1/186–7) We have sufficiently given you, dear friend,[2] during these past days the teaching on Christ our Lord in a way that is in keeping with the tradition of our blessed fathers. From now on, it is your task to carefully maintain the memory of what has been told you. For they have handed on to us a twofold way of speaking about the subject of Christ our Lord that is faithful to the sense of Scripture. For he was not merely God and not merely man, but is truly in both of them, being by nature also God and also man. It is God the Word who assumed, and the man who was assumed. That One who is the "form of God" has assumed the "form of a slave." But the "form of a slave" is not the "form of God." The One who is in the "form of God" is by nature God; he is the one who assumed the "form of a slave," whereas the "form of a slave" is by nature the man assumed for our salvation. Then the One who assumed is not the one assumed; nor was the one assumed the assuming One. The One assuming is God whereas the assumed one is human. For the One who assumed is so by nature; that is, He is God the Father as "He is God with God" (John 1:1) and, as such, He is in Him. But that one who has been assumed is so by nature, as he descended as a son from David and Abraham. But he is also [both] the Lord and son of David: a son of David by his nature but Lord because of the honor that he has [received]. For he was more exalted than David his father, because of the [divine] nature that has assumed him.

(8.13/204–5) Because of all this, let us learn then from the holy Scriptures the distinction of his natures and their union. Let us also firmly attach ourselves to this teaching and mentally embrace the distinction of the natures: that the One who assumed is God and the Only Begotten Son. But the "form of the slave" who was assumed is human; God assumed what is good in our race – that one who was assumed and dwells in the [divine] fullness and provides us with a way to share in his grace. But we must pay close attention to this indissoluble union. For never, not even for an instant, can this "form of a slave" be separated from the divine nature that has assumed him. For the distinction of natures does not nullify the exact union. Nor does this exact union void the distinction of natures. For these different natures dwell (206–7) in their substances (*ousiai*) with their union remaining [intact] out of necessity, because the assumed one is bound to his Assumer in honor and majesty. This is why God wanted to assume him.

(8.14) Although we affirm two natures, we are not forced to speak of two Lords – who would be so utterly naive [as to do so]? For in all those cases where two are one in a certain way, but each [differs] in another way, the bond making them one does not void the distinction of their natures. Nor is the distinction of natures opposed to their being one. He states: "We are one, I and my Father." This does not negate that "I" and "my Father" are two. Moreover he has said of a man and a woman that "They will be two but one single body." It is not because they are a single body that the man and the woman are not also two. But they remain as two insofar as they are two, but they are also one insofar as they are one and not two. So likewise, in the case [of the Word and the assumed man], they are two by nature because the natures differ so much. Yet they are one by their union [as shown by the fact] that there is not a separate adoration [shown them]. For the assumed one receives this [adoration] together with that One who has assumed him, because he is His Temple, seeing that it is absolutely impossible for him to be [ever] apart from that One who dwells in him.

(10.17/270–1) The church is called the "Body of Christ" in this world because of the second birth of baptism. For [the baptized] receive fellowship with [Christ in the flesh] by [their reception] of baptism in a typical way [that anticipates] the world to come. This [rebirth] will be truly brought to pass when "Our lowly body will be transformed and become like his body of glory" (Phil. 3:21). For just as in this world we are like Adam's body, by resembling also his body, so we also bear the name of the "Body of Christ our Lord," because we will be able to receive the glory of his likeness at the transformation of our lowly body.

(10.18) It is also what the blessed Paul says elsewhere: (272–3) "I now rejoice in my sufferings because of you, and in my flesh I am filling up what is lacking in Christ's tribulations for his Body that is the church, of which I, Paul, am a minister" (Col. 1:24). He clearly calls the "Body of Christ" his church, which he served by his ministry and for which he underwent many sufferings. It is in this way that [Paul] indicates that [the baptized] have become one Body by the unique power of the Holy Spirit, with all the faithful summoned to the unique future hope. Because of this, when writing to the Corinthians, [Paul] said: "You are the Body of Christ our Lord" (1 Cor. 12:27). Still our Lord in his discourse to his disciples said in the form of a prayer: "It is not only for these [disciples] that I pray but also for those who are going to believe in me because of their word, so that they all might be one, just as you, my Father, are in me, and I in you, in order that these also may be one in us" (John 17:20–21). For I want not only these, but also all those who are going to believe because of them, to be one with me by sharing in the same benefits as I do with you, because of our exact ineffable union. In this way all [believers] because of their faith will also be one with us, by the way they perfectly share in these benefits and possess a glory like my own, and a union with me whereby they will gradually attain the honor of being in the household of the divine nature.

(12.2/324–5) For every sacrament indicates invisible and ineffable realities through its signs and symbols. But such [spiritual] things need to be revealed and explained, if one is going to begin to understand the power [contained] in these mysteries. For if these [spiritual realities] were clear in such [signs and symbols], an [explanatory] word would be truly superfluous, since sight alone would suffice to show us [the power present in] each of the [mysteries]. But, since a sacrament contains signs of what will take place or has preceded this, something needs to be said to explain the meaning of the signs and the mysteries. For instance, as the blessed Paul states, the Jews "serve [God] as examples and shadows of what will take place in heaven [because] the Law contains a shadow of the goods to come, but it was not the image of the realities." For, as the shadow shows the closeness of an entire body, there cannot be a shadow without a body. But [the shadow] does not portray the body that it is revealing – which is what an image is naturally fitted to accomplish. For, when an individual sees an image, [this person] knows who is the one being represented, because the likeness is exact; that is, provided one knows who this is. However, one can never know whose shadow is represented. For the shadow has no representative (326–7) likeness to the body from which it comes.

(13.7/376–7) If then Satan is the one who has been waging war against us since our youth and the one who causes us harm, (378–9) it would suffice, as an example of how to profess our view of him, to say, "I renounce him," [signifying] that you will never accept friendship with him. But, although he is invisible, he knows nevertheless how to make war against us by visible realities, such as those men whom he has overcome and made instruments of his evil and who will strive to make others fail. Because of this you add [in your profession of faith] "and all his angels."

(13.8) Those named "his angels" are all those humans who glean from [Satan] some malice whereby they wrong others. At the beginning [of creation], since no one had yet fallen who would be fit to serve him by doing wrong to others, the serpent served as [Satan's] instrument to bring about the fall and human wallowing [in evil]. For, from the time he had caught humans in his trap and enslaved them, he continually availed himself of those who are suitable for his [plan] to cause evil to others. Also the blessed Paul states: "I fear that, as the serpent seduced Eve by his cunning, so your thoughts will be led astray, and your simplicity toward Christ will be lost" (2 Cor. 11:3). He shows that those now striving to seduce others from the good are fulfilling for the devil the same office that the serpent in the past filled to enslave men.

So, after you say [in your profession], "I renounce Satan," you continue on by adding, "all his angels." You name all those serving his will as men who stumble and err like Satan. We should, therefore, consider angels of Satan to be all who are immersed in profane wisdom, as well as those who introduce pagan error into the world. Partisans of Satan are clearly also all (380–1) the poets who have spread idolatry by means of their fables and have strengthened the erroneous beliefs of the pagans through their wisdom. Angels of Satan are also those who under the guise of philosophy have devised the dangerous teachings of the pagans and so corrupted many that they do not adhere [any longer] to what [the true] religion affirms. Angels of Satan, too, are the heretical leaders who have all spoken falsely, after Christ our Lord's coming, in the name of Christ and, although they are estranged from religion, have introduced their [heretical views] into the world. Angels of Satan are Mani, Marcion, and Valentinus, who have confined God's creative power to visible realities, when they assert that there is another cause beside God as the reason why visible realities subsist. An angel of Satan is Paul of Samosata, who says that Christ our Lord is a mere man, and denies that the Only Begotten [Son] existing before the ages is a divine Person (*hypostasis*). Angels of Satan are also Arius and Eunomius, who dare to say that the divine nature of the Only Begotten is created and does not exist from the very beginning, but that He has come into being from nothing, as it has been determined for [all] creatures. They imitate pagan stories when they insist that the Son's substance (*ousia*) is created and, like these [pagans], regard God as contrary to what He is by His nature. They imitate the failure of the Jews, who do not confess that the Son proceeds from the Father and that there is no beginning for his *ousia*, for He is truly the true Son. Rather they say that He is the Son in the same way that the Jews call those who are sons of God by grace and who do not possess sonship by *ousia*.

(13.9) An angel of Satan is also Apollinaris, who undermines our confession (382–3) in the Father, Son, and Holy Spirit. Under the outward appearance of orthodoxy he has made our salvation to be incomplete, when he asserts that our intellect (*nous*) has not been assumed, and does not participate as the body does in the reception of grace. Angels of Satan are those who lead astray and teach all the heretical errors, and are honored with an episcopal or a priestly title, and those too who direct as well as sustain erroneous debates. They are promoting error by proclaiming what Satan wills under the cloak of ecclesial matters. Angels of Satan are also those who, despite the fact that the Law has been abolished, strive to win over to Jewish observances those who believe in Christ. Angels of Satan are also those who give evil and impure advice against the divine laws and endeavor to entice these people to serve evil. For all of us who profess to renounce [Satan], it is no longer right, from this time on, to have any fellowship. Rather you are now presenting yourself to Christ, so that you may be inserted into the church of God. Because you are expecting, through your baptismal birth, to become a corporeal member of Christ and be associated with Christ your Lord by being attached to him as your head, separate yourself from all those who dare to break with the [true] profession of ecclesial faith.

(14.9/418–19) When this [anointing] is completed, then, as previously mentioned, "You descend into the water consecrated by the pontiff's blessing." But this is not simple ordinary water (420–1) in which you are baptized, but water [generating] a second birth. It cannot become such except by the descent of the Holy Spirit. Before this happens, the pontiff must use words established by the pontifical liturgical regulations to ask God for the Holy Spirit's grace to descend upon the water, [to] render it capable of engendering this [new] mysterious birth and turn it into a womb for a sacramental birth. For to Nicodemus' question, "Can one enter a second time into the womb of his mother and be reborn?" our Lord says in response: "If one is not born of water and the Spirit, one then cannot enter into the Kingdom of God" (John 3:5).

[The pontiff] is indicating that, just as when [a husband's] semen is received into [his wife's] maternal womb and physical birth occurs, the divine hand fashions it so that [this birth] accords with the ordinary way [in which life] begins. So also at [the time of] baptism water has become a womb for the one being born. It is then the grace [flowing] from the Spirit that molds the one being baptized, in such a way that this person is born anew, and that makes him a wholly other [person]. So likewise, just as the semen when it enters a mother's womb possesses no life, soul, and sensation [of its own], but when fashioned by the divine power an ensouled living human emerges, possessing sensation and a nature capable of every [kind of] human activity, so also the one being baptized descends into the water like semen into a womb that has no apparent sign of an immortal nature. But when [this person] is baptized and has received a divine spiritual grace, this one becomes entirely wholly other. (422–3) [This person] is changed from a mortal into an immortal nature; from a corruptible into an incorruptible one; from a mutable into an immutable one; and has become entirely and completely other in accordance with the sovereign power of the One forming him.

(14.10) And, just as one born of a woman possesses the power to speak, hear, walk, and work with his hands, but is completely impotent [to perform] all these actions, although after a time this one will receive these [powers] in accordance with the divine plan, so also the one born at baptism will possess the full powers of a nature that is immortal and incorruptible, though [such a person] is at this moment incapable of acting, performing, and revealing himself in these ways until God has determined for us to die. We will then rise from the dead and be given complete and perfect actualization of our incorruptibility, immortality, impassibility, and immutability. So, even though the [baptized person] obtains the power [to possess] these [powers] at baptism, this one receives the actualization of these when he will no longer possess a wholly natural body, but has become spiritual. For his body will be made incorruptible, and his soul immutable, by the operation of the Spirit.

(15.3/466–7) But at baptism it is presently in hope of this expected birth that we are born in a typical [anticipatory] way. Whereas we now possess the first fruits of the Spirit's grace, we will then have it fully. Today we acquire a title for the first fruits, whereas in the world to come we expect, at the time of our resurrection, to take it entirely, so that it will render us, we hope, immortal and immutable. We must also necessarily have a nourishment suitable for this life here below, that in a typical [anticipatory] way nourishes us with the grace of the Holy Spirit, as the blessed Paul says: "Every time you eat this bread and drink this chalice, it is the death of our Lord that you commemorate until I come" (1 Cor. 11:26). He thus shows that our Lord when he comes from heaven will visibly manifest the future life and bring resurrection to all. Then, from that moment on, we will be immortal in our bodies and immutable in our souls. Then, necessarily, the usage of symbols and types will cease, since the realities themselves are at hand. For then we will no longer have need of signs to evoke a remembrance of what is going to take place.

(15.4) In this world, two things enable us to be: namely, birth and nourishment. By birth, we acquire existence, whereas it is by nourishing ourselves that we obtain [the strength] to continue in our life. But, if our nourishment fails, inevitably those born will suffer dissolution. So too in the world to come, when we will be born [anew] at our resurrection, we will exist and continue thus in an immortal way. Consequently, the blessed Paul says: (468–9) "We know that, if our earthly home will be destroyed, we have a building made by God, a house not made by human hands, [but that will be] forever in heaven" (2 Cor. 5:1). In this world below, we procure our nourishment by the labor of our hands and can thereby continue, but when we come to be resurrected and have received our heavenly abode, we will no longer have need for this nourishment acquired by the labor of our hands. The immortality we will then have [acquired] will maintain us in existence by virtue of the grace [acting] to nourish us. This is the reason why "the house that is not the work of human hands" and "the edifice [made] by God" express what the blessed Paul affirms to be the kind of life that we will then have.

(15.5) Therefore, as I have stated, we will possess [this new life] at a future time when we are resurrected. But, because we are now born at our baptism by way of types and signs, we also need now to receive a nourishment that corresponds to what we have attained by means of these types, so that we can persist in the [new] existence of our self that we have received at baptism, as does every animal born naturally from another animal, by obtaining its nourishment from the body of its birth-giver. For God has ordained from the very beginning that this is the way this is to take place among created beings, namely that every female animal that gives birth will provide nourishing food for those who are born. It is necessary then that we who have received divine grace in a typical [anticipatory] way also receive nourishment from above in a way similar to how we have obtained it at birth.

(15.10/474–5) Then, when [our Lord] distributed the bread, he did not say that this is a type of my body, but that "This is my body"; and in like manner as regards the chalice [of wine], that this is not a type of my blood, but that "This is my blood." For, when we receive the grace coming from the Holy Spirit, [our Lord] wanted us no longer to regard the nature [of the body and blood] but accept them as the body and blood of our Lord. Also the body of our Lord did not naturally possess immortality and [the power] to give immortality, but this was given him by the Holy Spirit. At his resurrection from the dead, he attained to his [full] union with the divine nature, and then became immortal and the cause of others' becoming immortal.

(16.12/552–3) It is very necessary for the pontiff, in following the priestly ritual, to request and to supplicate God for the descent of the Holy Spirit, and for the grace flowing from on high upon the bread and wine that have been presented, so that one may see that it is truly the body and blood of our Lord that commemorate our immortality.[3] For the body of Christ our Lord, who is also from our nature, was first mortal by nature, but by means of the resurrection he has passed on to an immortal and immutable nature. When then the pontiff affirms that [this bread and wine] are the body and blood of Christ, he reveals clearly that they have become the body and blood of Christ by the descent of the Holy Spirit, and become immortal. For it is clearly seen that it is by means [of the Spirit] that the body of our Lord has been anointed and has received the Spirit. In the same way now, when the Holy Spirit comes, it is still a sort of anointing, coming by grace, that we think the bread and wine receive when they are presented. And from this we believe that the body and blood of Christ have become in their nature immortal, incorruptible, impassible, and immutable, as it happened to the body of our Lord at his resurrection.

(16.13/554–5) But [the priest] also asks that the grace of the Holy Spirit might come upon all those assembled, who have been similarly born again, in order to perfect them as a single, corporate kind of body that is in communion with the body of our Lord, and to bind them in harmonious peace and concern about what is right. We have come together and are united for this one [purpose] that, when we all regard God with a perfect conscience, we do not make our participation in the Holy Spirit a reason for punishment, because we are estranged because of our beliefs and are inclined to controversies, disputes, envy, and jealousy; rather [we need] to be seen to be worthy to receive [this union] in harmony, peace, and caring for what is good, with our rational mind regarding God with a perfect conscience. In this way we will be united to Him by participating in these holy mysteries and will thereby be conjoined to our head, Christ our Lord. For we believe that we are his Body and will participate by his means in the divine nature.

169

(16.30/582–3) We who are mortal by our nature are expecting to receive immortality. From being corruptible, we will become incorruptible; from being passible, become impassible; from being changeable, become utterly immutable. We will also rise above the earth and terrestrial evils to heaven and will delight in all the pleasurable benefits of heaven. We receive this hope because of the divine plan [fulfilled] by Christ, our Lord, who was assumed from our midst. For he is the first to receive this transformation from the divine nature, and to become in this way the one to lead us to a sharing in such [blessings] as these. It is for this reason that we zealously desire through these types to participate in the mysteries; that is, through signs that are greater than what we can state in words. But we are convinced we already possess these realities when we receive the first fruits of the Holy Spirit by participating in these mysteries; that is, when we are baptized we receive a new birth, and when we receive communion we believe that we are receiving nourishment and subsistence for our life.

19

CONCILIAR ANATHEMAS

[The following are the anathemas issued at the Second Council of Constantinople in 553 against Theodore's works and his person. They reveal that the Fathers believed that, despite Theodore's protestations to the contrary, he held that the Word and Jesus were two separate individuals. I have translated the canons from the Greek text found in Denzinger and Schönmetzer (1963). The number listed after the canon is where this canon can be found in Denzinger and Schönmetzer.]

Canon 2 (# 422) If anyone does not confess that God the Word was engendered twice, the [first] from the Father before the ages in a non-temporal and non-corporeal sense, and the [other] in these last days, with the very same [Word] descending from the heavens, becoming incarnate from the holy, glorious mother of God, the ever-virgin Mary, and being generated from the same, let such a one be anathema!

Canon 3 (# 423) If anyone says that the one who has done miracles is other than God the Word and that the Christ who has suffered is other, or says that God the Word was present in the Christ who has come to be from a woman or that He was in him as one is in another but was not the one and same our Lord Jesus Christ, God the Word, incarnated and made man, and that his miracles and the sufferings which He voluntarily submitted to in his flesh do not belong to the same one, let such a one be anathema!

Canon 4 (# 424) If anyone says that the union of the Word of God with the man took place by reason of grace, or activity, or equal honor, or absolute sway, or a relationship, or an external appearance, or power, or good pleasure, as if God the Word was pleased with the man, as Theodore says in his ranting, "on account of His being very well pleased with him," or on the level of a verbal identity, whereby the Nestorians call God the Word to be Jesus and the Christ, but call the man in a separate way as Christ and Son, clearly affirming two "persons" (*prosōpa*) when they designate one honor, dignity, and worship but say in reply that there is only one "person" and one Christ, but he does not confess that the union of the Word with the flesh – that is, animated with a rational and intellectual life – has taken place by reason of a synthesis, that is, hypostatically as the holy Fathers have taught, and that therefore there is only one *hypostasis*, that is, of the Lord Jesus Christ [who is] one of the holy Trinity, let such a one be anathema!

The union is, in fact, understood in many ways. [There are] those who follow the impiety of Apollinaris and Eutyches and have undertaken to undermine the combined [natures] by giving preference to a union by way of mixture, as well as those who, thinking like Theodore and Nestorius, have introduced a relational [kind of] union in which they revel in the separation [of the natures]. However the holy church of God rejects the impiety of both of these heresies and confesses that the union of God the Word [has occurred] with the flesh synthetically; that is, hypostatically. For, as regards the mystery concerning Christ, a union by synthesis not only maintains that the [two natures] come together in an unconfused way but permits no division.

Canon 5 (# 426) If one accepts the one *hypostasis* of our Lord Jesus Christ in the following way, as signifying the presence of many *hypostaseis*, and thereupon attempts to introduce into the mystery regarding Christ two *hypostaseis* or two *prosōpa*, and then, after having inserted two *prosōpa*, he speaks only of one *prosōpon* according to dignity, honor, and worship, as Theodore and Nestorius have written in their madness, and then falsely charges that the holy Synod in Chalcedon employed the phrase "one *hypostasis*" in the same sense as their impiety has done, without confessing that the Word of God is united to His flesh hypostatically and that, therefore, his *hypostasis* or his *prosōpon* is one – for this is the way that the holy Synod in Chalcedon has professed the one *hypostasis* of our Lord Jesus Christ – let such a one be anathema!

Canon 6 (# 427) If anyone says that [the term] *theotokos* is truly misapplied as regards the holy, glorious, and ever-virgin Mary, or [is appropriate] in the relative sense that it was a mere man whom she bore and not God the Word who became flesh from her, with the birth of the man being related to God the Word, as these [believe] in the sense that He was [joined] with the man when he came to be, and falsely charge that the Synod in Chalcedon has affirmed the mother of God to be the virgin in the identically contrived, impious sense, as Theodore has understood it, or if someone calls her the "man-bearer" or "Christ-bearer," as if Christ were not God, and confesses that she is not precisely and truly the mother of God, seeing that God the Word who has been generated from the Father before the ages has become incarnated in these last days from her – and it is in this sense that the holy Synod in Chalcedon has piously confessed her to be the mother of God – let such a one be anathema!

Canon 7 (# 428) If anyone, when speaking about the two natures, does not confess that our Lord Jesus Christ is known to be one in his divinity and humanity, and do not understand by this that the natures differ in this ineffable union in an unconfused way, seeing that the Logos has not been transformed into the nature of flesh, nor has the flesh been changed into the nature of the Word – for each remains according to its nature, for the union has taken place in a hypostatic way – but in regards to how both are divided, this one employs the same word [to express] the mystery of Christ by confessing a number of natures for our one Lord Jesus [who is] the incarnate Word of God, because he does not in theory understand how the different natures in the composite are not destroyed by the union (for he is one from both, and both are in one), but he has used the number [two] to separate the natures with each having its own *hypostasis*, let such a one be anathema!

Canon 9 (# 221) If anyone says that the Christ to whom two adorations are being offered is to be worshiped in his two natures, in a special way to God the Word and in a special way to the man, or if anyone [by holding] for a denial of the flesh or for a mixing together of the divinity and the humanity talks outrageously about one nature or *ousia* for the combined [natures], and worships Christ in this way, but does not worship by one adoration God the Word made man, together with His own flesh, as the church of God has held from the beginning, let such a one be anathema!

Canon 10 (# 222) If anyone does not confess that our Lord Jesus Christ who was crucified in his flesh is true God and the Lord of glory and one of the holy Trinity, let such a one be anathema!

Canon 12 (# 224) If anyone defends the impious Theodore of Mopsuestia, who said that God the Word is one and another is the Christ, who because he was troubled by the passions of the soul and the desires of the flesh, but after being gradually separated from what is inferior and having proven himself by progressing in good works and became pure in his way of life was baptized as a mere man in the name of the Father and the Son and the Holy Spirit, and through his baptism received the grace of the Holy Spirit, and became worthy of sonship, and was adored as the "Person" (*prosōpon*) of God the Word in a way similar to [how one worships] the image of a king, and after his resurrection became immutable in his thoughts and entirely without fault, seeing that the impious Theodore has said that the union of God the Word to Christ is just as the Apostle says of a husband and a wife, "The two will be one flesh," as well as there being innumerable other blasphemies, as when he dared to say that when the Lord breathed on his disciples after his resurrection and said, "Receive the Holy Spirit," he did not give them the Holy Spirit, but breathed [upon them] as only an outward sign (*schēmati*), and he also asserts that when Thomas touched the Lord's hands and side after (Christ's) resurrection, confessing "My Lord and my God," he was not speaking this [as referring] to Christ, but rather that Thomas, amazed at the wholly unexpected resurrection, was praising God for raising Christ, let such a one be anathema!

Canon 13 (# 225) Even worse, this same Theodore in his *Commentary on the Acts of the Apostles* has compared Christ to Plato, Mani, Epicurus, and Marcion, saying that, just as each of these has formulated his own teaching and his disciples are called Platonists, Manichaeans, Epicureans, and Marcionites, in the same way, as Christ has formulated his teaching, [his disciples] are called Christians after him. If anyone defends this aforementioned most impious Theodore and his impious writings, in which he spews out the aforementioned and other innumerable other blasphemies against our great God and Savior Jesus Christ, and does not anathematize him and his impious writings, and all those who have accepted these or defend him or say that he has expounded in an orthodox way, or write on his behalf, or on behalf of his impious writings, and think the same way or have thought so and persist until the end in this heresy, let such a one be anathema!

Canon 14 (# 227) If anyone defends the letter that Ibas is said to have written to Mari the Persian in which he denies that God the Word was incarnated by Mary the holy mother of God and ever virgin and became man, and states that it was only a man born to her, whom he calls a temple, as if God the Word were one and the man another; and, although Cyril, [presently] among the saints, proclaimed the true Christian faith, he attacks him as a heretic who has written like the ungodly Apollinaris, and censures the first holy synod of Ephesus on the grounds that it condemned Nestorius without a formal examination, seeing that this sacrilegious letter calls the twelve chapters of holy Cyril to be heretical and opposed to the right faith, and defends Theodore and Nestorius and their ungodly teachings and writings – if anyone now defends the said letter and does not anathematize it and all those who to defend it, saying that it, or a part of it, is correct, or [does not anathematize] those who have written or will write in support of it or the impieties contained therein, and those who are emboldened to defend it and the impieties contained there [as having been ascribed to] by the holy fathers or by the holy synod of Chalcedon, and persist in these positions until the end, let such a one be anathema!

(# 228) We confess, therefore, that we have received these teachings from holy Scripture, from the teaching of the holy fathers, and from the definitions regarding the one and the same faith that has been affirmed by the aforementioned four holy synods, and also by us against the heretics and their impiety, as well as against those who have justified or will justify the so-called "Three Chapters," and against those who have persisted or will persist in their own deceit. If anyone should attempt to hand on by teaching or writing anything contrary to what we have regulated in a God-fearing way, whether he be a bishop or one belonging to the clergy, then, insofar as such a one is acting contrary to what befits priests and those in the ecclesial orders, let him be stripped of his rank as bishop or cleric, and, if he is a monk or lay person, he will be anathematized!

NOTES

1 THEODORE'S LIFE

1 I am indebted for most of my details about Theodore's life to the article "Theodorus" in Smith and Wace (1877–78). H. B. Swete is believed to be the author of this article.

2 Ibid. In his article, Swete opines that Theodore "stands out among ancient expositors of Scripture almost alone – that of an independent inquirer, provided with a true method of eliciting the sense of his author, and considerable skill in the use of it" (p. 947).

3 For a contemporary study of Theodore and the sources of his life, see Guida (1994: 9–30).

4 Theodore was most likely educated at the academy of Libanius, one the elite rhetorical teachers in the Byzantine empire.

5 For a theological assessment of what happened at the Council of Ephesus, see Kelly (1978: 323–30). It is important to keep in mind that "Cyril's Twelve Anathemas were formally read out at the session on 22 June, but there seems to have been no move to canonize them along with his second letter" (p. 327).

6 For works that treat in some depth the historical and theological background of this period, see Murphy and Sherwood (1974) and Grillmeier (1975). For a general history of Antioch in antiquity, see Downey (1961).

7 The 71 excerpts and the creed attributed to him are found in the critical edition of the council's *Acta* in Straub (1971). In his *The Christology of Theodore of Mopsuestia*, Francis Sullivan (1956) shows that these excerpts are authentic, although three are not from Theodore but Diodore. Since the creed cited in the council does not agree with the one Theodore comments upon in his *Catechetical Homilies*, it is considered to be spurious.

2 HISTORY OF SECONDARY LITERATURE

1 Doran (2006: 171–2). "Hiba" is the Syriac equivalent of the Greek "Ibas."

2 For a treatment of Narsai's life and works, see McLeod (1979).

3 Birnie also notes that the East Syrian Synods in 484 and 605 condemned all those who spoke against Theodore and his writings.

4 The Pro-Oriente Foundation hosted these and three other meetings. Available at www.cired.org/east.html (accessed February 1, 2007).

5 I located this citation on the web. Available at www.earlychristianwritings. com/fathers/photios_03bibliothec.htm. It was listed as #4. The citation is interesting in that Photios esteems Theodore's arguments against Eunomius and that he seems only vaguely aware of who Theodore is.

6 The schism provoked in the Latin West by Constantinople II was not resolved until the late sixth century.

7 For the textual history of this commentary, see the Introduction to vol. 1 of Swete (1880, 1882).

8 Migne made these excerpts more readily available in the nineteenth century when he published in *PG* 66: 10–1020 what was then known of Theodore.

9 There were, of course, earlier times when Christ's humanity was stressed, for example by Francis of Assisi with his emphasis on the Christmas creche and Ignatius of Loyola when he urged his retreatants to imaginatively contemplate incidents in the human life of Christ.

10 Most of the excerpts published here are not contained in Migne.

11 Vosté (1940). The 71 excerpts are found on pp. 44–72. Nathaniel's confession is #26.

12 For a summary of these extracts, see McLeod (2005: 206–12).

13 The creed cited at the council also seems spurious. Norris sums up the literature on this point thus: "Considering that it most certainly is not the symbol which Theodore employs as the basis for his Catechetical Lectures, this Creed can be ascribed to him only with the utmost hesitation. Its source is best considered doubtful" (1963: 241n3).

14 For the last two exchanges, see McKenzie (1958) and Sullivan (1959).

15 He continued publishing on Theodore with his *The Captain of Salvation* (1973) and "The Analogy of Grace in Theodore of Mopsuestia's Christology" (1983). His other works on Diodore (1966a) and Nestorius (1966b) are also valuable studies for understanding Theodore.

16 She followed this up with *Biblical Exegesis and the Formation of Christian Culture* (1997).

17 I have been unable to obtain a copy at this time for an evaluation.

18 The programs for these meetings are available at www.cired.org/east.html (accessed February 3, 2007).

3 THEODORE'S EXEGETICAL METHOD

1 This passage raises the question of how much the traditional, conservative Jewish exegesis has affected the Antiochene exegesis.

2 Whereas Diodore's response to Julian has not survived, Theodore's *Reply to Julian* has only several brief abstracts, available in Guida (1994).

3 *Anagogē* literally means to refer one thing to another but connotes here what the English word *anagogy* signifies today, the discovery of a spiritual or mystical meaning for a text.

4 For a summary treatment of what may be the effect of a rhetorical
   education upon Theodore, see McLeod (2005: 25–7).

4 EXAMPLES OF THEODORE'S EXEGETICAL METHOD

1 As well as page numbers for Tonneau's edition, I give the homily and
   paragraph numbers. For example, CH 5.17 means paragraph 17 in *Catholic
   Homily* 5.
2 For a treatment of this topic, see McLeod (2005: 58–143).
3 Theodore also differs from his fellow Antiochenes, Diodore, John
   Chrysostom, and Theodoret over the meaning of "image." They associate
   image with the authority that God has bestowed upon humans over the
   material creation. For an extended study on this point, see McLeod
   (1999).
4 In ancient times, a ruler was considered to be symbolically present in a
   city by means of his prominently displayed image. To destroy or deface
   this image was considered to be an act of *lèse majesté*. Theodore is, of
   course, citing this as an analogy whereby cult can be seen to be shown
   not to the image itself, but to the one it represents. Since Theodore likens
   the union of Christ's natures to that between the body and the soul, he
   considers that the Word is revealing Himself through Christ's humanity
   as the soul does through the body. Christ's humanity as God's visible
   image, therefore, is not pointing to another separate reality but is one
   with the Word who permeates Christ's humanity as the soul does the
   body.

5 GOD'S INDWELLING OF GOOD PLEASURE

1 Theodore uses the term "body" to refer to Christ in his full humanity.
2 From the context, Theodore is referring to God's providential activity
   enabling all creatures to continue in their existence.
3 It seems strange that Christ is so suddenly introduced into the text by the
   pronoun "him." It raises the issue whether something has been omitted
   previous to this.
4 Luise Abramowski (1961: 293) translates the phrase "as in His true
   Son."

6 THEODORE'S UNDERSTANDING OF HYPOSTASIS AND PROSŌPON

1 This is, in fact, how the Arians argued. For, if the Word and Jesus are
   truly one, then what is said of one applies also to the other. So when Jesus
   asserts that "the Father is greater," then this justifies the belief that the
   Son is inferior to the Father.
2 For a study into the evolution of these terms, see Helmut Köster's
   detailed study into the meaning of *hypostasis* in Kittel (1968, vol. 8: 589).
3 The fathers at Nicaea probably chose to link the terms *hypostasis* and
   ousia together to make clear that the Word was not generated from the
   Person of the Father.

4 Perhaps when the fathers speak of the Trinity's "most perfect *hypostaseis*," they are simply asserting that no one Person is more perfect than the other two, as they all possess the very same substance.

5 I believe that the Latin *rationes* is a translation of the Greek *logoi*. It seems to me that it ought to be translated as "relations" in this context. It may simply mean that there are two "meanings" present.

6 The Syriac is probably a translation of the Greek, meaning "the same."

7 For a discussion of how Nemesius' explanation of how the spiritual soul can be united in love with its body and its implication for Theodore's teaching on an "indwelling of good pleasure," see McLeod (2005: 189–94).

7 THE FUNCTIONAL UNITY OF CHRIST'S NATURES

1 In the second part of his very lengthy article, John Romanides (1959–60) raises another possibility for how the divine and human natures can be united – that they can be joined on the level of substance. He argues that, since the divine nature transcends in an apophatic way every human way of trying to conceive its divine power, why then can freedom not reside in the divine nature and be able to freely act in a creative way upon Christ's human nature? Romanides believes that Theodore's approach to this question reveals that he is chiefly a moralistic metaphysician. Admittedly no one can definitively determine what the divine nature can and cannot do as regards becoming human flesh, above all in the present age when a nature's DNA can, at least in theory, be altered. Still a theologian can only argue on the basis of what he or she knows today by way of human experience. This may be an argument from analogy about how the divine can unite itself to a human nature – an argument that Theodore was convinced made sense of the New Testament witness. This meant for him that the only way to describe the union of Christ's natures is that the Word freely determined in love to dwell within Jesus' human nature. He strenuously opposed a union wherein the divine nature joined itself to human nature in a substantive way. This would necessarily result in one of the natures' being changed into the other.

9 GENERAL INTRODUCTION TO THE TEXTS

1 This has recently been translated into English by Robert Hill (2003).

2 Many of the excerpts used to condemn Theodore are available in J.-P. Migne's *Patrologia Graeca*, vol. 66, cols 10–1020.

3 Three other translations have been made of this work: Tonneau with Devreese (1949), Bruns (1994), and Gerber (2000).

4 George Kalantzis (2004), in a work that I have not seen, is reported to have translated this commentary into English, making a comparison between the Syriac version and the catenae.

5 Robert C. Hill has recently published an English translation (2006).

6 This work also contains fragments of Theodore's work *Against the Allegorists*.

7 These passages are also found in Migne.

NOTES

8 Probably the best works on this topic are Vosté (1925) and Swete (1877). This latter work is valuable as it cites the Greek and Latin passages from the sources on which he bases his comments.
9 Petavius thinks that this refers to Augustine (*PG* 66: col. 1005D); Swete (1882: 332), citing Photius, prefers Jerome.

10 IN OPPOSITION TO THE ALLEGORISTS

1 Origen of Alexandria (*c.* 185–*c.* 254) developed a school of theological thought on how to interpret the Christian Scriptures in a literal, moral, and especially allegorical way.
2 An allegory offers a point-by-point interpretation of a text that goes beyond what a text literally states, in order to uncover a deeper spiritual meaning.
3 This is a title acknowledging a person as one's superior.
4 This is probably a reference to those Arians who appeal to Origen as supporting their position.
5 For examples of this, see how Theodore introduces his interpretations of Psalm 8 (102) and John's Gospel (123).

11 PSALM 8

1 For an understanding of the restricted meaning that Theodore assigns to "type," see pp. 21–2 in Chapter 3, and pp. 49–53 in Chapter 6 for a "prosopic union."
2 Theodore is always careful to express Christ as signifying the unity of his two natures by referring to the Word as the One who has assumed Christ's humanity and to Jesus as the one who has been assumed. Both expressions indicate the union of one to the other. He is ever sensitive to the issue of how the creating Word can be joined to the created Jesus. Whereas Cyril stresses how Christ is actually a single individual, Theodore is wary that this can be interpreted to mean that Christ's humanity has in fact been assimilated and changed into the divine nature. To avoid this, he never ceases to assert an explicit role for the existence of the humanity in the union.

12 THE CREATION OF ADAM AND EVE

1 This is most likely either Augustine or Jerome.
2 Theodore regards the spiritual powers residing in the created universe as encompassing the angels and any other similar powers that God may have created. He believes that they are all united to the spiritual soul of humans and that the material worlds are also joined to the human body. As such, humans serve as the bond that unites the created spiritual and material worlds to one another and to God. As such, Adam first and then Christ's humanity later function as mediators in creation.

3 Theodore is, of course, referring here to the role that he sees Christ's humanity playing in salvation as the one who recapitulates all creation within his human nature and unites it to God because of his inseparable union with the Word. When this is achieved in a future immortal and immutable life, all will be at peace.

13 COMMENTARY ON JOHN'S GOSPEL

1 Asterius (+ c.341) was initially a non-Christian orator in Cappadocia who converted to Christianity. Although he offered sacrifice during the persecution of Maximian, he later repented. His early Christian writings were Arian, but his later homilies are considered to be orthodox, representing a pre-Nicene christological outlook.
2 Porphyri is probably the bishop appointed at Antioch after the death of Flavian in 404. If so, this strongly suggests that Theodore's commentary on John was written after this date.
3 Theodore is referring here to his monumental dogmatic work *On the Incarnation*.
4 If this soul–body analogy is taken seriously, Theodore intends his bonding to be more than a mere functional union. His intent is to express a strict union.
5 Because the common "ego" is the mysterious union combining Christ's human will with that of the Word, Theodore can assert that Christ was actively involved in creation. Since this is being said on the level of will, this does not mean that Theodore held that Christ's human nature became one with that of the Word. Theodore avoids once again any implication that Christ's natures are one on the substantial level.
6 Theodore is alluding here to his belief that baptism has made a person one with Christ and a participant, sharing in an inchoative way in the immortal life that Christ's humanity now shares.

14 COMMENTARY ON PHILIPPIANS 2:5–11

1 Theodore holds that because Christ's two natures are united in one common *prosōpon*, Christ's humanity can be said to share on this level in the creative activity of the Word.
2 This may be a reference to Matt. 8:29.
3 Because Theodore is sensitive to the charge that he holds Christ to be merely human, he will almost always refer to the Word and Jesus by their roles in the union as either the One who has assumed Christ's humanity or the man who has been assumed by the Word. These titles highlight the union of both natures.
4 Theodore is doubtless referring to Apollinaris or one of his followers.
5 Theodore is referring here to the charge that when he speaks of "one" and the "other," he is expressing that the Word and Jesus are two separate individuals. Theodore is actually speaking about Christ's two natures being "one" and "the other."

15 SELECTIONS FROM THEODORE'S COMMENTARIES ON THE EPISTLES TO THE GALATIANS, EPHESIANS, AND COLOSSIANS

1 Theodore explains the sacraments of baptism and the eucharist as types that enable a baptized person to share in Christ's human death and resurrection in an inchoative way that guarantees that one will achieve after his or her resurrection an immortal life, provided one has lived a virtuous earthly existence.

16 ON THE INCARNATION

1 The Latin is: "sed unum eundemque dic, hominem dicens connaturalem mihi Deum." This is a significant line, as it expresses how Theodore regarded the unity between the Word and Jesus as "one and the same."

2 This clause is likely to be the translator's interpolation.

3 Miletus was the bishop and leader of the moderate Nicene community at Antioch during the 370s, when the Arians, Semi-Arians, strict Nicenes, and moderate Nicenes vied for ecclesial control at Antioch. John Chrysostom and Theodore belonged to Miletus' group.

4 Theodore is distinguishing here between the overall kind of unity that an "indwelling of good pleasure" effects and the various degrees to which individuals can share in this divine good pleasure. Theodore maintains that there is a radical difference between the way that Christ's humanity is personally blessed by God and that of the saints and the virtuous who are also recipients of God's good will.

5 Theodore is arguing that, because God is the Creator of everything that exists, He can then be thought to be present in each being by reason of His substance. But this would not suffice to distinguish His unique union with Christ's humanity from His relationship with all creatures. Theodore, moreover, is wary of maintaining a substantial union, as this would mean, in his theological framework, that either the Word's divine nature has changed into Jesus' human nature or vice versa.

6 Theodore is emphasizing here that the Word enters into an exact union with Christ's humanity because this is what He freely and fully desires to do in His love.

7 See especially pp. 61–3 in Chapter 6 for a treatment of this citation.

8 Theodore is doubtless responding here to Apollinaris, who called his union of the Word with Christ's flesh one *hypostasis*. It may explain why Nestorius believed that Cyril's stress on one *hypostasis* revealed that he was infected with Apollinarism.

9 Theodore seems to be arguing here that the title "Savior" can be applied to Christ's humanity. For Jesus' name, like that of Joshua, has this meaning. If this name was to be applied only to God, Moses would never have chosen it for Joshua.

10 In ancient times, a ruler was considered to be symbolically present in a city by means of his prominently displayed image. To destroy or deface this image was considered to be an act of *lèse majesté*. Theodore is, of course, citing this as an analogy whereby cult can be said to be due not

to the image itself, but to the one it represents. Because Theodore likens the union of Christ's natures to that between the body and the soul, his thought here should be understood as affirming that Christ's humanity "images" the Word in a way similar to how one's body reveals the soul that permeates it.

11 Theodore wants to stress the spiritual passions here against Apollinaris, who claimed that the Word has supplanted Christ's human rational soul. If Apollinaris were right, then there would be no possibility for the Word to experience such passions.

12 The Greek is ἰσότητος νόμῳ. I have translated νόμος in its later musical meaning as "a composition including both words and melody." It is a term also used in opposition to "nature."

13 The Greek is ἐνδιάθειον οἰκείωσιν.

14 The Greek word is ἑνώσις.

15 The reference here seems to be to Apollinaris, who so stressed the singular unity of the Word with Christ's flesh that the Word can be said to be both the merciful One and the one seeking mercy.

17 IN OPPOSITION TO APOLLINARIS

1 This is a favorite way for Theodore to express how the Word and Christ's humanity are one and the same. He skillfully asserts that they are singularly one, while still being two.

2 The Greek term *nous* is to be taken in the sense of being the human rational soul and its activities. Theodore rejects Apollinaris' view that the Word supplanted this soul on the grounds that it destroys the integrity of Christ's human nature, especially his freedom of will.

3 Paul lived between 200 and 275 and served as bishop of Antioch from 260 to 268. He is believed to have taught a strict Unitarianism, holding that the Son of God and the Spirit were simply names for the inspired man Jesus Christ. He was formally condemned at the Synod of Antioch in 268.

4 Theodotus lived at Rome around the beginning of the third century and became a principal exponent of Adoptionism.

5 Artemon was a prominent Adoptionist teacher in third-century Rome. Little is known of his life.

6 Theodore at times uses the term "body" to express Christ's full humanity.

18 CATECHETICAL HOMILIES

1 Theodore is distinguishing here between the life principle of an animal's mortal soul and that of a human immortal soul. He sees the life principle as always being coupled with a real nature.

2 Theodore is addressing each member of his congregation here with a greeting of personal respect.

3 Theodore believes that the transformation of the bread and wine into the body and blood of Christ takes place at the descent of the Holy Spirit.

BIBLIOGRAPHY

Primary sources

PG   Migne, Jacques-Paul (1856–66) *Patrologia Graeca*. 241 vols.
PL   Migne, Jacques-Paul (1844–64) *Patrologia Latina*. 221 vols.

Denzinger, Henry and Schönmetzer, A. (eds.) (1963) *Enchiridion Symbolorum, Definitionum et Declarationum de Rebus Fidei et Morum*, 3rd edn. Freiburg: Herder.

Diodore of Tarsus, ed. Jean-Marie Olivier (1980) *Diodori Tarsensis Commentarii in Psalmos*. Corpus Christianorum Series Graeca 6. Turnhout: Brepols.

Doran, Robert (trans.) (2006) *Stewards of the Poor: The Man of God, Rabbula, and Hiba in Fifth-century Edessa*. Cistercian Studies 208. Kalamazoo: Cistercian.

Facundus of Hermiane, *PL* 67:527–878.

Narsai, ed. and trans. Frederick McLeod (1979) *Narsai's Metrical Homilies on the Nativity, Epiphany, Passion, Resurrection and Ascension*. Patrologia Orientalis 40.1, No. 182. Turnhout: Brepols.

——, trans. F. Martin, (1899 and 1900) "Homélie de Narsès sur les trois Docteurs nestoriens." *Journal Asiatique* 14: 446–92 and 15: 469–525.

Nemesius of Emesa, ed. and trans. William Telfer (1955) *Cyril of Jerusalem and Nemesius of Emesa*. Library of Christian Classics 4. Philadelphia: Westminster.

Straub, Johannes (ed.) (1971) *Concilium Universale Constantinopolitanum sub Justiniano Habitum*. Acta Conciliorum Oecumenicorum. Tome 4, vol. 1. Berlin: De Gruyter.

Tanner, Norman P. (ed.) (1990) *Decrees of the Ecumenical Councils*, vol. 1: *Nicaea to Lateran V*. Washington, DC: Georgetown University Press.

Theodore of Mopsuestia. *Opera Omnia*. PG 66: 10–1020.

——. *Commentary on Obadiah*. PG 66: 303–18.

——. *Commentary on Haggai*. PG 66: 474–94.

——. *Commentary on Genesis*. PG 66: 633–46.

——. *Commentary on the Epistle to the Romans*. PG 66: 787–876.

——. *Commentary on the Incarnation. PG* 66: 971–94.

——. *Fragment of a Work against Apollinaris. PG* 66: 994–1002.

——. *Epistle to Domnus. PG* 66: 1011–14.

——, ed. Luise Abramowski (1958) "Ein unbekanntes Zitat aus *Contra Eunomium* des Theodor von Mopsuestia." *Le Muséon* 71: 97–104.

——, trans. Peter Bruns (1994) *Theodor von Mopsuestia Katechetische Homilien.* 2 vols. Fontes Christiani 17/1. Freiburg: Herder.

——, ed. Robert Devreese (1939) *Commentaire sur les Psaumes I–LXXX.* Studi e Testi, 93. Vatican City: Vaticana.

——, trans. Simon Gerber (2000) *Theodor von Mopsuestia und das Nicänum: Studien zu den katechetischen Homilien.* Leiden: Brill.

——, trans. Augusto Guida (1994) *Teodoro di Mopsuestia: Replica a Guiliano Imperatore.* Firenza: Nardini.

——, trans. Robert Hill (2003) *Commentary on the Twelve Prophets.* Fathers of the Church. Washington, DC: CUAP.

——, trans. Robert Hill (2006) *Theodore of Mopsuestia: Commentary on Psalms 1–81.* Society of Biblical Literature, Leiden: Brill.

——, trans. Sebastia Janeras and Joseph Urdeix (2000) *Homilies Catèquetiques.* Clàssics del Christianisme 70. Barcelona: Fundació Enciclopèdia Catalana.

——, trans. George Kalantzis (2004) *Theodore of Mopsuestia (Gospel of John).* Strathfield, Australia: St. Pauls.

——, ed. William Macomber (1968) "Newly Discovered Fragments of the Gospel Commentaries of Theodore of Mopsuestia." *Le Muséon* 81: 441–7.

——, ed. and trans. A. Mingana (1932 and 1933) *Commentary of Theodore of Mopsuestia on the Nicene Creed and Commentary of Theodore of Mopsuestia on the Lord's Prayer and on the Sacraments of Baptism and the Eucharist.* Woodbrooke Studies 5 and 6. Cambridge: Heffer.

——, ed. and trans. Françoise Petit (1987) "L'homme créé à l'image de Dieu: quelques fragments grec unédits de Théodore de Mopsueste." *Le Muséon* 100: 269–77.

——, ed. and trans. Lucas van Rompay (1982) *Fragments syriaque du Commentaire des Psalmes (Psaume 118 et Psaumes 138–148).* CSCO 189–190. Louvain: Peeters.

——, ed. and trans. E. Sachau (1869) *Theodori Mopsuesteni Fragmenta Syriaca.* Leipzig: G. Engelmann.

——, ed. Karl Staab (1984) *Pauluskommentare aus der Griechischen Kirche*, 2nd edn. Münster: Aschendorff.

——, ed. H. B. Swete (1880 and 1882) *Theodori Episcopi Mopsuesteni in Epistolas B. Pauli Commentarii.* 2 vols. Cambridge: Cambridge University Press.

——, trans. Raymond Tonneau with Robert Devreese (1949) *Les Homélies Catéchétiques de Théodore de Mopsueste.* Vatican City: Vaticana.

——. R.-M. Tonneau (1953) "Théodore de Mopsueste, Interprétation (du Livre) de la Genèse (at. Syr. 120, ff. I–V)." *Le Muséon* 66: 45–64.

——. R. P. Vaggione (1980) "Some Neglected Fragments of Theodore of

Mopsuestia's 'Contra Eunomium'." *Journal of Theological Studies*, n.s. 30: 403–70.

——, ed. and trans. J.-M. Vosté (1940) *Theodori Mopsuesteni Commentarius in Evangelium Johannis Apostoli*. Corpus Scriptorum Christianorum Orientalium 115–16/Syr. 62–63. Louvain: Officina Orientali.

Secondary sources

Abramowski, Luise (1961) "Zur Theologia Theodors von Mopsuestia." *Zeitschrift für Kirchengeschichte* 72: 263–93.

—— (1981) *Drei christologische Untersuchungen*. Beiheft zur Zeitschrift für die neutestamentliche Wissenschaft und die Kunde der älteren Kirche 45. Berlin: de Gruyter.

Amann, É. (1946) "Théodore de Mopsueste." *Dictionnaire de Théologie Catholique* 15.1 col. 258–80. Paris: Letouzey.

Anastos, M. V. (1951) "The Immutability of Christ and Justinian's Condemnation of Theodore of Mopsuestia." *Dumbarton Oaks Papers* 6: 126–60.

Anastos, M. V. (1962) "Nestorius was Orthodox." *Dumbarton Oaks Papers* 16: 119–40.

Arnou, R. (1936) "Nestorianisme et Néoplatonisme." *Gregorianum* 17: 122–31.

Birnie, M. J. (1996) "The Church of the East and Theodore of Mopsuestia: The Commitment to his Writings and its Implications for Dialogue." *Journal of the Assyrian Academic Society* 10.1: 14–9. Online. Available at <www.JAAS. Org/v10n1/birnie.PDF> (accessed 1 February 2007).

Bultmann, Rudolf (1984) *Die Exegese des Theodor von Mopsuestia*, ed. H. Field and K. Schelke. Stuttgart: W. Kohlhammer.

Devreese, Robert (1946) "La méthode exégétique de Théodore de Mopsueste." *Revue Biblique* 55: 207–41.

—— (1948) *Essai sur Théodore de Mopsueste*. Studi e Testi 141. Vatican City: Vaticana.

de Vries, Wilhelm (1941) "Der 'Nestorianismus' Theodors von Mopsuestia in seiner Sakramentenlehre." *Orientalia Christiana Periodica* 7: 91–148.

Dewart, Joanne McWilliam (1971) *The Theology of Grace of Theodore of Mopsuestia*. Catholic University of America Studies in Christian Antiquity 16. Washington, DC: Catholic University of America Press.

—— (1975) "The Notion of 'Person' Underlying the Christology of Theodore of Mopsuestia." *Studia Patristica* 12: 199–207.

Dorner, I. A. (1863–66) *The History of the Development of the Doctrine of the Person of Christ*. 5 vols. Edinburgh: Clark.

Downey, Glanville (1961) *A History of Antioch in Syria from Seleucus to the Arab Conquest*. Princeton: Princeton University Press.

Galtier, Paul (1957) "Théodore de Mopsueste: Sa vraie pensée sur l'incarnation." *Recherches de science religieuse* 45: 161–86 and 338–60.

Greer, Rowan A. (1961) *Theodore of Mopsuestia: Exegete and Theologian.* Westminster: Faith.

—— (1966a) "Antiochene Christology of Diodore of Tarsus." *Journal of Theological Studies* 17: 327–41.

—— (1966b) "Image of God and the Prosopic Union in Nestorius' *Bazaar of Heracleides*," in *Lux in Lumine: Essays for W. N. Pittenger*, ed. Richard A. Norris, Jr. New York: Seabury, pp. 46–59.

—— (1973) *The Captain of Salvation: A Study in the Patristic Exegesis of Hebrews.* Tübingen: Mohr.

—— (1983) "The Analogy of Grace in Theodore of Mopsuestia's Christology." *Journal of Theological Studies* n.s. 34: 82–98.

Grillmeier, Aloys (1975) *Christ in Christian Tradition from the Apostolic Age to Chalcedon (451).* 2 vols. 2nd rev. edn., trans. J. Cawte and P. Allen. Atlanta: John Knox.

Harnack, A. (1958) *History of Dogma.* 7 vols. New York: Russell and Russell. Vols. 1–2 trans. Neil Buchanan, vols. 3 and 5 trans. J. Millar, vol. 4 trans. E. B. Speirs, vols. 6–7 trans. W. McGilchrist.

Jugie, M. (1935) "Le 'Liber ad baptizandos' de Théodore de Mopsueste." *Echoes d'Orient* 34: 257–71.

Kelly, J. N. D. (1978) *Early Christian Doctrines.* Rev. edn. San Francisco: Harper.

el-Khoury, Nabil (1990) "Der Mensch als Gleichnis Gottes: Eine Untersuchung zur Anthropologie des Theodor von Mopsuestia." *Oriens Christianus* 74: 62–71.

Kittel, G. (1968) *Theological Dictionary of the New Testament*, ed. and trans. Geoffrey W. Bromiley. Grand Rapids, MI: Eerdmans.

Koch, Günter (1965) *Die Heilsverwirklichung bei Theodor von Mopsuestia.* Münchener Theologische Studien 2. Systematische Abteilung 31. München: Hueber.

Köster, Helmut (1968) *Theological Dictionary of the New Testament*, ed. Gerhard Friedrich, trans. Geoffrey W. Bromiley. Grand Rapids, MI: Eerdmans.

Lera, José Maria (1991) "Théodore de Mopsueste." *Dictionnaire de Spiritualité* XV. Paris: Beauchesne.

McGuckin, John (1990) "Did Augustine's Christology Depend on Theodore of Mopsuestia?" *Heythrop Journal* 55: 39–52.

McKenzie, John L. (1949) "A New Study of Theodore of Mopsuestia." *Theological Studies* 31: 394–408.

—— (1953) "The Commentary of Theodore of Mopsuestia on John 1:46–51." *Theological Studies* 14: 73–84.

—— (1958) "Annotations on the Christology of Theodore of Mopsuestia." *Theological Studies* 19: 345–73.

McLeod, Frederick (1979) *Narsai's Metrical Homilies on the Nativity, Epiphany, Passion, Resurrection and Ascension.* Patrologia Orientalis 182, vol. 40.1. Turnhout: Brepols.

—— (1999) *The Image of God in the Antiochene Tradition*. Washington, DC: Catholic University of America Press.

—— (2000) "Theodore of Mopsuestia Revisited." *Theological Studies* 61.3: 447–80.

——(2002) "The Theological Ramifications of Theodore of Mopsuestia's Understanding of Baptism and the Eucharist." *Journal of Early Christian Studies* 10.1: 41–50.

—— (2005) *The Roles of Christ's Humanity in Salvation: Insights from Theodore of Mopsuestia*. Washington, DC: Catholic University of America Press.

McNamara, Kevin (1952 and 1953) "Theodore of Mopsuestia and the Nestorian Heresy." *Irish Theological Quarterly*, 46: 254–78 and 47: 172–91.

Martin, Josef (1974) *Antike Rhetorik: Technik und Method*. Münich: Beck.

Murphy, F.-X., and P. Sherwood (1974) *Constantinople II et Constantinople III*. Histoire des Conciles Oecuméniques 3. Paris: L'Orante.

Nassif, Bradley (1996) "Spiritial Exegesis in the School of Antioch," in *New Perspectives in Historical Theology: Essays in Memory of John Meyendorff*, ed. Bradley Nassif. Grand Rapids, MI: Eerdmans, pp. 343–77.

Norris, Richard A. Jr. (1963) *Manhood and Christ: A Study in the Christology of Theodore of Mopsuestia*. Oxford: Clarendon.

—— (1966) "Toward a Contemporary Interpretation of the Chalcedonian Definition," in *Lux in Lumine: Essays for W. N. Pittenger*, ed. Richard A. Norris, Jr. New York: Seabury, 62–79.

—— (ed. and trans.) (1980) *The Christian Controversy*. Sources of Early Christian Thought. Philadelphia: Fortress.

O'Keefe, John J. (2000) "'A Letter that Killeth': Toward a Reassessment of Antiochene Exegesis or Diodore, Theodore, and Theodoret on the Psalms." *Journal of Early Christian Studies* 8.1: 83–104.

Oñatibia, I. (1954) "La vida christiana, tipo de las realidades celestes. Un concepto basico de la teologia de Teodore de Mopsuestia." *Scriptorum Victoriense* 1: 100–33.

Patterson, Leonard (1926) *Theodore of Mopsuestia and Modern Thought*. London: Society for Promoting Christian Knowledge.

Poppas, Harry S. (2002) "Theodore of Mopsuestia's Commentary on Psalm 44 (LXX): A Study of His Exegesis and Christology." *Greek Orthodox Theological Review* 47.1–4: 55–79.

Richard, Marcel (1943) "La tradition des fragments du Traité Περί ἐνανθρωπήσεως de Théodore de Mopsueste." *Le Muséon* 46: 55–75.

Romanides, John (1959–60) "Highlight in the Debate over Theodore of Mopsuestia's Christology and Some Suggestions for a Fresh Approach." *Greek Orthodox Theological Review* 5: 140–85.

Schäublin, Christoph (1974). *Untersuchungen zu Methode und Herkunft der Antiochenischen Exegese*. Theophaneia 23. Cologne: Hanstein.

Sellers, R. V. (1953a) *Two Ancient Christologies: A Study in the Christological Thought of the School of Alexandria and Antioch in the Early History of Christian Doctrine*. London: Society for Promoting Christian Knowledge.

—— (1953b) *Council of Chalcedon: A Historical and Doctrinal Survey*. London: Society for Promoting Christian Knowledge.

Simonetti, Manlio (1992) "Diodore of Tarsus," "Exegesis, Patristic," "Theodore of Mopsuestia," and "Three Chapters," in *Encyclopedia of the Early Church*, ed. Angelo Di Berardino, trans. A Wolford. 2 vols. New York: Oxford.

Smith, W. and H. Wace (eds.) (1877–78) *The Dictionary of Christian Biography, Literature, Sects and Doctrines*. 4 vols. London: Murray.

Sullivan, Francis (1951) "Some Reactions to Devreese's New Study of Theodore of Mopsuestia." *Theological Studies* 12: 179–209.

—— (1956) *The Christology of Theodore of Mopsuestia*. Analecta Gregoriana 82. Rome: Gregorianae.

—— (1959) "Further Notes on Theodore of Mopsuestia." *Theological Studies* 20: 264–79.

Swete, H. B. (1877) "Theodorus," in *Dictionary of Christian Biography, Literature, Sects and Doctrines*, ed. W. Smith and H. Wace. London: J. Murray, 4: 934–48.

Viciano, Albert (1996) "Das Formale Verfahren der Antiochenischen Scriftauslegung: Ein Forschungüberblick," in *Stimuli: Exegese und ihre Hermeneutik in Antike und Christentum: Festschrift für Ernst Dassman*, ed. Georg Schöllgen und Clemens Schulten. Munster: Aschendorff, 370–405.

Vogt, Herman J. (1997) "Bemerkungen zu Exegese und Christologie des Theodore von Mopsuestia," in *Synodos*. Paderborn: Schöninger.

Vööbus, Arthur (1964) "Regarding the Theological Anthropology of Theodore of Mopsuestia." *Church History*, 33: 115–24.

Vosté, J.-M. (1925) "La chronologie de l'activit de Théodore de Mopsueste au II Councile de Constantinople." *Revue Biblique* 34: 54–81.

—— (1929) "L'oeuvre exégétique de Théodore de Mopsueste au II Councile de Constantinople." *Revue Biblique* 38: 382–95 and 542–54.

Warne, Graham J. (1995) *Hebrew Perspectives on the Human Person in the Hellanistic Era: Philo and Paul*. Lewiston, NY: Mellen.

Wickert, Ulrich (1962) *Studien zu den Pauluskommentaren Theodors von Mopsuestia: Als Beitrag zum Verständnis der Antiochenischen Theologie*. Berlin: Töpelmann.

Young, Frances M. (1989) "The Rhetorical Schools and their Influence on Patristic Exegesis," in *The Makings of Orthodoxy: Essays in Honor of Henry Chadwick*, ed. Rowan Williams. Cambridge: Cambridge University Press, pp. 182–99.

—— (1997) *Biblical Exegesis and the Formation of Christian Culture*. Cambridge: Cambridge University Press.

Zaharopoulos, Dimitri Z. (1989) *Theodore of Mopsuestia on the Bible: A Study of his Old Testament Exegesis*. New York: Paulist.

INDEX

Abramowski, Luise 12, 52, 72, 178

Adam: effects of his sin 24–8, 58, 85–93; as God's image 29–30, 92–3; as the head of mortal existence 11, 16, 24–7, 86–9, 106; as the mediating bond of the universe 27–8; as a type 21, 27, 73, 102

adoration *see* person (one common *prosōpon*), adoration of

allegory: Origen's understanding of 18, 120, 180n1; pagan origin of 18; Theodore's opposition to 18–20, 75–9, 120–1

Amann, Émile 13

anagoge 21, 177n3 (2)

Anastos, M. V. 13–14

Apollinaris of Laodicea/ Apollinarianism 13, 34–5, 44, 46, 72–3, 126, 148–57, 160, 166, 172, 175, 182n8, 183n2, 183n11

Aristotle 11–12, 23

Arius 4, 73, 148, 165, 178n1 (3), 182n3

Arnou, Robert 11

Artemon 153, 183n5

assumens/assumptus see union of Christ's natures

Asterius 95, 181n1

Augustine 15, 24, 180n9

baptism: as a type ix, 12, 21, 101–2, 106, 118–19, 135, 168, 182n1 (1); effects 101–2, 106, 119, 163, 166–8, 181n5; Spirit's role 140, 152, 166, 174

Birnie, M. J. 9, 177n3 (1)

body/Body: expressing Christ's complete humanity 35, 137, 146, 156, 168–9, 178; in relation to the material non-rational world 27–8, 92, 121, 180n2 (3), 181n4 (1), 183n10; in relation to its soul 11, 28, 45, 51–2, 56–8, 61, 79, 104, 121, 136, 142, 153–5, 157, 160, 176n4 (2), 179n7

Boethius 42

bond of the universe: Adam as 27–8; Christ's humanity as 27–9, 33, 40, 64–5, 92–3, 118, 121–5, 180n2 (3)

Bruns, Peter 15

Bultmann, Rudolf 15, 20

Chalcedon, Council of (451) 5, 7–10, 13–14, 47–8, 64, 67, 172–3, 175

Children of God, adopted 40, 62–3, 65, 101, 124, 135, 138–9

Christ's humanity: as bond of the universe 27–9, 33, 40, 64–5, 92–3, 118, 121–5, 180n2 (3); as the divine *plerōma* (divine fullness) 31, 39–40, 102, 122–3, 125, 134, 162; as firstborn of creation 26, 31, 124, 139, 158–9; as first fruits 88, 118, 124, 127, 132, 167, 170; growth in knowledge 35, 60–1, 68, 132, 155–6; as head of his

Body, the church 27–8, 40, 65,
105–6, 108, 118–19, 122–3, 125,
163–4, 169; as head of immortal
existence 24, 27–8, 30, 33, 58, 65,
88–9, 119, 122, 169–70, 181n1
(1) and n6, 182n1 (1); as the
head recapitulating the cosmos
28, 40, 64–5, 118, 121–2, 181n3
(1); as mediator 26, 35, 40, 60,
64–5, 68, 102, 181n2 (1); as the
perfect image of God 26, 29–33,
68, 72, 89, 118, 123–4, 141, 174,
178n3 (1) and n4 (2), 182n10;
possessing free will 10–11, 13–15,
35, 53–4, 57–60, 64, 66–7, 88–9,
179n1 (1), 182n6, 183n2 (1);
sharing in the Word's honors 39,
41, 65, 83–4, 102, 112, 126; sinless
10, 35, 58, 64–5, 89, 132–4, 142,
159; subject to passions 60, 127,
142–3, 155, 159, 174, 183n11
christological terms *see* nature
(*physis*); person (*hypostasis/
qnōmā*); person (*prosōpon*);
person (one common *prosōpon*);
substance/essence (*ousia*)
Church as the Body of Christ *see*
Christ's humanity
Constantinople I, Council of (381)
4, 47
Constantinople II, Council of (553)
8–10, 12–13, 48, 67, 71, 171–5,
177n6
Cyril of Alexandria 4, 13–14, 46–7,
53, 64, 66–8, 175, 176n5, 180n2
(2), 182n8

Devreese, Robert 12–13, 80
de Vries, Wilhelm 12
Dewart, Joanne McWilliam 15
Diodore of Tarsus 3–4, 13, 15, 20–1,
72, 176n7, 177n2 (2), 178n3 (1)
Dioscorus, Patriarch of Alexandria 5
Dorner, Isaak August 10, 14, 30
Downey, Glanville 176n6

enoikēsis see indwelling of good
pleasure
Ephesus I, Council of (431) 4, 8, 67,
175, 176n5

Ephesus II, Council of (449)
("Robbers' Council") 4–5, 8, 21
eucharist 11–12, 16, 158, 168–9,
182n1 (1)
Eunomius 9, 148, 156, 165, 177n5
Eusebius of Emesa 18
Eustathius of Antioch 18
Eutyches 5, 172
exegesis *see* Theodore of Mopsuestia,
exegetical method and examples

Facundus of Hermiane 9
'Form of God' and 'form of the
slave' (intermingled treatment)
49–50, 52, 109–16, 154, 162
free will *see* grace and free will;
Christ's humanity, possessing
free will

Galtier, Paul 13, 64, 67–8
Gerber, Simon 15
grace and free will 12, 14–15, 35,
54, 57, 60, 65, 106–18; *see also*
Christ's humanity, possessing
free will; indwelling of good
pleasure; Spirit of God
Greer, Rowan 14
Grillmeier, Aloys 15
Guida, Augusto 72, 176n3

Harnack, August 10–11, 14
Hill, Robert Charles 15
historia (narrative account) 19–21
homo assumptus see union of Christ's
natures
human nature *see* nature (*physis*)
hypostasis see person (*hypostasis/
qnōmā*)

Ibas, bishop of Edessa 5, 8–9, 174,
176n1 (2)
image of God *see* Adam, as God's
image; Christ's humanity, as the
perfect image of God
indwelling of good pleasure 34–41,
129–32, 136, 140; *see also* Spirit
of God
intellect *see nous*

person (*prosōpon*): early church
usage 47; relation to *hypostasis*
135–6, 144, 172; Theodore's
understanding 47–9
person (one common *prosōpon*):
49–55, 65, 67, 109–16, 136, 181n1
(2); adoration of 32, 53, 56, 85,
112, 115–16, 139–44, 151–2, 163,
173–4; common "ego" 56–9,
66–7, 143–4; Theodore's three
analogies 51–3; *see also* union of
Christ's natures
Petit, Françoise 12
Philo 77–8
Photius, patriarch of Constantinople
9, 177n5, 180n9
physis see nature
plerōma (divine fullness) *see* Christ's
humanity, as the divine *plerōma*
Porphyry, bishop of Antioch 79,
181n2 (1)
prosōpon see person (*prosōpon*)

Rabbula, bishop of Edessa 4
rational soul *see nous*
recapitulation *see* Christ's humanity,
as the head recapitulating the
cosmos
resurrection 11, 27–8, 68, 78, 85–7,
101–2, 106, 108, 110, 112, 118–19,
122, 126, 140, 150, 167–9, 174,
182n1 (1)
Richard, Marcel 12–13
Robber's Council (Latrocinium) *see*
Ephesus II, Council of
Romanides, John 14, 179n1 (1)

Sabellius 47
Sachau, Edward 10–11, 71, 74
sacraments *see* baptism; eucharist
salvation 10–11, 14, 24, 27–30, 33–5,
37, 49, 54, 57–64, 91, 101, 103,
112–18, 134, 136, 138, 141, 160–2,
166, 181n3 (1)
Schäublin, Christoph 15
schēma (outward appearance) 49–50,
174
Sellers, R. V. 12
sin 10–12, 24–6, 28, 33, 58, 64, 73,

86–92, 101, 104, 121, 131, 137,
143, 159–60
Son and sonship: adopted children
40, 62–3, 65, 101, 124, 135,
138–9; charge of two sons 61,
138, 142, 144, 149, 157, 161, 172;
Christ as the Son by grace 37,
54–5, 61–3, 65, 82, 84, 102, 104,
107, 113, 128, 138–9, 153, 156–7,
161, 174; as God's visible image
26, 31, 119; "as in God's S/son"
32, 38–40, 132, 135, 137–9, 178n4
(3); Word as the only Begotten
Son by nature 34, 46, 52, 54,
61–3, 79, 97–101, 105, 124, 128–9,
132, 138, 141, 143–4, 153, 156,
158–9, 161–2, 165–6
Spirit of God: a divine inspiring
hypostasis 4, 17–19, 22, 32, 34,
79–82, 102–4, 116–17, 126, 129,
141, 143–5, 166; indwelling and
assisting Christ's humanity 32,
35, 39–40, 58, 61, 63, 102–3, 106,
108, 120, 123, 129, 132–5, 140–1,
143, 149–53, 159; role in baptism
63, 101–2, 105–6, 118, 135, 160,
163, 166–7, 174; role in the
eucharist 167–70, 183n3 (2)
Straub, K. 176n7
substance (*ousia*) 34, 36, 41–4, 47–8,
97, 99, 130–1, 135, 143–4, 150,
153–4, 162, 165, 173, 178n3 (3),
179n4 (1) and n1 (1), 182n5
Sullivan, Francis A. 13–14, 176n7
synapheia akribēs see union of
Christ's natures
Swete, H. B. 4, 10–11, 71–3, 86, 109,
118, 176n1 (1) and n2 (1), 177n7,
180n8 and n9

temptations of Christ 59–60
Theodore of Mopsuestia:
christological terms of
see christological terms;
condemnation of 4–10, 13, 48, 64,
72, 171–5; distinction between
"beginning" and "first" 96–8;
exegetical method and examples
17–33, 49, 72, 86, 177n1; as

Related titles from Routledge

Evagrius Ponticus

A. M. Casiday

'Casiday's Evagrius remains an excellent introduction to an elusive yet important father of the desert.'

Bryn Mawr Reviews

Evagrius Ponticus (c. 345–99) was a seminal figure for Eastern monasticism and had a strong influence on Western monasticism as well. He left more writings than any other father from the Egyptian desert. However, many of his writings were lost as he was condemned as an Origenist in the sixth century. During the twentieth century, numerous works were recovered (especially in ancient oriental translations from the original Greek) but very few of these works are available in English translation; many of them are not readily available at all.

This collection presents complete works drawn from the full range of his writings, many of which have not previously appeared in English, offering translations of some of Evagrius' letters, his notes on various books of the Bible, his treatises and his 'chapters' (a genre popularised by Evagrius that consists of condensed, interconnected sentences). All of the works included here are translated in full.

The translations aim to present the material accurately and accessibly. The volume is prefaced by a substantial introductory essay that presents Evagrius, his works and influence, and modern scholarship about him in a way that is of great use to students and also comprehensible to beginners.

For students dealing with Evagrius for the first time, they could not find a better book to begin their exploration of this figure in late antique history and theology.

ISBN10: 0-415-32446-7 (hbk)
ISBN10: 0-415-32447-5 (pbk)
ISBN13: 978-0-415-32446-5 (hbk)
ISBN13: 978-0-415-32447-2 (pbk)
ISBN13: 978-0-203-35697-5 (ebk)

Available at all good bookshops
For ordering and further information please visit:
www.routledge.com

Related titles from Routledge

Gregory of Nazianzus

Brian Daley

Gregory of Nazianzus, a complex and colourful figure in a crucial age (fourth century AD), when it was permissible for the first time to be a public Christian intellectual, was well placed to become one of the outstanding defenders and formulators of Church doctrine.

A gifted and skilled rhetorician, poet and orator, as well as a profound theologian, Gregory was ordained a bishop and served, for almost two years, as head of the orthodox Christian community in Constantinople, where he played a crucial role in formulating the classical doctrines of the Trinity and the person of Christ. Under fire from opponents in the Church, the enigmatic Gregory eventually retreated into a quiet life of study and simple asceticism in his native Cappadocia, concentrating there on bringing the broad canon of his own writings to their present form. The body of his works, including poetry, letters, sermons and lectures on religious themes, and written with the precision and elegance of classical Greek literature, was recognised in the Byzantine age as equal in quality to the achievements of the greatest Greek writers.

A collection of new translations of a selection of these works, with an extensive introduction to Gregory's life, thought, and writings, *Gregory of Nazianzus* presents to us a vivid portrait of a fascinating character, who deserves to be regarded as one of the Christian tradition's outstanding theologians, and as the first true Christian humanist.

ISBN10: 0-415-12180-9 (hbk)
ISBN10: 0-415-12181-7 (pbk)
ISBN13: 978-0-415-12180-4 (hbk)
ISBN13: 978-0-415-12181-1 (pbk)
ISBN13: 978-0-203-02197-2 (ebk)

Available at all good bookshops
For ordering and further information please visit:
www.routledge.com

Related titles from Routledge

Theodoret of Cyrus

István Pásztorik Kupán

Theodoret of Cyrus lived during the stormy decades of the third and fourth
ecumenical councils of Ephesus (431) and Chalcedon (451), when many
important doctrinal questions (including the mode of interpreting Chirst
as God and man) were in dispute. Being the champion of the so-called
Antiochene tradition and an opponent of Cyril, the mighty patriarch of
Alexandria, Theodoret left behind a fascinating legacy. His biography shows
that he was immersed in the highly tense dogmatic and ecclesiastical-political
battles of the fifth century, whilst remaining a truly pious churchman, who
had distributed his inheritance to the poor and lived a very modest life even
as bishop.

The larger part of his extant writings still remains untranslated, which provides
a fragmented representation of his thought and has led to his misrepresentation
by ancient, medieval and some modern scholars.

Theodoret of Cyrus offers a fresh collection of texts from all periods of his
career, including two complete treatises (*On the Holy and Vivifying Trinity*
and *On the Inhumanation of the Lord*) as well as representative selections
from two others (*A Cure of Greek Maladies* and *A Compendium of Heretical
Mythification*) so far unpublished in English, with a critical introduction
concerning his life, legacy and place in the history of Christian doctrine. This
book provides the reader with a more balanced picture of Theodoret's often
neglected, deprecated and largely inaccessible theological legacy.

ISBN10: 0-415-30960-3 (hbk)
ISBN10: 0-415-30961-1 (pbk)
ISBN13: 978-0-415-30960-8 (hbk)
ISBN13: 978-0-415-30961-5 (pbk)
ISBN13: 978-0-203-08855-5 (ebk)

Available at all good bookshops
For ordering and further information please visit:
www.routledge.com